Worse than Watergate

Also by John W. Dean

Warren G. Harding

Unmasking Deep Throat — History's Most Elusive News Source

*The Rehnquist Choice: The Untold Story of the Nixon Appointment
That Redefined the Supreme Court*

Lost Honor

Blind Ambition: The White House Years

Worse
than
Watergate

The Secret Presidency of George W. Bush

John W. Dean

Little, Brown and Company
New York • *Boston*

Little, Brown and Company
Time Warner Book Group
1271 Avenue of the Americas, New York, NY 10020
Visit our Web site at www.twbookmark.com

First Edition

Library of Congress Cataloging-in-Publication Data
Dean, John W. (John Wesley).
   Worse than Watergate : the secret presidency of George W. Bush /
John W. Dean. — 1st ed.
       p.   cm.
   Includes bibliographical references and index.
   ISBN 0-316-00023-X
   1. United States — Politics and government — 2001–   2. Bush, George W.
(George Walker), 1946– — Political and social views.   3. Cheney, Richard
B. — Political and social views.   4. Bush, George W. (George Walker),
1946– — Ethics.   5. Cheney, Richard B. — Ethics.   6. Official secrets —
United States.   7. Deception — Political aspects — United States.
8. United States — Foreign relations — 2001–.   9. National security —
United States.   I. Title.

E902.D42 2004
973.931 — dc22   2004001413

10 9 8 7 6

Q-FF

Printed in the United States of America

Secrecy — the first refuge of incompetents — must be at bare minimum in a democratic society, for a fully informed public is the basis of self-government. Those elected or appointed to positions of executive authority must recognize that government, in a democracy, cannot be wiser than the people.

— House Committee on Government Operations,
1960 Report

Contents

Preface

George W. Bush and Richard B. Cheney have created the most secretive presidency of my lifetime. Their secrecy is far worse than during Watergate, and it bodes even more serious consequences. Their secrecy is extreme — not merely unjustified and excessive but obsessive. It has created a White House that hides its president's weaknesses as well as its vice president's strengths. It has given us a presidency that operates on hidden agendas. To protect their secrets, Bush and Cheney dissemble as a matter of policy. In fact, the Bush-Cheney presidency is strikingly Nixonian, only with regard to secrecy far worse (and no one will ever successfully accuse me of being a Nixon apologist). Dick Cheney, who runs his own secret governmental operations, openly declares that he wants to turn the clock back to the pre-Watergate years — a time of an unaccountable and extraconstitutional imperial presidency. To say that their secret presidency is undemocratic is an understatement.

I'm anything but skittish about government, but I must say this administration is truly scary and, given the times we live in, frighteningly dangerous. This conclusion is not that of a political partisan, for those days are long behind me; rather, it is the finding of a concerned observer, with something of a distinct understanding and appreciation of the modern presidency.

I was initially astonished watching the Bush-Cheney presidency, not certain they realized the very familiar path (at least to me) that they were taking. Richard Nixon, who resigned his presidency thirty years ago, had many admirable strengths and qualities. His secrecy, which shielded his abuses of presidential power, was not among them. Thus, from time to time, I fired off flares, hoping to throw a bit of light — if not a warning — on where they were headed. I did so by raising these matters in my regular *FindLaw* column. For one such column, in which I discussed the potential of impeachment if the Bush administration had intentionally manipulated government intelligence on Iraq's weapons of mass destruction, an editor at *Salon*, which reprinted the column, used the title "Worse than Watergate" — drawing his own conclusion from the material.* Three months later, Chris Matthews of MSNBC's *Hardball* described the Bush administration's revengeful act of leaking the name and CIA identity of the wife of an administration critic, former ambassador Joseph Wilson, as "worse than Watergate" (for the leak was potentially life-threatening, given her undercover status, as well as against the law). Matthews made this comment in an exchange with the chairman of the Republican National Committee, Ed Gillespie, who to my surprise did not disagree.** So while I can't claim original authorship for the title, when my editor suggested it for this book, I could not deny that it describes perfectly what I have to say in more ways than I had anticipated.

This book began as an admonition, an approach both "beware of Bush" and "Bush beware." Only ignorance or bliss, I figured at the time, could lead another president and White House to make the same kind of mistakes we made during Nixon's presidency. As I proceeded, however, and the post-9/11 activities and

---

*See "Worse than Watergate," *Salon* (June 11, 2003).
**See *Hardball* transcript, MSNBC Television (September 30, 2003).

operations of Bush and Cheney unfolded, it was evident that these were carefully calculated policies and plans. No longer was I writing a warning, but rather an indictment, for I could not write and publish fast enough to get in front of the abuses of power and the emerging ends-justify-the-means mentality, and even if I could have, it would not have made any difference, for they understood exactly what they were doing and why. Stated a bit differently, I've been watching all the elements fall into place for two possible political catastrophes, one that will take the air out of the Bush-Cheney balloon and the other, far more disquieting, will take the air out of democracy. Allow me to explain.

To compare the Bush-Cheney presidency with Nixon's tenure and Watergate and assert that it is worse than Watergate is not a charge to be made lightly. Nor do I. Watergate symbolizes totally unacceptable presidential behavior. Dictionary definitions of the term *Watergate* typically describe this unacceptable conduct as the abuse of presidential power, or high office, for political purposes.[1] Watergate, of course, was a very messy presidential scandal and a political disaster for Nixon. Certainly no comparable scandal has occurred during the Bush-Cheney tenure — at least not yet. Scandals have a way of smoldering before erupting, as has occurred with every major presidential scandal — Teapot Dome, Watergate, Iran-Contra, and L'affaire Lewinsky. There are simply too many problems rumbling just below the surface of the Bush-Cheney presidency to avoid making the comparison.

Former attorney general (and later secretary of state) William Rogers once advised that "the public should view excessive secrecy among government officials as parents view sudden quiet where youngsters are playing. It is a sign of trouble."[2] Woodrow Wilson, based on his long study of statecraft, concluded that "everybody knows that corruption thrives in secret places, and avoids public places, and we believe it a fair presumption that secrecy means impropriety."[3] Thus, undue secrecy not only is undemocratic, denying the public its right to know, but also schools scandal by concealing and protecting errors, excesses, and all manner of impropriety. And we have a presidency that seeks to control, if not suppress, everything.

Political pollster John Zogby tells us that Democrats are from Venus and Republicans are from Mars, and based on my examination of the Bush II White House vis-à-vis his predecessor, I'm inclined to agree.[4] In short, nothing suggesting a sex scandal blipped on my screen.* On the other hand, the potential for a serious financial and/or power scandal, as I discovered, is quite real.

In addition, there is another state of affairs with the Bush-Cheney presidency that is worse than any scandal and far worse than Watergate. In General Tommy Franks's first interview as a civilian shortly after he departed as four-star head of Central Command, when discussing what he thought Americans should be thinking about concerning terrorism, he asked rhetorically, "What is the worst thing that can happen?" His answer is chilling. Franks has no doubt whatsoever that upon obtaining a weapon of mass destruction, a terrorist organization will use it. If that should happen, Franks believes the Western world may lose "what it cherishes most, and that is freedom and liberty we've seen for a couple of hundred years in this grand experi-

---

*Unless it should happen that Bush's brother Neil starts hanging around the White House. Neil Bush is busy at work embarrassing his brother as he did his father when he was president, with titillating headlines: BUSH BROTHER'S SHOCKING SEX AND BIZ LIFE (*New York Daily News*), SEX AND SWEET DEALS: BUSH BRO'S ASIAN ROMP (*Boston Herald*), HOTEL SEX CLAIMS OF BUSH BRO (London *Sun*), to name a few of the stories from the world press recounted by Rick Casey in the *Houston Chronicle* (December 3, 2003).

ment that we call democracy." He has reached that conclusion because he feels that there exists "the potential of a . . . massive casualty-producing event somewhere in the western world — it may be in the United States of America — that causes our population to question our own Constitution and to begin to militarize our country in order to avoid a repeat of another mass, casualty-producing event. Which in fact, then begins to unravel the fabric of our Constitution."[5]

I agree with General Franks, but I suspect for very different reasons. Watching the responses of Bush and Cheney to 9/11, their obsessive secrecy, their endless political manipulation and exploitation of 9/11, their blatant suppression of rights and liberties of foreigners, their taking our nation to its first "preventive war" as aggressors in Iraq, their distortion of intelligence gathering, their Nixon-like rationalizations, I realized that — with the near certainty of a catastrophic terrorist attack against America one day — we have the wrong leaders. Not because they are not able or well motivated or "real Americans," as President Lyndon Johnson used to say — for they are all those things. But they are also zealots who are convinced of their own wisdom, oblivious to not only what Americans think but the opinions of the entire world. Former Supreme Court justice Louis Brandeis once spoke of this problem: "The greatest danger to liberty lurks in the insidious encroachment by men of zeal, well-meaning but without understanding." If the dreaded event that General Franks has raised occurs (and as I explain, this presidency may actually attract such an event), there is good reason to fear for the fabric of our Constitution.

It goes without saying that it would be best to have neither a scandal nor something far worse. There is, however, only one antidote: an end to the obsessive, unjustified, and disproportionate secrecy that defines the Bush-Cheney White House. In addressing these matters, I seek only to make the prima facie case, to show that these potential problems are very real, not fanciful concerns, and should not be ignored. In thinking about how best to set forth the disquieting circumstances, I selected the only form of discourse that seems fitting, a polemic. *Polemic* comes from the Greek word *polèmikos* — "of or relating to war." That, of course, is the current situation. By tradition, polemics are first-person, strongly felt, and relatively brief. Though polemics often indict, those that simply trash are worthless. Whether one accepts or rejects his argument, an example of a classic polemic is Christopher Hitchens's *The Case Against Henry Kissinger.* Hitchens's case is powerfully presented, compellingly and closely argued, and ardent without being strident or unduly nasty. On the other hand, Peggy Noonan's polemic, *The Case Against Hillary Clinton*, provided me with a perfect model of what I did not want to do: invent facts, appeal to emotions rather than intelligence, engage in vicious name-calling, and fail to provide documentation. Hitchens's work must be taken seriously, whereas Noonan's effort is easily dismissed.

By way of preface I must add that I do not believe in conspiracy theories. I use terms such as "shadow national security council," "secret government," and "hidden agenda" because they are descriptive of actual facts, not theory. In addition, I have provided detailed documentation (as chapter notes, along with occasional footnotes) not only to show where information was found but to provide access to it for others. As noted in the Acknowledgments, I have talked (or exchanged e-mails) with a lot of people while working on this project, and many wished to remain off-the-record, for reasons I understand and explain. I decided to make virtually all these sources off-the-record because they were not necessary to state my case, so only in rare instances have I quoted from any of these sources, and never for any point of particular significance. Rather, this information was used as leads, confirmation, insights about Bush or Cheney, and background about their secretive ways, or to find answers to the myriad questions that arise with such widespread secrecy.

In the chapters that follow, I begin where this inquiry started, with my discovery of the surprising Nixon-like traits of George W. Bush. When looking at him closely, though, I noted the early-warning signs of the undue Bush-Cheney secrecy. What at first appeared only a penchant for secrecy I soon realized was a policy of concealment that they exercised throughout the 2000 campaign. I've used examples of their campaign stonewalling because they have morphed into White House stonewalling. Once ensconced in their offices at 1600 Pennsylvania Avenue, they quietly closed their doors, pulled the shades, and began making themselves increasingly inaccessible to the media and Congress while demanding complete control over government information. Government under a virtual gag order became their standard operating procedure.

In looking at the Bush-Cheney White House, I found it not unlike Nixon's in that it spends far more time crafting the president's public image and working on the politics of reelection, than on truly addressing the business of the American people. But what clearly distinguishes this presidency is its vice president, a secretive man by nature whose unmatched power is largely veiled but whose secret governmental operations have changed the world — and not for the better. Dick Cheney, effectively a co-president incognito, works behind closed doors and does not answer to Congress or the public. His partner, the president, is not sufficiently knowledgeable about their policies to answer questions about them adequately, if and when he does occasionally make himself available. It is not that he is stupid, only ignorant — and apparently by design. Yet time and again, their principal public policies — both foreign and domestic — are laden with hidden agendas.

The Bush-Cheney hidden agenda I have focused on relates to their national security policies, given their critical importance. Equally worthy of attention is their hidden agenda to end federal entitlement programs by running up budget-busting deficits while hiking military spending, which is bleeding the federal treasury and will ultimately result in there simply being no money available to pay for social programs after this administration is gone. These, of course, are programs — such as Social Security and Medicare — that they dare not eliminate. But economic and fiscal policy is not my forte, so rather than merely repeating the conclusions of others whose judgment I respect, I have stayed with matters that I fully understand.

I have made no effort to write a history of all their sorry activities. Instead, I have merely drafted a bill of particulars, setting forth a sampling of their secrecy indicative of their policies and practices that demand the public's attention. This material, found in chapters two to five, provides overwhelming evidence that their secrecy is out of hand and that it has become so pervasive and troubling that it must be called sinister, for it has dreadful potential consequences for all Americans.

Perhaps, as one historian mentioned to me, the best model for a polemic is Thomas Paine's *Common Sense*. After all, Paine's tract blasted a monarchy headed by a fellow named George, and he called it as he saw it. Both Paine's undertakings are certainly compatible with my intentions. First, by calling attention to the surprisingly Nixonian nature of the Bush presidency, then by proceeding through a number of particularly disquieting instances of the Bush-Cheney secrecy — not a complete catalog but more than sufficient to establish their mentality — which started with the 2000 campaign, progressed at the White House, and has resulted in the most abusive use of secrecy in the modern presidency. My hope along the way is not to scandalmonger, but rather to spray as much antiscandal disinfectant — called light — as I possibly can. And my goal is to raise several important, if not critical, issues now being hidden from the public and place them on top of the table of public discussion, particularly matters like those raised by General Tommy Franks that could end "this grand experiment that we call democracy." In short, my plea is really for a little common sense.

Nothing is secret that shall not be made manifest.

— Luke 8:17

Worse
than
Watergate

Chapter One

Surprisingly Nixonian

This [Bush-Cheney] administration is the most secretive of our lifetime, even more secretive than the Nixon administration. They don't believe the American people or Congress have any right to information.

— Larry Klayman, chairman, Judicial Watch

Nothing about George W. Bush struck me as secretive, dangerous, or the slightest bit Nixonian when he first ambled onto the national political scene. On the contrary, I saw an easygoing, back-slapping son of a former president, a hail-fellow-well-met politician whose family name and pleasing manner had landed him in the Texas governor's mansion, where he employed his considerable people skills as a onetime prep-school cheerleader and college fraternity president. He presented himself in the early 2000 presidential primaries as a nice guy, not deep, not too bright, and not terribly serious. We've not had a lot of presidential candidates playing doofus, as he did regularly for the press.[1] Bush appeared anything but driven in seeking the nation's highest office, seeming actually rather uninterested in power. I had the impression he was running for the hell of it or because so many others thought he could be elected.

My first impression was altered slightly during South Carolina's presidential primary in February 2000, when the Bush folks went after Arizona senator John McCain. Molly Ivins, the Texas columnist who has followed Bush for years, later called it Karl Rove's "East Texas special," a barrage of false rumors that chased McCain like storm troopers around the state.[2] First it was rumored that McCain was gay, then that he was a tomcat who cheated on his first wife. (Inconsistency is not a problem for political gossipmongers and mudslingers.) Next came a pamphlet claiming that McCain's wife, Cindy, was "a drug addict." When cruelly exploiting Cindy's brief addiction to prescription painkillers didn't work, they said McCain was crazy — too long at the Hanoi Hilton as a POW. But that was a tough sell, so finally they played the race card. Since some South Carolinians still salute the Stars and Bars, a picture of McCain's adopted daughter, a beautiful dark-skinned girl born in Bangladesh, was circulated to sons and daughters of the Confederacy in rural areas. Rove's "East Texas special" worked and Bush knocked off his only real Republican rival.

The South Carolina contest made clear that Bush wanted the Republican nomination much more than his casual manner suggested. Dirty political tactics, even when done in a way that provides deniability for the candidate, in fact always have the blessing of that candidate; anyone who thinks otherwise is not merely naive but uninformed. Thus, it was clear after South Carolina that Bush played hardball, that he played dirty, and that he was playing for keeps.

Suffice it to say that all this piqued my interest. I knew a little bit about Karl Rove, for I'd first learned about him decades earlier when I was working with the Watergate Special Prosecutor's Office. Even back then they were asking questions about him. I had never heard of Rove, but assistant Watergate special prosecutor Richard Davis — who was investigating political dirty tricks such as leaking stolen campaign information, infiltrating an opponent's campaign operations during the presidential primaries, and using unidentified negative campaign advertisements — had Rove on his radar. The questions Davis and his assistants asked me suggested that Rove was a political operator who played at the edge of the rules, if not beyond them.[3]

More political shenanigans surfaced after the November 2000 deadlock, when Bush's operatives were openly trying to disrupt the recount in Florida's Dade County; young people were flown in from Washington, D.C., to chant and stomp in the hallways of the building where the recounting was being conducted, to bang threateningly on doors, and to agitate mobs in the Miami streets with bullhorns — all to intimidate the Florida election officials. Watching these political high jinks made me think of my former Nixon White House colleagues, for they too believed in such down and dirty, if not corrupt, electioneering. Anyone familiar with the operations of a presidential campaign must appreciate that this well-financed and covertly directed activity had been blessed by the top of the Bush campaign. Had George Bush wanted to stop it, such activity would have been stopped.*

By pure chance, at the outset of the new Bush administration I happened to read a column by William McKenzie, a *Dallas Morning News* editorial writer, who noted that Bush's presidential campaign was highly reminiscent of Nixon's 1968 campaign.[4] McKenzie, alluding to Nixon's theme of bringing the

---

*To distinguish George Walker Bush, the forty-third and incumbent president, from his father, George Herbert Walker Bush, the forty-first president, I typically refer to the father as Bush senior, Poppy Bush, or the Bush I administration, as opposed to the Bush II administration of the son. Throughout, unless otherwise indicated, I simply use *Bush* when referring to the son and incumbent president, George W. Bush.

country together, concluded that "Bush probably won't like thinking of himself as Richard Nixon's potential heir. But the unifying, constructive [perhaps he meant *compassionate*] conservatism he favors seems similar to the government Nixon envisioned." McKenzie's piece struck a chord for me. From what I had seen of Bush's campaign and the vote recount, I wondered if there were more similarities between Nixon and Bush than McKenzie, or anyone else, realized.

Nixon Vis-à-Vis Bush

During the early months of Bush's presidency, I read his campaign autobiography, *A Charge to Keep*, which was ghosted by Karen Hughes (his longtime press aide), a work described by the *Texas Observer* as "a political memoir so bad that reviewers have been calling around looking for ghost readers to review it." Indeed, this selective history is almost useless. But I had accumulated material about Bush during the 2000 campaign, which I went through — newspaper and magazine profiles and reports, plus *Shrub* by Molly Ivins and Lou Dubose.[5] Additionally, I spoke with friends who knew the Bush family, or Junior, but was surprised to discover widespread concern, if not genuine fear, of speaking openly about Bush or his family. Repeatedly I was told that Bush is known for taking revenge against those who fail to hold the family's confidences.

Others, I discovered, were noticing Bush's Nixonian traits, too. On August 9, 2001, Bush announced his controversial decision to limit federal support of stem-cell research (which effectively meant ending it). After much purported moral anguish and agonizing, he claimed there would be "more than sixty" cell lines available for this life-saving federally funded research, but no more. A *New York Times* Op-Ed piece on Bush's decision appeared the next day by Richard Brookhiser, a senior editor of the *National Review*. In examining the new president's decision making, Brookhiser concluded that "George W. Bush's strategies seem most like those of Richard Nixon, who knew the conservative temperament and was willing to summon it." Brookhiser added: "For pro-lifers and other conservatives, George W. Bush may be Richard Nixon, without the restless intelligence or the paranoia."[6] Later, of course, a bit of what might be considered good ol' Nixonian duplicity became evident in Bush's decision, since there are, in fact, only ten cell lines, not sixty.[7]

Time and additional information have reinforced my initial reaction of Bush vis-à-vis Nixon. Several journalists who cover the White House, those old enough or astute enough to be familiar with Nixon, have also recognized the pronounced patterns of similarity of these men.[8] Without seeking to make more of this fact than it deserved but finding it impossible to ignore, I began comparing the two men seriously.

With today's presidents, what you see is not what you actually have; rather, it is what they want you to see. Both Nixon and Bush invested greatly in projecting carefully crafted public images. In fact, Bush picked up where Nixon left off in attention to presidential imagery, far exceeding even the image-crafted presidency of Ronald Reagan. Nixon's image, for example, was that of a hardworking, brainy world leader who was constantly upgrading to "new Nixon" editions. Bush, on the other hand, has stayed with basically one image, which he latched onto as governor of Texas but has refined as president. He projects the plain-talking CEO of American, Inc., just a regular and likable guy from Midland, Texas. While there is some truth to these Nixon and Bush images, they are also deceptions — for neither man is really his crafted picture, just as no actor is the character he or she portrays onstage or before the camera.

Take Nixon. Though highly intelligent, he did not have the raw brain power, for example, of his chief of staff Bob Haldeman (with a Mensa-level IQ) or the intellectual prowess of his national security advisor, Henry Kissinger. Yet it was important to Nixon to be seen as something of a closet intellectual. Indeed, he was bookish and intellectually curious, but more important, he was highly disciplined, if not driven. Nixon was a grinder — as a student, as a member of Congress, as a vice president, as a lawyer appearing before the U.S. Supreme Court, and as a president. He pored through mountains of papers, studied issues deeply, and worked hard to understand matters before publicly addressing them or making decisions. Because of his years of hard work, his long experience with government, and his focus and interest, Nixon as president was able to assimilate large amounts of raw data and synthesize it quickly and accurately. He appeared the master of extemporaneous speaking, when in fact such talks were the product of great diligence, for he had all but memorized his material. Through sheer determination, he made himself "smart." Yet his countless hours of privately taped conversations reveal that without preparation, he was not a particularly fast study of unfamiliar subjects, nor naturally articulate. Most damning, of course, his tapes show him to be highly manipulative, dishonest, distrusting, and always able to say something nasty about everyone with whom he dealt.

Bush, on the other hand, is not as intellectually handicapped and inarticulate as many "misunderestimate" him to be. No question he is mentally shallow, intellectually lazy, and incurious.[9] He reads little more than his speeches, since his staff briefs him orally on the news, and he demands very short memos and as little homework as possible. Yet he has an abundance of natural intelligence, which he is willing to employ when interested in a subject. He was the only pledge at his Yale fraternity who could flawlessly recite the names of all fifty of his pledge brothers. He has a vast knowledge of baseball. Behind closed doors, when talking with those with whom he is comfortable, his malaprops are rare and he is surprisingly articulate.[10] When he has been interested or deeply concerned about a matter, he is a very fast study. If so inclined, he can also quickly rehearse a speech, and when he concentrates he can deliver his written speeches with eloquence. But seldom does he want to dig or focus or work hard. He has succeeded in life without doing much mental heavy lifting, and only on rare occasions has he done so as president. All the CEOs I know — and I know a number who have run Forbes 500 organizations — work much harder than our CEO-in-chief — plus they know far more about their business and its operations and policies than does Bush.

Like Nixon, Bush is also a bit of a loner. This is not to say these men don't have many and good friends, for they do. But their friends are all pretested, for these are men who don't want strangers around and feel safe only with people who are known to keep their mouths shut. While Bush has far more natural people skills than Nixon, he is actually more antisocial than Nixon. "He doesn't socialize a whole lot," noted Jeanne Cummings of the *Wall Street Journal*.[11] This has caused the Washington social scene to come to a screeching halt during his administration. "It's part of the pathological secrecy they have," Diana McClellan, a veteran social observer and former Washington society-page columnist, said, adding, "They don't want to go out and blab things about. He's [referring to Bush] like Greta Garbo — 'to talk about me is to betray me.'"[12]

Also like Nixon, Bush holds a rather formal view of the presidency. For example, Nixon refused to wear anything other than a white shirt, believing to do otherwise would be unpresidential. "The president doesn't wear a blue shirt," he once roared at a media adviser. Bush demands that he and his staff always wear a coat and tie in the working areas of the White House. Bush, like Nixon, is a decidedly punctual and highly scheduled president (with both giving themselves private time each day: Nixon to nap, Bush to exercise). Both men developed their view of the presidency from watching up close presidents they greatly respected: Nixon as Eisenhower's vice president, Bush as the son of a president. Nevertheless, there is a certain hypocrisy about the straitlaced formality of both the Nixon and Bush presidencies, for both men are known to be privately profane and to enjoy locker-room language to show that they are also one of the guys (with Bush even using the f-word in front of female staff, something Nixon did not do).[13]

Although Bush is capable of far more empathy for others than was Nixon, and his emotions are closer to the surface than Nixon's, he is not really the hail-fellow-well-met guy he pretends to be (but he has felt he must play this game in public much of his life). White House correspondents traveling with Bush have noticed his aloofness. "He's very lofty. He views the presidency as lofty, and he uses the power of the presidency and the position itself to enhance his goals," Jeanne Cummings said in a statement that could just as easily have been made about Nixon. Cummings, who has traveled abroad with Bush (as well as with Clinton, who enjoyed meeting the ordinary people when in foreign countries), has further reported that Bush has "no interaction with the everyday people in the [foreign] countries"; rather, he meets only with kings, queens, prime ministers, and ambassadors — those he apparently feels befitting his visiting potentate status.[14]

Both Nixon and Bush learned their presidential politics from the inside. Nixon from in the arena. Bush apprenticed as an aide on his father's many campaigns: the unsuccessful runs for the

U.S. Senate (1964 and 1970), his successful run for the House of Representatives (1969), and his runs for the presidency or vice presidency (1980, 1984 and 1988, and 1992). In addition, Bush worked as a political consultant on several U.S. Senate campaigns in Florida and Alabama. He ran his own campaigns, for Congress unsuccessfully (1978) and twice successfully for governor of Texas (1994 and 1998).

Along the way, Bush was tutored in the world of mud politics by a master: Lee Atwater. When Atwater, who directed George H. W. Bush's 1988 presidential campaign (said to be the dirtiest in American history to that date), died at age forty with a brain tumor, the press was as gentle as possible under the circumstances in describing his campaigning style: "He relished operating on the edges of propriety and to members of his party he was a genius in defining and exploiting the weaknesses of his opponents. To his critics, however, he was a symbol of the dark side of American politics."[15] His legacy is being perpetuated by Bush and his political adviser, Karl Rove, a longtime friend and associate of Atwater's. Indeed, in using Rove, Bush may have stepped up a notch over Nixon. When I asked one of my former colleagues who has had dealings with Rove what he was like, I was given a shorthand answer: "He's Haldeman and Ehrlichman, all in one."*

No doubt because much of my focus on the Bush II presidency has been on what is going on behind the scenes, I have taken notice of Cheney's powerful role. In fact, this presidency cannot be understood without taking into account Cheney's influence on Bush, for in many ways it is a co-presidency. Cheney, however, prefers the shadows. As a dozen *Time* magazine

---

*Those who say Karl Rove is Bush's political brain are wrong, but both men like the arrangement, for it flatters Rove while getting Bush off the hook for the hardball dirty campaigns he runs.

reporters focusing on Cheney discovered, "he loathes . . . [the] retail kind of politics, the gripping-and-grinning, baby-kissing, self-aggrandizing, self-abnegating politics. Cheney loves and flourishes in a different political arena. It is the one that few outsiders see, the one in which, particularly in this Administration, all decisions are made. It is the politics of governance at the highest level, in the White House, where the art of guiding the decision-making process is practiced by some of the most skilled inside-the-room players in Washington. And it is the politics at which Cheney is unrivaled."[16]

It was pure curiosity about the Nixon parallels that started my inquiry, but it was the troubling Nixonian secrecy that kept it going, because I did not want to believe where the Bush II presidency was headed. By the time former *Los Angeles Times* reporter Jack Nelson, a seasoned Washington correspondent, reported that "no president since Richard Nixon has been as secretive or as combative about leaks as George W. Bush," I had become sufficiently concerned about Bush and Cheney to have written several columns and a *New York Times* Op-Ed piece about it, as well as an open letter to Karl Rove.[17] After Rove told the *New York Times* there was nothing to be learned from the Nixon presidency, I wrote him that I couldn't imagine the Bush administration wanted to risk repeating the mistakes of the Nixon presidency. I pointed out that "the continuing insistence on secrecy by your White House is startlingly Nixonian. I'm talking about everything from stiffing Congressional requests for information and witnesses, to employing an executive order to demolish the 1978 law providing public access to presidential papers, to forcing the Government Accounting Office to go to Court to obtain information about how the White House is spending tax money when creating a pro-energy industry Vice Presidential task force. The Bush Administration apparently seeks to reverse the post-Watergate trend of open government."[18] Not surprisingly, there was no response.

•   Worse than Nixon's Secrecy

There has been little study of presidential secrecy and even less study of its consequences. Presidential secrecy is typically examined by looking at the uses (or abuses) of "executive privilege" in withholding information from Congress, the uses (and abuses) of the national security classification system, or how the First Amendment's press freedom has fared under given presidents. All these are certainly manifestations of presidential secrecy, but they are anything but its full measure.

No president can govern without some secrecy (better described as confidentiality or privacy). Confidentiality is essential to developing and implementing both domestic and foreign policy.* Without privacy a president could not gather necessary information, explore options and alternatives, obtain unfettered advice, or undertake such deliberations as needed to make proper decisions. No one seriously doubts a president's need for appropriate operating space for himself and his staff. Nor is there real dispute that the government is justified in many situations in withholding information if its distribution or publication will harm the national security, improperly invade personal privacy, unjustly publicize trade or commercial secrets, or negatively jeopardize the government's law enforcement responsibilities. These are all justifiable uses of secrecy, although they can be

---

*American philosopher Sissela Bok, who explores secrecy in public and private contexts in her classic work *Secrets: On the Ethics of Concealment and Revelation*, has found "concealment, or hiding, to be the defining traits of secrecy," while privacy is "the condition of being protected from unwanted access by others — either physical access, personal information, or attention."

(and often are) abused. But in a democratic society, all use of secrecy must be questioned, and if it cannot be justified, it is antithetical to a self-governing society. As James Madison famously put it, "a popular government without popular information, or the means of acquiring it, is but a prologue to a farce or tragedy, perhaps both. Knowledge will forever govern ignorance; and a people who mean to be their own governors must arm themselves with the power which knowledge gives."[19]

Presidential secrecy has been closely associated with the role of commander in chief. Early presidents limited their secrecy mostly to matters of war, treaty negotiations, and covert military operations (which I have largely excluded from coverage, although Bush and Cheney have made the most aggressive use of the CIA and intelligence community of any presidency). Presidential secrecy expanded with Abraham Lincoln and Woodrow Wilson, because of war. Ironically, before becoming president, both men had been outspoken critics of such secrecy. As a young Illinois congressman, Lincoln took President James Polk to task for his secrecy during the Mexican War. As president, Lincoln employed extraordinary and extraconstitutional powers to preserve the Union. Woodrow Wilson, writing as a young scholar, declared, "Light is the only thing that can sweeten our political atmosphere." As a candidate for president in 1912 he made secrecy a campaign issue, contending that "government ought to be all outside and no inside. I, for my part, believe there ought to be no place where anything can be done [by government] that everybody does not know about." As president, however, Wilson was highly secretive. He was less than forthright when campaigning for reelection in 1916, promising to keep the United States out of the European war, yet in 1917 he asked Congress for a declaration of war, along with some of the most repressive secrecy laws ever written, the Espionage Act of 1917 and the Sedition Act of 1918. After suffering a debilitating stroke in 1919, Wilson used secrecy (with the help of his wife and a few aides) to maintain his presidency, hiding his almost total incapacity to govern effectively.

Presidential secrecy was further expanded during World War II. Franklin D. Roosevelt used secrecy for personal, political, and governmental purposes. His love affair with Lucy Mercer was kept a secret, and he concealed his various government actions for purely political and personal reasons. He was the first of several presidents to be seduced by the queen of Washington secrecy, FBI director J. Edgar Hoover. For Hoover, secrets were coinage of the realm, and he offered, and FDR accepted, secret information from the FBI's files. FDR used the Bureau to secretly investigate everyone from his potential political opponents to his wife.[20]

Following World War II, the Cold War years became the dark ages of government secrecy. Of all the Cold War presidents, none was more secretive than Nixon, who admitted, after leaving office, that as his presidency progressed, he became "paranoiac, or almost a basket case with regard to secrecy."[21] Nixon's White House was so secretive that the Joint Chiefs of Staff believed it necessary (for military preparedness and national security) to plant a spy in the National Security Council, who literally pilfered information from Henry Kissinger's briefcase, made copies, and sent relevant documents to the Joint Chiefs. When Nixon's aides uncovered this spy operation (which was also leaking information to the news media), nothing was done other than to end it, because further action might have revealed the pervasive nature of Nixon's secrecy. So tight was information held that Secretary of State William Rogers and Secretary of Defense Melvin Laird were not aware of Kissinger's back-channel negotiations with the North Vietnamese to end the war and didn't have a clue about his plans with China until just before Nixon made the information public. Such secrecy prevailed in every part of Nixon's highly compartmentalized White House, with information available only on a "need to know" basis. (The counsel's office, as it happened, learned a lot from its mid-level perch in the hierarchy.) Suffice it to say, with secrets being kept from insiders who had every right — indeed, responsibility — to know, the prospects of the public being informed were nil.

"Deception, including frequent concealment and resorting to covert operations, as well as misleading the public in large ways, was a hallmark of Nixon's handling of foreign policy throughout his presidency," notes William Bundy in his study of Nixon's foreign policy.[22] Robert Gates, who served in the Nixon administration and went on to work for five additional presidents at the National Security Council or Central Intelligence Agency, describes the Nixon years as "a time of secret deals and public obfuscation (and deception), reflecting more accurately than they imagined the personalities of its principal architects [referring Kissinger and Nixon]."[23] While Bundy acknowledges that other Cold War presidents used deception and similarly savored secrecy, with Nixon "the taste for acting secretly was obsessive." Bundy too finds that Nixon paid dearly, for his potentially great foreign policy accomplishments "were in large measure offset or made worthless by his consistent practice of deception, through secret actions and especially through actions inconsistent with his public positions."[24]

Ironically, Nixon's practices resulted in serious attempts to end unnecessary government secrecy. Even before Nixon had left office, Congress enacted the Federal Advisory Committee Act to open the doors of the executive branch to otherwise private advisory committee meetings. With Nixon departed, the once toothless and often ignored Freedom of Information Act

(FOIA), first adopted in 1966, was amended over President Ford's veto. Also in late 1974, Congress passed the Privacy Act, which gives citizens the right to information the government may have in its files about them. In 1976, Congress enacted the Government in the Sunshine Act, which requires all agencies headed by more than one presidential appointee to open their meetings to the public. And in 1978, Congress adopted the Presidential Records Act, giving Americans ownership of papers and records of all presidents and their staffs and making this information publicly available no later than twelve years after a president leaves office. These new laws, which have had a profound impact on government secrecy, are a start but do not deal with the large problem of years of overclassification of national security information.

Bill Clinton, the first post–Cold War president, sought to end that problem and did so, with Democrats controlling Congress, until Newt Gingrich took over in 1995. Gingrich pretty much ended the joint presidential and congressional efforts to open government, but by then, New York senator Patrick Moynihan, a former member of the cabinet or subcabinet of Presidents Kennedy, Johnson, Nixon, and Ford, managed to get legislation enacted to create a bipartisan government-funded study of secrecy, the Commission on Protecting and Reducing Government Secrecy. Moynihan, who chaired the three-year undertaking, changed his thinking about secrecy because of this experience, realizing the undemocratic and senseless mess existing policies had created — for example, literally mountains of highly classified documents that have little to do with national security, long outdated information going back to World War I, World War II, Korea, and Vietnam. Moynihan's work found a receptive president in Clinton, who by executive order started declassifying the enormous backlog of information, forcing the automatic release of literally *billions* of classified documents. His order made all national security classifications expire after twenty-five years, unless the head of a department or agency with jurisdiction over the subject matter claimed that continued classification was necessary for a particular document. By shifting the burden in favor of declassification, Clinton's order turned the old system upside down. As overwhelming evidence in the following chapters shows, Bush and Cheney seek to reverse this trend toward open government. They are once again closing government, and their practice and policy started long before the September 11, 2001, terror attacks. In fact, 9/11 merely provided an additional excuse for more concealment.

Again, there is a parallel. Nixon's secrecy became obsessive after Daniel Ellsberg leaked the so-called Pentagon Papers, a forty-volume collection of highly classified information found in a Defense Department study of the origins of the Vietnam War. For Nixon, this was an act of information/disclosure terrorism, threatening his ability to govern. It changed the Nixon White House, as 9/11 changed the Bush White House. Because of the Pentagon Papers leak, Nixon adopted an ends-justifies-the-means approach to government. His thinking, as he headed his presidency toward what would prove its resulting ruin, is revealing if not instructive:

> In hindsight I can see that, once I realized the Vietnam war could not be ended quickly or easily [which became evident when the North Vietnamese slammed the door on his secret peace talks following the Pentagon Papers leak] and that I was going to be up against an anti-war movement that was able to dominate the media with its attitudes and values, I was sometimes drawn into the very frame of mind I so despised in the leaders of that movement. They increasingly came to justify almost anything in the name of

forcing an immediate end to a war they considered unjustified and immoral. I was similarly driven to preserve the government's ability to conduct foreign policy and to conduct it in the way that I felt would best bring peace. I believed that national security was involved. I still believe it today, and in the same circumstances, I would act now as I did then. History will make the final judgment on the actions, reactions, and excesses of both sides; it is a judgment I do not fear.[25]

If any historian has favorably judged Nixon's actions, rationalizations, justifications, and thinking favorably, I have been unable to find it. His most sympathetic biographer/hagiographer is Jonathan Aitken, an admiring former member of Parliament and minister of state for defense in Great Britain who had met the retired Nixon and was deeply impressed. (Aitken wrote his Nixon paean before his own conviction and imprisonment for perjury.)[26] Yet even Aitken, who fills his work with distortions and misinformation, is unable to muster a favorable appraisal of Nixon's reaction to the Pentagon Papers. "Thus, the slide toward Watergate began with the misconceived reaction to the Pentagon Papers," Aitken writes, adding, "The reality was that the importance of Ellsberg's theft of the Pentagon Papers was wildly exaggerated. Both the press and the White House were at fault here. For his part, Nixon was unbelievably badly advised about the national security implications of Ellsberg's grave misconduct. On the basis of that advice he overreacted and his responses had the unforeseeable knock-on effects of transforming the underground of the White House from a juvenile sideshow to a sinister force."[27] So too, as I will show, for 9/11 — but with even greater overreaction.

Such presidents as Franklin Roosevelt, Truman, Eisenhower, Reagan, and Clinton have filled the presidential office, happily exercising their temporary grant of the great powers and fully enjoying themselves, notwithstanding the demands of the office. Even when times were grim, it was clear they wanted to be exactly where they were. But like Nixon, rather than truly becoming the president, Bush plays the role of being president (sometimes well and other times poorly). Note the telling way both men have talked about their jobs. Nixon constantly referred to "the president" doing this or that, as if the president were someone other than himself. Similarly, Bush discusses his job in the third person, as did Nixon: "First of all, a president has got to be the calcium in the backbone," "The job of the president is to unite a nation to achieve big objectives," "A president likes to have a military plan that will be successful," "I'm the commander — see, I don't need to explain — I do not need to explain why I say things. That's the interesting thing about being the president."[28] Seldom have other presidents talked this way, for they saw themselves as president.

This tendency to separate self from title is more than a verbal tic, and anything but an act of humility. For both Nixon and Bush it reflects a kind of inoculation and immunization from the impact of their decisions, and a further buffer and rationalization from disclosing those decisions. It is almost as if they are saying that it wasn't them who did it, but rather someone else, that presidential character. At the same time, they give themselves a distance and implied fruitlessness in trying to find out what was really done, a sort of "don't ask me — I wasn't involved." Big clues evolve from little ones. When a president separates himself from his actions — his official actions — it reveals a fear both of being identified with those actions and of officially taking responsibility but privately shirking it. With George Bush, the fear and dodging is understandable. He and his administration have engaged in some of the most deplorable activities in modern American political history. And they know what they're doing, using secrecy and its handmaidens — obfuscation, deception, stonewalling, and lying — to remain unaccountable, when possible, which is merely further evidence of dissonance between the man and his high office. Dick Cheney, on the other hand, appears to find the sort of pleasure in power that medieval warlords once did.

Never before have we had a pair of rulers — it is difficult to call them leaders — like Bush and Cheney, men whose obsession with control of information, and spin, is so strong that they are willing to subvert the democratic process for their own short-term personal political gain. Not since Nixon left the White House have we had such greed over presidential power, and never before have we had such political paranoia. When I first began to compare Nixon and Bush, I assumed that their similarities would be superficial. Unfortunately, they are not. History never exactly repeats itself, but it does some rather good imitations. It is remarkable that Nixon and his past are prologue for the Bush and Cheney presidency. But so it is. And as I show, the echo resonating through time is coming from the lower notes of Nixon's era.

Chapter Two

Stonewalling

I don't give a shit what happens, I want you all to stonewall it.

— Richard Nixon

Stonewalling is one of secrecy's more truculent servants. Bush and Cheney started stonewalling during their 2000 run for the White House; they haven't stopped yet, either running or stonewalling. At first, they stonewalled only matters they claimed to be personal and private and, therefore, off-limits. When they succeeded with this ploy, even though the public by all prior standards had a right to the information that both Bush and Cheney insisted on withholding, it emboldened them and they carried their stonewalling into the White House, where it has grown even more encompassing.

Understandably, presidential candidates (and presidents) do not like talking about matters they consider personal and private, particularly when the information reveals problems or prior misconduct. But to seek and attain the presidency (or vice presidency) is to voluntarily give up much of one's privacy. The *National Review* has flatly stated that "a presidential candidate, in the role he aspires to, is not a private person."[1] Hardly less can be said about those who attain the office. When private matters become public business, privacy must yield. This certainly did not seem to be an issue for Republicans when they recently insisted that the then president reveal whether or not his erect, and very democratic/Democratic, penis had "distinguishing characteristics." Indeed, with such demands Republicans obliterated all the remaining areas of personal presidential privacy.[2] Notre Dame University professor of journalism, ethics, and democracy Robert Schmuhl has said that presidential aspirants are (or should be) told by their political advisers that "prominence and power notwithstanding, presidents . . . have to cope with the probable — yes probable — disclosure of any fact or rumor that suggests 'a dark side' or murky motive" regarding any and all aspects of their private and public lives.[3] Obviously, some disclosures are relevant and some are not. Equally obvious, some can be used unfairly against a candidate or president. But when the U.S. Supreme Court looked at the question, they held that a president's privacy must be balanced against the right of the public to know.[4]

However, the Court provided no real guidance whatsoever, since for all practical purposes, it has consistently held that the public has the right to know anything the news media deems "newsworthy" about public figures (and public officials), as long as the information is understood by the publisher of the information to be true.[5] Common sense guides journalists and public judgment, and it is widely agreed that matters relating to character, such as honesty and integrity, and a candidate's background are appropriate areas for exploration. Another area that has consistently been deemed not only fair but necessary is the health of a candidate for the highest office. From the outset of the Bush-Cheney 2000 campaign, and throughout their first term, questions relating to background, character, and health have been consistently stonewalled. Thus, they have refused to provide information that the public, by all prior standards, has the right to know.

The Character Issue

Voters believe that good character is the first essential for presidents (and vice presidents).[6] Accordingly, when presidential candidate Gary Hart invited scrutiny of his private sex life in 1987 by challenging the news media to catch him fooling around, reporters from the *Miami Herald* did just that and ended his candidacy. Character inquiries regularly probe a candidate's (or president's) financial dealings. In 1992, for example, the *New York Times* initiated its inquiry into President Clinton's pre-presidential business affairs, focusing on his investment in a failed land deal at Whitewater, Arkansas. That inquiry prompted an independent counsel investigation, which took on a life of its own and spanned the entirety of his presidency — only to find no financial impropriety by the president or his wife. Journalists regularly look for conflicts of interest, graft, shady dealings, hypocrisy, and duplicity.

Bush made character an issue in his 2000 campaign, and by doing so he asked voters to judge his character. It started when Bush, and his campaign, questioned the character of Senator John McCain in the primaries, and then Vice President Al Gore's character in the general election. Yet Bush simply refuses to answer questions about his own background and character. More remarkably, he has gotten away with it. For example, Bush ran repeated television ads questioning Gore's character, claiming that Gore had switched his position on debating, with his ad proclaiming: "If we can't trust Al Gore on debates, why should we trust him on anything?"[7] Yet when forced to admit his own long concealed drunken-driving arrest, which he said he had wanted "to keep secret so he would not be a bad role model for his teenage daughters and other children," Bush refused to elaborate. Instead, he went on the attack, making the issue who had reported his drunk-driving arrest so late in the campaign, so the messenger became the issue, not his actions. No modern president has risen so high revealing so little information about himself.

Bush's Hidden Background

While Bush claims to be independent of dynasty, before being elected president, he was both running on his family name and being given a pass because of it. For the public and reporters, Bush's formative years — which he extends to age forty — are out of bounds. Yet those are the years when one's character and values are formed. During his 1994 campaign for governor of Texas, Bush acknowledged that as a "young man" he had on occasion overindulged with alcohol and been a bit of an irresponsible youth. Asked in 1999 if he had been an alcoholic, he said he did not think he was "clinically an alcoholic," although one of his close friends countered that "there's a fine line between heavy social drinking and alcoholism" — close enough for a friend to have raised it with Bush.[8] During the 2000 campaign, he was asked if he had ever used marijuana or cocaine. Bush said, "I'm not going to talk about what I did as a child," adding, "What's relevant is that I have learned from any mistakes I made."[9] And yet it was impossible to know what he learned, since he refused to explain what he had learned from, and once again he turned the issue from the allegations against him to who was making them.

Before launching his presidential campaign, Bush hired a private investigator to snoop into his own past to see what others might discover about his personal life and financial activities.[10] Knowing his worst-case downside, during the campaign he told the news media, "I will not play the game of political 'gotcha.' I will not respond to the rumor du jour. I have told people what they need to know about me."[11] But his defiance has only raised more questions: Was he just a party guy until he turned forty, or does he have a serious problem with alcohol? What about that missing time during his military service — was Bush AWOL? Has he truly replaced abusive substances with healthy running, making endorphins his new drug of choice? And what about the rumors that Prozac is for Bush what Dilantin was for Nixon?[12] Or the rumors he has been nipping a bit? Does alcohol remove inhibitions and show the real, albeit darker, inner self (who had no problem calling a *Wall Street Journal* columnist, accompanied by his wife and young child, a "fucking son of a bitch")?[13]

Clearly, Bush is ashamed and embarrassed by his personal behavior during the first four decades of his life. But why refuse to talk about one's business affairs as well? Business conduct is a good way to judge character, if not a person's acumen. "When Bush is asked to cite the career accomplishments of which he is most proud," the *Washington Post* reported, "they begin at the age of 42, when he led an investment group that bought the Texas Rangers."[14] His official White House biography is notable in that between his graduation from Harvard Business School in 1975 and his work helping run the Texas Rangers baseball team, his only reported activity is working on his father's 1988 presidential campaign. There is a reason for this.

When questioned about his business dealings, Bush bristles at the suggestion that his family name and father's prominence were significant factors in his business success (or stated differently, in repeated saves from serious business and financial failures).[15] But one need only look at his record, which he has been unable to bury, to see that such was not the case. Bush had only *one* business success in his entire career; the rest, which he will not discuss, were a string of failures. Virtually every reporter who has examined Bush's business career has found that his father's influence was pervasive and decisive. "Bush's entire business career was built on little more than the kindness rich men often bestow on the children of powerful politicians," Richard Cohen concluded after his investigation at the *Washington Post*.[16] Byron York, an investigative writer for the *American Spectator* (not exactly a Republican-hostile publication), similarly concluded that "if one superimposes a timeline over the Bush career path, one sees that his rise in business coincides with his father's rise to the highest levels of government. . . . But it may be that — provided no evidence of wrongdoing emerges — there's little more to say than the obvious: Of course Bush benefited from his connections, but that's just the way the world works."[17] There is, however, more to say, because there is evidence of wrongdoing.

Bush's claims about his one successful venture with the Texas Rangers are well known. He used it to run for governor and featured it prominently in his 1999 campaign biography, in which he recounts how he was working on his father's 1988 presidential campaign when he had a call from Bill DeWitt Jr., a Cincinnati businessman. He leaves out the part about how four years earlier, DeWitt (a Yale and Harvard graduate like himself) bailed him out of his first business venture — Arbusto (Spanish for "bush"), later renamed Bush Exploration. After going through millions, in 1984 the Arbusto/Bush Exploration operation had one asset left — the unsuccessful son of the vice president of the United States. Bill DeWitt merged Bush's company into Spectrum 7. With Bush serving as chairman and CEO, Spectrum 7 quickly failed. But another oil-exploration company, Harken Oil, was eager to have George W. Bush's name on its board.

George Soros, a part owner of Harken, who was not active in the management of the company but was aware of its activities, later told Washington journalist David Corn, "We were buying political influence. That was it. [Bush] was not much of a businessman."[18] David Rubenstein, the cofounder and managing director of the Carlyle Group, a group of top-level former Washington officials who until recently touted Bush's father as one of their high-profile advisers, has shared an account of Bush as a director. In 2001, Rubenstein gave a public speech to the Los Angeles County Employees Retirement Association, not aware the event was being recorded.

Rubenstein explained that in 1991 one of Bush's friends said, "Look, there is a guy who would like to be on the board [of Caterair]," an airline-catering company the Carlyle Group had just acquired from Marriott. Rubenstein continued, "[So] we put [Bush] on the board and [he] spent three years. Came to all the meetings. Told a lot of jokes — not that many clean ones. And after a while I kind of said to him, after about three years, you know, I'm not sure this is really for you. Maybe you should do something else. Because I don't think you're adding that much value to the board. You don't know that much about the company." (Of course, the punch line to this story is that Bush did do something else — he became the president of the United States. Rubenstein said that he has not "been invited to the White House for any things.")[19] Savvy business people such as Rubenstein know talent when they see it, and Bush didn't have it.

At Harken, Bush was relieved of day-to-day management responsibility but still served on the board of directors. So when Bill DeWitt called in 1988, during the campaign, who can really doubt he was looking for a bit more of that magic Bush name? DeWitt, whose family once owned the Cincinnati Reds baseball team, told Bush when he called that he had heard from others in baseball that the Texas Rangers might be for sale.* "This could be a natural for you," Bush quotes DeWitt as telling him.[20] It was, for Bush loves baseball and, as a matter of fact, just happened to know the owner of the Texas Rangers, Eddie Chiles, a longtime supporter of his father. Chiles's widow has said that when Eddie learned of Bush's interest, he didn't want to deal with anyone else. This fact made Bush instrumental to the deal. But neither Bush nor DeWitt (apparently) nor the other potential partners Bush rounded up had the $86 million that Chiles wanted to sell his ball club. According to the *Wall Street Journal*'s account (which differs significantly from Bush's autobiography), following "a pattern repeated through his business career, Mr. Bush's play did not quite make the grade." Rather, "Baseball Commissioner Peter Ueberroth stepped in, brokering a deal that brought Fort Worth financier Richard Rainwater together with the Bush group. Mr. Ueberroth's pitch to Mr. Rainwater was that he join the deal partly 'out of respect' for President Bush."[21] Also brought in was a successful Harvard MBA, Edward "Rusty" Rose III (who'd made his millions in the nasty business of short selling overvalued companies).[22] It was agreed that Rusty would crunch numbers and run the club's finances, and Bush would be the front man. The deal went through, and Bush had his baseball team while DeWitt and the others could now further leverage the presence of the president's son. Their next step was to get a new stadium built. The stadium would

---

*In October 2003, Bush appointed his friend William O. DeWitt Jr. to the sixteen-member Foreign Intelligence Advisory Board, which requires a clearance so high that it is classified. The FIAB is supposed to keep an eye on the intelligence community and let the president know if they are doing their job. See *Cincinnati Enquirer* (Oct. 10, 2003).

turn out to be the source of the money Bush made with the Texas Rangers, and making that money would involve a fair bit of very dubious wheeling and dealing with public money.

Karen Hughes describes the spin placed on the deal in Bush's autobiography. It is called "a public-private partnership, in which the Rangers put up part of the money to construct a new stadium, and the citizens of Arlington would put up the rest, using a half cent of the sales tax allocated for economic development" — an arrangement Bush says he was "comfortable with . . . so long as taxpayers of Arlington knew all the facts and were allowed to vote on the proposition."[23] Bush says this "ingenious plan" was embraced by "another big thinker, the mayor of Arlington, Richard Greene." But keep your eye on the shell covering the part of the deal "in which the Rangers put up part of the money to construct a new stadium."

According to the *American Spectator*, it was, in fact, nothing short of a bait and switch on Texas voters. Bush and his partners were to receive $135 million from the city of Arlington, of an estimated $189 million needed to build a new stadium. "Arlington Mayor Richard Greene aggressively promoted the deal," the *American Spectator* reported, by explaining the alleged benefit to the city, justifying the half cent sales tax and promising that "the Rangers would put in $30 million 'up front, like a down payment on a house,' to get the deal going." Not until voters had overwhelmingly approved the deal was it revealed that "the Rangers would *not* produce the money up front, rather over time, in the form of a $1-a-ticket surcharge, paid by the fans." And the Rangers, who would pay $5 million a year in rent for twelve years (or $60 million), could then purchase the stadium at the end of their lease — for nothing![24] So for every dollar Bush and his fellow partners put into the stadium, they got to take more than two dollars back from every Arlington taxpayer. And the money that Bush and his new business associates put in was actually money they garnished from inflating the prices paid by Ranger fans for tickets. At the end of the day those fans and the city would not have a single asset to call their own.

In addition, Bush and his partners arranged for the state of Texas to condemn the land around the stadium so it could be commercially developed, another sweet deal for the Rangers partnership. Remarkably, most of this information was ignored during the 2000 presidential campaign, although the *American Spectator*, which ferociously investigated Bill and Hillary Clinton's business affairs (under a grant from Richard Mellon Scaife) for years, thought "a healthy inquiry [of Bush's business affairs would be] a good thing." It never happened.*

To participate in the Rangers deal, Bush borrowed $500,000 from the United Bank of Midland (Texas), where he had earlier served as a director. It appears he collateralized this loan with his shares of Harken stock, which had about the same value. (He had been given 212,000 shares of Harken when it acquired Spectrum 7, plus he had acquired additional shares through a special offering to directors.) Harken paid Bush an annual consulting fee that ranged between $42,000 and $120,000 (dropping when he was off working on his father's campaign, which would have paid him as well, or certainly covered all his expenses — again, he will not discuss or reveal such matters). In 1989 and 1990, when Bush was working on the Rangers deal, he

---

*It might not have been a happy story for the folks of Arlington, but it was for Bush and former mayor Richard Greene, whom Bush appointed as an administrator of the Environmental Protection Agency. See U.S. Environmental Protection Agency at www.epa.gov/region6/6xa/greene2.htm.

was still on the board of directors of Harken, as well as being on the board's audit committee. In June 1990, he sold 212,140 Harken shares at $4 each in a private transaction for $848,560.* Eight days after the sale, Harken reported a $23.2 million loss, and the share price fell to $2.37. Bush used his proceeds to pay off his half-million-dollar loan and pocketed almost $350,000 from the deal. Bush parlayed his Rangers investment into a staggering $14.5 million when he sold his interest in 1998.

Did Bush take advantage of his insider information when selling his Harken stock? Of course he did. But when the Securities and Exchange Commission looked at the transaction and Bush's late filings of his insider trade, they said no enforcement action was called for against him, nor did any U.S. attorney convene a grand jury to look at the potential federal offenses. Of course, all those people worked for his father. Incredibly, Bush actually touts the fact that he was not charged as evidence of his exoneration, which is like O.J. saying the fact he is free proves he did not murder his wife.

Many of the facts surrounding Bush's sale of his Harken stock remain buried, and Bush has stonewalled all efforts to find out more. If this information could withstand scrutiny, it would have been spread out for all to see. The SEC chairman had been appointed by Bush's dad and was also a partner from the law firm of James Baker, Bush senior's White House chief of staff and later secretary of state. Bush's attorney during the SEC investigation just happened to be a former partner of the lead SEC investigator. The lead investigator at the SEC into Bush's Harken trade just happened to be Bush's former personal attor-

---

*The private purchaser has never been revealed, and the stockbroker who handled the transaction refuses to discuss it. The broker has not yet received a federal appointment, but anything is possible in a second Bush administration.

ney who had helped put together the Texas Rangers deal. These conflicts of interest — or worse — troubled no one. Notwithstanding these serious problems and less-than-satisfactory results from Freedom of Information Act inquiries, Bush's stonewalling has kept the truth hidden.

This I can say after having gone through the available record.* With the exception of the Texas Rangers deal, which screwed lots of little people but otherwise appears clean, Bush's business background has remained buried in order to conceal either sleaze or stupidity, or both. Bush the businessman would not qualify to sit in any president's cabinet, and it is even doubtful he could withstand an FBI background check, which you need to work for a president but not to be president.

Few potential presidents could carry the baggage Bush does — filled with dirty laundry — right into the Oval Office with no one stopping to check it. Now, with the powers of the presidency, he is even better able to keep his past hidden. And with Dick Cheney as a partner, Bush found more than a soul mate, for Cheney is a man more secretive than Bush, as well as a wonderful mentor in the workings of government secrecy and stonewalling. Cheney has shown his mettle in refusing to reveal important information about his precarious health throughout the 2000 campaign, and as his condition has deteriorated as vice president, his secrecy has become only more pronounced — now at the risk of the nation.

---

*I spent many years in the merger and acquisitions business, including over five years studying accounting and taking business courses. I have examined and/or participated in countless business transactions. Though I have retired from the world of commerce, I mention this because I believe by experience (and training) I am fully qualified to talk about Bush's (and Cheney's) dubious business affairs.

Cheney's Health Secrets

Before Bush named Dick Cheney as his running mate, Bush senior requested that a heart doctor friend check with Cheney's physicians to determine if Dick "was up to a strenuous campaign."[25] Soon word came from Poppy Bush's friend, renowned Texas cardiologist Dr. Denton Cooley, that Cheney's "health problems in the past should not interfere with a strenuous political campaign."[26] Cheney, then fifty-nine years of age, had suffered his first heart attack in 1978, when still in his thirties, and he had two additional heart attacks, in 1984 and 1988. After the last attack, he had quadruple-bypass surgery. Cheney's cardiologist, Dr. Jonathan Reiner, later clarified that Dr. Cooley had overstated things by saying Cheney had normal cardiac function. That was not the case, for Cheney's heart attacks had destroyed his heart muscle cells, and he has a severely damaged heart. Nonetheless, Dr. Reiner assured the public that his patient was up to the task (not that his patient would have permitted him to say otherwise), regardless of his condition. When asked for more details, Dr. Reiner said he could provide no further information until he received permission.[27] He never got such permission. Karen Hughes, as communications director of the Bush campaign, released a letter from another doctor, Cheney's primary-care physician, confirming that Cheney was otherwise in good health. Hughes promised more details would be released later. They never were.[28] And several *New York Times* reports by Dr. Lawrence K. Altman, its medical expert who reports on such matters, noted that the medical information that had been provided was useless, totally insufficient for any other medical professional to draw any conclusions.[29] Still, throughout the 2000 presidential campaign no further information on

Cheney's health was made available, even though it was regularly requested.

During the chad and vote counting in Florida, Cheney was taken from his McLean, Virginia, home at 3 A.M. on the morning of November 22, 2000, to George Washington University Hospital, suffering from chest pains. Bush, who was at his ranch in Texas, later announced that it was nothing serious, that Cheney had not suffered another heart attack. But Bush's information was wrong. Cheney *had* suffered another heart attack.[30] In addition, as a so-called precautionary procedure, Cheney's doctors had performed an angioplasty (which involves threading a small balloon-tipped wire into the clogged heart artery to open it) and inserted a stent (a metal mesh tube) to brace and keep open the narrowing artery. Putting the best face on a bad situation, Bush's campaign assured all that Cheney would be back on the job within days, working on the transition. Yet again, no detailed information about Cheney's condition was provided. Instead, the Bush campaign played pure public relations, having Cheney call into the *Larry King Live* show from his hospital bed. "I can report that when they got in there today, they didn't find any pregnant chads at all," a less-than-chipper Cheney quipped in a pathetic effort at Reaganesque humor, trying to convince everyone that when he and Bush were elected, he would be ready to serve.[31] As the Bush campaign and American journalists played it as a minor matter, an eminent British heart specialist pointed out, "No heart attack is minor."[32]

Dr. Altman, reporting for the *New York Times*, once again noted that Cheney's physicians had consistently been less than forthcoming with meaningful information, even though the *Times* and several other news organizations again made repeated requests for more relevant medical information. Cheney declined to be interviewed or to permit his doctors to be questioned. "American culture holds that public figures surrender much of their privacy," Dr. Altman wrote, "and no one is forced to run for office." Though there is no legal requirement that a candidate disclose health information, Dr. Altman observed that "the way health information is disclosed has become a test of a campaign. The public as an employer has come to expect timely information about the health of a candidate just as shareholders do about the health of a top corporate executive."[33] The next day the *Times* editorial board added its voice by asserting that "the public deserves a fuller medical accounting." Even Bush-Cheney supporter *New York Times* columnist (and former Nixon speechwriter) Bill Safire wrote, "Throughout the campaign, Cheney [has] ducked detailed questions about his heart disease. His blood pressure and daily medications were not revealed. We now know that our toleration of his brushoffs was a mistake." As for Cheney's effort to defuse the matter with an interview on Cheney-friendly *NBC Nightly News*, Safire said, "Cheney stonewalled again."[34]

Given the obvious importance of this information, other journalists continued to press the issue. *Los Angeles Times* reporter Marlene Cimons quoted the concern of Douglas Zipes, president-elect of the American College of Cardiology: "This guy is the potential vice president, and they're not really telling us anything about his cardiac status." Dr. Zipes said it was important to know whether Cheney had any heart-rhythm problems, because arrhythmias are often fatal.[35] *USA Today* noted that "Cheney refuses to release comprehensive medical data that is crucial to any independent assessment of his health."[36] Even Republican officials recognized the problem. Former New Hampshire governor Stephen Merrill bemoaned the failure of Bush to "truly grasp how significant Dick Cheney is perceived to this presidency" and predicted (incorrectly) that they would "eventually release every document to prove this is not a significant health issue. It is a political issue."[37] Although other newspapers across the country joined the chorus, Bush and Cheney refused to provide more information.

Stonewalling is a stall, the hope that with time or an intervening event, the matter will be forgotten as new issues become current. Few reporters (and their editors) want to harp, even when the matter is important. Politicians know this, and it encourages their stonewalling. The issue of Cheney's heart might have faded in the light of other problems, except Cheney was headed back to the hospital, now as the vice president of the United States, not as a candidate — and a uniquely powerful vice president. By March 2001, three months into the new presidency, Beltway insiders appreciated that Cheney was doing what he did best, operating out of sight but running the White House. "Bush [is] the nation's chairman of the board, Cheney [is] America's chief executive," the *Washington Post* explained.[38] *USA Today* columnist Susan Page described the inner workings at Bush's White House even more bluntly: "You name it, [Cheney] runs it." He "quietly has become prime minister, the go-to guy on everything from appointments to budget to congressional relations."[39] Cheney resolves disputes between cabinet officers without having to take the issues to Bush; he is the dominant man on the National Security Council, the only person capable of mediating between the high-horsepower players like Colin Powell and Don Rumsfeld; and Cheney heads key policy task forces (on everything from terrorism to energy) and even resolves departmental budget disputes. In addition, Cheney has become the White House's key lobbyist on Capitol Hill (with offices in both the Senate and the House), where legislators and party leaders prefer to meet with him rather than the president to get matters resolved. Cynics say that if anything happened to Cheney, Bush would become president.

Karl Rove and Karen Hughes, worried that Bush was being treated as a joke, put out the word to downplay Cheney's latest visit to the hospital. Cheney, a shrewd political operator who told Bush he has no interest in being president (given his health and age), understood his power would be greater if he acted as if he had none at all. As a result, he has increasingly downplayed his bad health and made himself as consciously subservient to Bush as possible.

Cheney broke his silence, or pretended to, by suddenly appearing in the White House briefing room on Friday, June 29, 2001. No advance notice was given, however, so no news organizations had time to dispatch reporters with medical knowledge (or appropriate medical briefing) to ask questions. Cheney told the reporters, those who hang around the White House for such unexpected events, "I thought it was important to come down because there obviously is great interest, for understandable reasons, in the health of the vice president." He said, "I'm going to undergo a test tomorrow at George Washington University Hospital. It's called an electrophysiology study. And it specifically is performed for the purpose of determining the prospective risk for me going forward in terms of abnormal heart rhythms." He explained that if the test indicated irregular heartbeats, he was likely to have a pacemaker-type device installed. But he maintained that he would still be able to serve, that he was exercising regularly and watching his diet.[40]

Cheney entered the hospital the next morning and the tests showed irregular heart activity, so he had an implantable cardioverter defibrillator (ICD) placed in his chest, which his doctor said could run for five to eight years before it needed replacing. While Cheney and his physicians were all very sanguine, downplaying it all, other heart specialists noted that Cheney's ICD was typically used with "high risk" patients, that it was there for a dire emergency but did nothing to reverse Cheney's chronic problems.[41] Dr. Alan Moss, a University of Rochester cardiologist and a leading authority on the ICD device Cheney had implanted, had earlier published a study in the *New England Journal of Medicine*, reporting that "heart patients fitted with an [ICD] had a 1-in-9 chance of dying within two years, compared with about a 1-in-100 chance for a healthy man Cheney's age."[42]

Cheney, in a staged departure from the hospital, walked rather than use a wheelchair as required by all other patients being discharged after similar surgeries. Following the pattern, little information was provided. The *Christian Science Monitor* scolded: "Instead of politicians deciding in secret whether they are fit to serve, the voting public — armed with health information — should make the call." The *Monitor* called for more "transparency."[43] The *New York Times* asked Harry J. Pearce, the new chairman of Hughes Electronics, a General Motors subsidiary, "What would a Fortune 100 company say publicly if a top executive suffered from a heart condition like that of the vice president, and what should be disclosed?" Pearce responded, "There is an absolute requirement to make full disclosure. And by full disclosure I mean full public disclosure."[44] The vice president of the largest organization in the world, however, had no intention of making full disclosure and has refused to do so.

Since 9/11, Cheney has increasingly disappeared from public view, causing those inside the Beltway to speculate about his heart. All that is known about Cheney's heart condition is that it has become progressively more serious. It is known, for example, that a mammary arterial bypass like Cheney's lasts "at least 20 years," according to Dr. Stephen Siegel, a cardiologist at

NYU Medical Center.[45] Cheney's twenty-year period will end in 2004, during the campaign. Cheney's doctors have refused, because Cheney refuses, to discuss his restenosis, which is the renarrowing of an arterial vessel due to scarring from angioplasty. Yet this occurs in a significant number of cases, because the angioplasty cracks the vessel wall and causes damage. None of these are matters that can be solved by diet and exercise; rather, they are a natural biological process.[46]

I have gone on at some length about Cheney's health because few people realize how little we know about a vice president who is, in fact, sick. He is not a healthy man. It is difficult to imagine any candidate, or recruiting team, who would select a vice president in Cheney's poor health. Of course, we all hope Cheney beats the odds and lives to a ripe old age. But the stakes are too high to ignore the gamble, which is what Bush and Cheney are demanding that Americans do. This is not an issue that should be brushed aside, as it raises questions about the 2004 election and any possible second term:

- Why have Bush and Cheney refused to provide full medical information?
- The Bush-Cheney administration does most of its planning based on "worst-case scenario" situations. What plans have they made should Cheney not be able to complete his next term?
- Who is on Bush's short list of potential men or women he would nominate to fill any vacancy in the vice presidency, should that be necessary?
- Is Cheney's health going to be used *after* the election — assuming reelection — as a ploy to select another vice president? Is Cheney really going to stay on the ticket throughout the 2004 campaign?

For anyone who has considered the potential problems, one looms larger than all others. Bush's health appears to be a non-issue, as long as he stays away from pretzels. Presidential protection, however, is never easy, and it has become aggravated in an era of terrorism. Given the condition of Cheney's heart, the true "worst case" would be for a terrorist to kill the president, and the strain of the event also prove fatal to Cheney (recall that he had a heart attack during the strain of the Florida recount) without his having yet selected and confirmed a new vice president. Are we really ready for Illinois congressman Denny Hastert, the Speaker of the House, to be president of the United States? Or more likely, Texas congressman Tom DeLay, the power behind Hastert, who could easily insist under such circumstances that Hastert step down (as Speaker temporarily), with the former exterminator being elected Speaker, then proceeding to the White House?

Even before the threat of terrorism, assassinations and physical assaults of presidents were all too common. Four presidents have been killed by assassins: Lincoln, Garfield, McKinley, and Kennedy. Reagan and Ford had close calls. Less well known is that almost half of all the presidents during the past century have been physically assaulted.[47] Having served as liaison between the White House and Secret Service, I have the greatest respect for the work they do, but it is an impossible task to totally protect the president (and other high officials). In fact, unless Bush and Cheney move into one of the emergency assistance centers, the government's huge underground facilities, and live like moles, they are highly vulnerable. Recent scholarly analysis of presidential protection, in the post–September 11 world of "nerve gas, dirty bombs, biological agents and shoulder-held missiles, to name only a few" of the new threats, is anything but reassuring: "No one yet knows whether the Secret Service's improvements in protective methods — which they cannot, of course, reveal — have kept pace with the increased severity of threats."[48] But with Bush it is more than terrorism. He is the most hated president in recent history. As columnist Nicholas von Hoffman points out, "Whenever President George W. Bush ventures abroad to meet foreign officials the question is not what will he get accomplished but whether or not he will be murdered."[49] Dick Cheney does not evoke warm and fuzzy feelings around the world, either. These men are greater targets, I'm sad to say, than any of their predecessors.

Regrettably, the denial of such fundamental information about the vice president's medical condition is consistent with his denial of information about his character, as revealed by his business conduct. After leaving government service and thinking he would never return, Dick Cheney picked up some baggage filled with ugly stuff, as well as a few unsavory friends, all of which he has managed to keep hidden during the 2000 campaign and while serving as vice president. No one realizes better than Cheney that as long as he keeps all this concealed, not only can he operate as the most powerful vice president in American history, but when he completes that assignment (his heart willing), he can become even richer with part-time visits to the corporate boardrooms and the folks he is now taking such good care of as our first co-president. He has proceeded from poster boy of the military-industrial complex to the godfather of almost every industry providing services to the American military (and many foreign ones).

Cheney's Halliburton Secrets

Dick Cheney served as chief executive officer, and later as chairman of the board also, of Halliburton Company from October

1995 to August 2000. He was running this energy-industry giant when Bush asked him to be his running mate. (Actually, he was heading a search committee for a vice presidential running mate for Bush and had promised the Halliburton board that he would not be leaving "any time soon.")[50] Cheney's selection proceeded on "a track so secret" that no one other than Bush and his campaign manager, Joe Allbaugh (who vetted Cheney); Bush senior; and probably Karl Rove and Karen Hughes knew that Bush had actually made his choice. It was not announced until mid-July 2000.[51] Had he vetted himself as he was other candidates for vice president, Cheney would likely have vetoed himself because of his medical condition, if not because of his financial and business dealings.

Clearly, Cheney had never contemplated returning to politics and public service, and had acted accordingly. Cheney was hired by Halliburton not for his business skills (for he had none) but rather for his Rolodex (no one has a better one), given his career and extensive contacts, particularly in Arab oil nations, from his tenure as secretary of defense. Cheney's contacts gave Halliburton "a level of access that [no one] else in the oil sector [could] duplicate," according to Halliburton's president, David Lesar.[52] Cheney told *Business Week* in 1998 during an interview at Halliburton, "This is where I expect to spend the rest of my career."[53]

In 1998, after three years in the oil business, Cheney shared with a group of oil-industry executives the essence of his business philosophy. For Cheney, it all boiled down to business: "You've got to go where the oil is," he told them.[54] That meant trading with the enemy, and regimes ruled by leaders who employ unspeakable horrors against their people proved to be good places to do business. Under Cheney, Halliburton did business with Iraq, Iran, Libya, Indonesia, Saudi Arabia, and Azerbaijan — to name a few of the countries that use its oil to exploit its people, countries notorious for violating human rights. Several of them are avowed enemies of the United States. This issue arose only fleetingly during the 2000 campaign. In late July the *New York Times* reported that "Mr. Cheney's company has already done business in countries still facing American sanctions, including Libya and Iraq, the enemy Mr. Cheney helped vanquish in the gulf war."[55] It was a question Cheney had to have known was coming when he appeared on ABC's *This Week* a few days later, and he was ready:

> Sam Donaldson: I'm told, and correct me if I'm wrong, that Halliburton, through subsidiary companies, was actually trying to do business in Iraq?
>
> Dick Cheney: No. No. I had a firm policy that we wouldn't do anything in Iraq, even — even arrangements that were supposedly legal. What we do with respect to Iran and Libya is done through foreign subsidiaries, totally in compliance with U.S. law. . . . Iraq's different, but we've not done any business in Iraq since the sanctions [were] imposed, and I had a standing policy that I wouldn't do that.[56]

It was a lie, but there was no follow-up from Donaldson. The *New York Times*, however, stayed on the story and a month later removed all doubt about the untruthfulness of Cheney's statement. The *Times*, quoting Halliburton's vice chairman, Donald Vaughn, reported that Halliburton's subsidiary did, in fact, have "business relations" with Iraq.[57] Not until after the campaign had ended did the *Washington Post* obtain records from the United Nations showing that Halliburton's subsidiaries had sold more than $73 million in oil-production parts and equipment to Iraq.

In fact, *no one* did more oil-related equipment business with Saddam. The *Post* also noted that Cheney had managed to compound his initial false statement to ABC's *This Week* by later adding, during another appearance, a bit of obfuscation in claiming that he was unaware of the business they had "inherited" but that they had "divested ourselves of those interests." That was a real stretch, since the divestiture did not take place until Halliburton's subsidiary completed some $30 million in business with Saddam.[58] By then, *New York Times* columnist Nicholas Kristof also discovered that the Cheney-led Halliburton had "sold more equipment to Iraq than any other company did."[59]

"Principle is okay up to a certain point, but principle doesn't do any good if you lose," Cheney once advised one of his White House associates during a campaign.[60] This appears to be the guiding philosophy of Cheney's political and business careers. For example, not much principle was involved in Cheney's courting and befriending the notoriously cruel and cunning dictator and former Soviet apparatchik Heydar Aliyev, the late leader of Azerbaijan. Lawrence Kaplan, senior editor at the *New Republic*, was one of the few journalists who found Cheney's relationship with Aliyev sufficiently offensive to write about it. Aliyev, who was first dispatched to the former Soviet republic of Azerbaijan by the KGB to run the country, later staged a successful coup against the country's elected president when the USSR fell apart. As president of Azerbaijan, Aliyev "presided over" the final phases of "a vicious war and blockade" of the Armenian enclave of Nagorno-Karabakh, Kaplan reported. Aliyev, who was known for his "the ethnic cleansing of Azerbaijan's Armenian population" and disposing of personal enemies by treason trials or simply through brutal detention, was befriended by Cheney.

The U.S. Congress, recognizing the atrocious mistreatment

of Armenians by Aliyev, enacted legislation making it illegal for the United States to provide financial aid to Azerbaijan, in section 907 of the Freedom Support Act. Kaplan pointed out that the reason for this legislation — Aliyev's inhumanity — "seems not to have made the slightest impression on Cheney, who has become one of Aliyev's biggest backers in the United States, schmoozing with the aging dictator when he comes to Washington."[61] Clearly, Azerbaijan's oil was irresistible to Cheney. The Caspian Sea area oil reserves are believed by many to equal, if not exceed, the reserves of Saudi Arabia. Cheney was positioning Halliburton to have a significant role in recovering this landlocked oil.

Rather than using Halliburton's (and other American companies') money to build the necessary pipeline to get Azerbaijan's oil to the West, Cheney wanted American taxpayers to take the risk. (Just as Bush had done with Arlington, Texas, Cheney hoped to do with all of America.) As a result, Cheney lobbied Congress to repeal the aid embargo against Azerbaijan, section 907, but he had not succeeded before Bush called him to run and serve. Even then he did not resign from the Azerbaijani front organization in Washington, which is devoted to "educating" Americans and their officials about the wonders of this Caspian seaside nation — the United States-Azerbaijan Chamber of Commerce (USACC).[62]

What Cheney as chairman of Halliburton could not accomplish for Heydar Aliyev, however, he could as vice president. In January 2003, Bush quietly sent a letter to Congress exercising his authority, as president, to waive section 907, thereby starting a flow of U.S. government financial assistance to Azerbaijan.[63] And in late February 2003, Bush invited Heydar Aliyev to visit the Oval Office to chat about terrorism, strengthening global energy security, and the endless Nagorno-Karabakh conflict.[64]

Not surprisingly, the dictator's troops were (alphabetically, anyway) at the top of the list of the "coalition of the willing" for America's war in Iraq — all 150 men (designated for law enforcement and protection of religious and historic monuments).[65] In October 2003, Heydar Aliyev gave his personal fiefdom to his son, Ilham, through a rigged election that would have made Joe Stalin proud. But these "irregularities" did not trouble Bush (although his State Department gagged and had to hold its nose), as the president quickly sent Ilham, described by the *New York Times* as a "businessman, playboy and novice politician," his hearty congratulations upon receiving what the *Times* called "a nice gift from his father." Clearly, Bush could identify with Ilham. On a more serious note, the *Times* added that "President Bush has said he went to war in Iraq in part to create democratic models in Islamic nations. But America's support for the Aliyevs suggests the administration has not learned the lessons of its oil-inspired support for the shah of Iran, Saddam Hussein and successive Saudi governments."[66]

Given that he simply upped and unexpectedly walked out on Halliburton in July 2000, Cheney's severance package was stunning. Rather than hold Cheney to his agreement, Halliburton's board swapped it for a futures contract, betting that Cheney would become vice president and that when he did, it would be good for Halliburton and the oil industry. It proved a very smart investment.

Cheney's departure from Halliburton should have been treated as a "resignation"; instead, Halliburton called it an "early retirement," which enabled Cheney to keep his options for shares of the company earned earlier. By any norm, the deal Cheney cut when he left was exceptional for a CEO with a "mixed record" at best. Halliburton had given other senior executives (those who did not happen to be running for vice president of the

United States) rather shabby treatment. In fact, at the time they fashioned the deal for Cheney the company was being sued for denying the former president of Dresser Oil Tools (a subsidiary of a company that had merged with Halliburton) his Halliburton options.[67] CNN reported that Cheney's "golden parachute" gave him stocks and options with a market value of an astonishing $62.6 million, plus deferred income and supplementary benefits. Others guessed it to be less, around $45 million. No one really knows, because only the bare minimum of information, that necessary to comply with vague ethics laws, has been made public. And Bush and Cheney have done all they can to make sure that no further clarification will be forthcoming.

During the campaign Cheney refused to talk about his business career, but in a prepared statement he promised that if elected, he would sell his Halliburton stock and "forfeit any options that have not vested by the time I assume office."[68] (He did sell his stock but not his options — which apparently had restrictions or were below the strike price — rather, he purportedly gave them to a charity, so it was a half-truth.) But his business career did come up in a forum where he could not dodge it completely. During the vice presidential candidates debate, Joe Lieberman said, "And I'm pleased to see, Dick, from the newspapers, that you're better off than you were eight years ago, too." Cheney stiffened his back slightly and shot back, "And most of it — and I can tell you, Joe, that the government had absolutely nothing to do with it."[69] To say that this was a disingenuous response would be disingenuous, if not farcical. Within a few hours, John Rega of *Bloomberg News*, after a quick fact check, blew Cheney's throwaway line out of the water as false.[70] Of course, neither Cheney nor the Bush-Cheney campaign issued a correction.

Had Enron not imploded, proving itself to be a colossal accounting scam, aided and abetted by its auditor Arthur Andersen, followed by Global Crossing, WorldCom, etc., Cheney's stonewalling about Halliburton might have succeeded and his business career faded from public concern. But as the contagion of corporate corruption unfolded in the summer of 2002, the *New York Times* learned that Halliburton, under Cheney, had employed its own Enronesque accounting practices. Rather than take a hit on its corporate earnings in the last quarter of 1998, after the Dresser Industries merger (which Cheney had engineered) Halliburton changed its accounting method in a manner that covered the potential loss — and did so without reporting this fact to the SEC as required.

In late December 2002, the SEC went from an informal to a formal investigation (giving it subpoena power). It is not clear where the SEC is going, or why it is taking so long; as of this writing, it has remained silent. But if it is doing its job, Cheney's problems appear to run potentially much deeper than failing to report a change in accounting practices to the SEC. (Even a Bush/Cheney-friendly *National Review* thinks that it was a violation and that the remaining question is whether it was fraudulent and thus criminal.)[71] I believe even more is involved. Once the SEC investigative camel gets its nose in the tent, so to speak, it has been known to smell other problems cooking. Time has shown that Cheney's sweetheart severance deal may have been too sweet. Cheney sold his Halliburton shares at over $50 per share. By July 2002, Halliburton's stock was trading at just over $13 per share.[72] So precipitous was this decline in value, it is impossible not to wonder if Cheney made himself "available" to serve as vice president (knowing the job was his if he wanted it) because it gave him a unique way to escape from Halliburton —

and cash out — before the collapse. Bush had used his insider knowledge to cash out of Harken, leaving other investors behind for the red ink. Greedy minds think alike.

If Bill and Hillary Clinton's relatively small, money-losing investment in an Arkansas land deal at Whitewater was justification for a special counsel investigation (with the special counsel investigation later becoming an independent counsel investigation when the IC law was revived), by taking the standards of that IC law — whether there are "reasonable grounds to further investigate" — then a special counsel investigation of Cheney's financial relationship with Halliburton is in order. There are also questions about war profiteering by Halliburton that a special counsel should explore.* There is certainly evidence strongly suggesting the possibility of securities fraud regarding Cheney's sale of his Halliburton stock, for it is unlawful to trade shares based on nonpublic (and material) information. Indeed, a person with insider information who undertakes such trades can be fined up to $1 million and sent to prison for up to ten years.[73] Martha Stewart's purported insider-trading activities have resulted in a massive investigation to which she has been exposed and charged. Her trades are inconsequential in comparison with Cheney's.

Obviously, there is the matter of the accounting change. David Lesar, Cheney's successor, who had run the day-to-day operations for Cheney, told *Newsweek* that Cheney was well

---

*News stories of Halliburton's secretly awarded multibillion-dollar no-bid contracts (the contents of which are also secret) and overbilling have been front-page news. The Center for Public Integrity, a nonpartisan organization, has reported that so far some seventy American companies and individuals who were substantial campaign contributors to the Bush-Cheney campaign have been awarded billions of dollars in contracts in Iraq, all with secrecy clauses prohibiting the companies from disclosing their profits, and the White House has direct (if not exclusive) oversight over most of this activity.

aware of the accounting practice changes that prompted the SEC investigation.[74] In addition, Cheney was very close to the Arthur Andersen partner in charge of the Halliburton account, with Cheney even providing the accounting firm with a personal videotaped endorsement of its practices (before it was criminally indicted because of those practices at Enron). Cheney would not be the first CEO to play accounting games and get caught. But he would be the first CEO to use the vice presidency to escape an approaching boardroom disaster. That is an accurate description of what the deal with Dresser became — a disaster.

Cheney initiated this merger when salmon fishing with Dresser's top man. The two competing companies had been warily eyeing each other for years, but the two men got along so well that they decided to do the deal. Cheney spent $7.7 billion to merge his rival, but Dresser was a time bomb. *Time* reported that Cheney knew of this developing crisis, which was asbestos litigation at a former Dresser subsidiary.[75] When reporting the merger with Dresser, Halliburton stated that the asbestos litigation would have no material financial impact on the business. Later, when the significance of this litigation became clear, Halliburton officials claimed that they had been kept in the dark about the Dresser problem until *after* the merger. The *New York Times*, however, reported that "undisclosed court documents show Dresser was notified a month *before* the merger that it might face greater asbestos liability from its former subsidiary than it had disclosed," and the *Times* also quoted a spokeswoman from Halliburton, who acknowledged that the "asbestos litigation environment deteriorated after 1998."[76]

Not until March 2000, when Cheney was getting ready to help Bush vet running mates, did Halliburton disclose that it had a whopping 107,650 asbestos claims against it. The company blithely said the claims were no big deal, and would be resolved without significant financial harm. Yet in May 2000, Cheney unloaded 100,000 shares of his stock at $50.97 a share, bagging almost $5.1 million. It is not clear when he put himself in play as vice president, but it was certainly sometime in May or June, for he and Bush agreed on it as a done deal over the July 4 holiday. In August, Cheney resigned from Halliburton (with his sweetheart "retirement" deal) and promptly sold another 660,000 shares of the stock, at between $50 and $54 a share, collecting nearly $36 million. Three months later, Halliburton reported another 10,000 asbestos cases but still claimed they would have no significant impact on the company's finances.

In fact, the 117,000 pending asbestos claims were (and remain) a financial disaster for Halliburton. This problem, when the truth became known, sent the company's stock value plummeting. According to SEC filings, since Cheney's departure, Dresser's asbestos claims are going to cost Halliburton an estimated $3.4 *billion*. If Cheney was not aware of the problem he was sitting on as chairman of Halliburton, he is not half as smart as people give him credit for. Indeed, he could have been unaware of the potential problem only if he had stopped reading the newspaper about 1998 (when journalists began reporting significant verdicts in asbestos cases), stopped talking with other CEOs (who trembled at the potential of asbestos claims), and failed to notice that Congress was holding hearings and considering various proposals to deal with the problem. In fact, Dick Cheney operated one of the most sophisticated intelligence operations of any CEO in America, even hiring former CIA agents to serve as superspooks for him while at Halliburton.[77] And he was known for asking his accountants and lawyers and insurance carriers and others penetrating questions about everything. It is thus extremely unlikely he could have truly believed that the asbestos claims were "no significant" financial problem for his company. One need only look at a chart of Halliburton's stock value for years 1999 through 2002 to realize that Cheney — either miraculously or maliciously — sold his shares at the height of the market. Maybe miracles do happen. And miracle of all miracles will be if Cheney can get the Republican Congress to pass the pending legislation that will solve much of Halliburton's asbestos problem and if the SEC somehow simply looks the other way at Cheney's relationship with Halliburton. What a remarkable coincidence all that would be.

What does Cheney have to say about all this? Nothing. To paraphrase Nixon, Cheney doesn't give a shit, so he's going to just keep right on stonewalling. It has worked too well to consider doing otherwise. After all, stonewalling is gamesmanship, which both Bush and Cheney play with gusto. But the game of stonewalling could not begin to satisfy their need to conceal their White House activities and the workings of their presidency, where their demand for secrecy has become nothing less than obsessive.

Chapter Three

Obsessive Secrecy

*I'm a Republican and George W. Bush is one of my heroes. . . . [But]
I believe a veil of secrecy has descended around the administration
and I think that's unseemly.*

— Congressman Dan Burton, chairman,
Government Operations Committee

Well before the final ruling by the U.S. Supreme Court in
Bush v. *Gore*, Dick Cheney was confidently at work on the presidential transition. It was his sixth, and this time his own.[1] Cheney's fishing buddy and former secretary of state James Baker, a
hard-nosed but respectable political fixer, was supervising the
Florida recount and related legal actions. With Bush's brother
John Edward "Jeb" Bush in the Florida governor's chair, Cheney had good reason to feel confident. Although Jeb's behind-
the-scenes activities to deliver Florida's electoral votes to his
brother — both the work actually undertaken as well as various
contemplated contingency plans — have remained secret (of
course), we can get an inkling of Jeb's thinking, for it is known
that he was prepared to defy the Florida Supreme Court, if necessary, to ensure his brother's election.[2]

Cheney's inside knowledge of White House operations went
back to his tenure as Donald Rumsfeld's aide at the Nixon

White House in 1969. Cheney later served as deputy chief of staff under Rumsfeld at the Ford White House before taking over himself as chief of staff when Rumsfeld became secretary of defense.* Ford later wrote that he selected Cheney, a "bright young political scientist . . . still in his early thirties," to be his chief of staff because he was "low-key" and a pragmatic problem solver who "worked eighteen-hour days" and was "absolutely loyal."[3] The new chief of staff had his hands full getting control of the leak-prone, highly splintered Ford White House (with factions of former Nixon aides who remained, Ford's old cronies who had come in, and new people like Cheney). With time, however, Cheney became known as "Grand Teuton," the name being "a complex pun referring to his mountainous home state of Wyoming and the Germanic style of his predecessor, H. R. Haldeman."[4]

Despite a laid-back demeanor, Cheney was (and is) a steely, cold-blooded man of strong beliefs and few words. Cheney has never been a showboat, preferring to work out of public sight, which during the Ford years earned him the Secret Service code name "Backseat." During his six terms in Congress representing Wyoming, Cheney continued (with a remarkably low profile) to have extensive dealings with the Reagan White House, effectively shielding his friend Vice President George H. W. Bush during the Iran-Contra scandal. Later he served as Bush senior's secretary of defense. In short, Cheney knew White House procedure, practice, and protocol from the inside out and vice versa. His running mate, though not as familiar as Cheney with the ways of Washington, certainly was no naïf about govern-

---

*President Ford used the title *staff coordinator* rather than *chief of staff* because of the bad name H. R. Haldeman had given the title *chief of staff* under Nixon, but the post was truly that of staff chief.

ment and politics. While Cheney worked on their new administration in Washington, the soon-to-be president-elect was taking care of business in Texas and getting ready to move out of the governor's office.

Illegally Hiding Gubernatorial Papers

As his last act as governor of Texas, and one of his first acts as president-elect, George Bush demonstrated his utter disregard for the law when it comes to secrecy. In December 2000, as the cliff-hanging Florida presidential vote recount was sorting itself out and heading for the U.S. Supreme Court, Bush was in Austin, Texas, away from the spotlight. As soon as he got word of the U.S. Supreme Court's favorable ruling, he arranged for his gubernatorial records to be gathered, placed on sixty large pallets, shrink-wrapped in heavy plastic, and, with no announcement, quietly shipped off to his father's presidential library at Texas A&M University. Actually, this effort to bury his records had started in 1997, when Bush sought and obtained a change in Texas law to permit a governor to select a site for his papers, within Texas, other than the Texas State Library. But such an alternative site was permissible only after "consultation" with the state's library and archives commission. This consultation was mandatory, obviously required to make sure any alternative arrangement satisfied the state's stringent open-access law regarding the records. Bush, however, removed his papers with no consultation whatsoever; rather, he dispatched an aide to inform the head of the Library and Archives Commission that he was sending his records to his father's library, like it or not.[5]

Well, she didn't like it. With one of the nation's strongest public information laws (much to Bush's chagrin), Peggy Rudd, the director and librarian of the Texas State Library and Archives

Commission, took exception to his unilateral action. Under Texas law, gubernatorial papers are immediately indexed by archivists and then made publicly available. All requests for these records must be answered within ten days under the Texas statute. Bush senior's presidential library is run by the U.S. government's National Archives and Records Administration, however, which quickly advised those seeking access to Bush's gubernatorial records that his papers were no longer subject to Texas law and that the federal archivists were too busy with the father's papers to process the son's. Bush had effectively federalized his papers, hiding them in a legal limbo in his father's library, where no one could have access to them. His handpicked successor, the newly installed Texas governor Rick Perry, agreed with Bush.

But Ms. Rudd did not cotton to being bullied by the former governor, even if he was president of the country, and refused to accept Bush's designation of his father's library. It took her over a year, but in May 2002 she prevailed, forcing the Texas attorney general, who would have been hard-pressed to read the Texas law any other way, to rule against Bush, making his gubernatorial papers subject to the Texas Public Information Act. Given the clarity of Texas law, Bush's claim that Ms. Rudd's office had no role other than the ministerial one of recording the governor's designation of an alternative location was beyond Philadelphia lawyering. It was a flagrant violation of the law.

News accounts reported that Bush's ploy had not violated the law,[6] but a close reading of the attorney general's formal opinion shows that these reports are incorrect.[7] There are no sanctions for such a violation other than to make the papers available as the law requires. No telling how much scrubbing Bush's gubernatorial papers received, both before he left office and while in limbo at his father's library.

However, Bush appears to have the last laugh in this tale. His papers were sent to Austin, Texas, for processing — slowly. And Governor Perry, along with a new attorney general (both Bush supporters), has found new exceptions in the state's information law that give him the keys to the filing cabinets with Bush's records.[8] In short, secrecy wins, and good luck to anyone seeking Bush's gubernatorial records (as a few did before Perry got the keys; such access resulted in Bush's embarrassment, like showing that Bush and his counsel Alberto Gonzales processed death-row commutations on incomplete information and faster than Bush could say, "Execute her").[9] It is difficult to believe one would go to so much trouble to hide his records unless he had something he really did not want people to know about.

Shrink-Wrapping the White House

Bush, once a leak chaser (and discipline enforcer) for his father's campaigns and presidency, understood how leaks had hurt his father's vice presidency, implicating him in the Iran-Contra scandal, and his presidency, with rumors of extramarital infidelity. Bush's distaste for leaks and need for information control, while great, was surpassed only by Cheney's, who had been burned badly by leaks when he first became Ford's chief of staff. His scars were deep. Surely it had to have been exceedingly unpleasant when charges of his incompetence erupted in the *New York Times*, accusing him of running an "inept" White House operation, with a personal staff that was characterized for its "political naiveté" by other Ford White House insiders.[10] Then another leak to the *Times* reported that while life at the White House was more relaxed and pleasant under Ford and Cheney than under Nixon and Haldeman, the unidentified source said, "Sometimes I wish that we had some of the old Haldeman discipline back. These days things are hardly ever ready on time and the staff work is often sloppy and incomplete. There are just too many mistakes."[11] Even more serious public charges reported that Cheney (and Ford) had no control over the National Security Council or Secretary of State Henry Kissinger, who was making foreign policy without informing the president.[12]

Cheney had been appalled as a member of Congress at leaks during the Iran-Contra investigations, and when he took charge of the Pentagon in 1989, his fully developed anathema and his related obsession for controlling information were quickly put into action. A week after he arrived as defense secretary, he publicly reprimanded the air force's chief of staff for privately briefing influential members of Congress. A year later, he fired another air force chief of staff for discussing contingency plans relating to the Gulf War without clearance. So tight-lipped is Cheney that he seldom briefs his own aides about his activities, his dealings with others, or his knowledge on given subjects.[13] Not surprisingly, Cheney's strong feelings about information control are reflected in the operational structure, functioning, and staffing of the Bush II White House.

To leakproof their new presidency, Bush and Cheney first selected a White House chief of staff who not only shared their views but, more important, understood how the place worked. Cheney recommended that Bush hire a longtime Bush family friend, Andrew H. Card Jr., who had worked with Bush senior and had known Bush since 1979, when they met as Card was visiting the family's compound at Kennebunkport. Card, a former Massachusetts state legislator and unsuccessful candidate for governor, ran the critical New Hampshire primary for Bush senior in 1988 and then became the deputy chief of staff at senior's White House in 1989, under White House chief of staff John Sununu. Card, nothing like the acerbic, high-profile Sununu, has received high marks from the outset, praised as a prudent choice by Bush. "Andy brings street smarts, firmness, yet humility, to that post," a knowledgeable source informed the *Washington Post.* "It's a perfect fit," said another.[14] "He's not a sparkling personality," Brent Scowcroft, Poppy's national security advisor, observed; rather, "he's a very quiet, down-to-earth person. He's a workhorse not a show dog, absolutely."[15] During the 2000 campaign, Card had helped prepare Bush for his debates with Al Gore, purportedly playing Gore, so he knew both Bush's limits and his potential. To take the job at the Bush II White House, Card gave up his lucrative work as a Washington lobbyist for the automobile industry, explaining to the *New York Times,* "I would do anything to help [Bush's] parents . . . I have an infinite amount of love for them." The feeling was mutual, as former First Lady Barbara Bush noted in her memoir.[16]

Cheney and Card planned the White House out of the spotlight, which remained focused on the Florida recount, not the transition, contrary to what typically occurs. The two men took advantage of the opportunity, creating a highly compartmentalized White House. Power in the White House generally comes from access to the president. Many presidents permit their chief of staff to determine who should and should not have access and when. Bush and Cheney decided at the outset that Cheney would have open access to Bush, as would a few other senior aides, such as political adviser Karl Rove, press secretary Ari Fleischer, and Karen Hughes (before she returned to Texas). That Card cannot control access dilutes his power, but this was acceptable to him, and his only condition for taking the job was an assurance from Bush to "keep him informed of all briefings, whether or not [he was] included."[17] In truth, Card is more a staff coordinator (as once contemplated by Ford) and White House operations manager than a power center like his predecessors.

Three years into the Bush II presidency, the *Wall Street Journal* described the White House operations under Card: it found "tightly centralized power inside the White House's West Wing" and "a nearly leakproof system to shield the president from scandal and distraction — keeping secrets from the media, Congress and even cabinet members until Mr. Bush decides to reveal them, if ever."[18] The Bush-friendly *Journal* observed that this system has its downside, for it has resulted in Bush's being significantly out of touch with reality. In addition, the structure and arrangement has frustrated agency and cabinet department heads, who are "kept out of the loop" (not to mention in a state of trepidation regarding their jobs).* For example, the *Journal* reported that the attorneys in the office of White House Counsel Alberto Gonzales "deliberately avoided asking [others] about the state of the West Wing debate" regarding the University of Michigan's affirmative action program when the issue was before the U.S. Supreme Court and before the administration had determined its position. Why keep yourself in the dark? So the aides could "secure some deniability in case news leaked," the *Journal* said.

---

*Former secretary of the treasury Paul O'Neill, who was one of the few members of Bush's cabinet to have regular access to the president, found Bush consistently disengaged and uninformative. Bush kept all but a very small group of White House aides and Cheney guessing about everything. American Enterprise Institute chairman Christopher DeMuth confirmed O'Neill's finding about the tight ranks at the White House, particularly after O'Neill left. The "circle around this president is smaller and tighter than any we've seen in recent times . . . and I was in the Nixon White House." O'Neill, with two decades of White House–level experience — as well as that of a successful CEO — found that the absence of policy process resulted in department and agency heads "acting, in many cases on little more than hunches about what the President might think . . . or what he might, someday, be convinced was the right path, long after the U.S. government had already embarked on it." See, e.g., Ron Suskind, *The Price of Loyalty: George W. Bush, the White House, and the Education of Paul O'Neill* (New York: Simon & Schuster, 2004), 98, 321.

The highly compartmentalized, need-to-know White House employs another Cheneyesque firewall to prevent leaks. Early in the Ford administration, Cheney had found that excluding speechwriters (many of them former journalists) from key scheduling and decision-making meetings helped to stem the leaks.[19] Given their facility with words, speechwriters are also the most likely to write books. In Bush's White House, speechwriters have been strictly contained and are relied upon as wordsmiths, not thinkers, not policy makers. Bush's top speechwriter, Michael Gerson, a devout evangelical Christian, is not a journalist by trade; rather, Gerson was hired and trained ("appropriately politicized" may be a better description) by former Nixon White House hatchet man and political schemer Chuck Colson, who read a column in the Wheaton College newspaper that Gerson had written on Mother Teresa when he was a theology student. Colson, who has been running a prison ministry since Watergate, hired Gerson as a staff writer (and ghostwriter) upon his graduation from Wheaton in 1986. Before Bush snagged him for the 2000 campaign, Gerson had also worked for Senator Dan Coats (R-Ind.) and had written speeches for such other Republicans as Steve Forbes, Jack Kemp, and Bob Dole.[20] So he knew the GOP gospel, and he was not likely to be found hanging out at the National Press Club bar or any other journalistic watering hole (although he is known to leave the White House and work at a Starbucks nearby).

There is a dearth, but not total absence, of journalists on the staff of the Bush II White House, and ironically the first insider account of Bush's presidency is by one of them, David Frum, who was on the White House staff from January 2001 to February 2002. A former speechwriter, Frum published his largely laudatory book about Bush in 2003. A striking feature of his book, *The Right Man: The Surprise Presidency of George W. Bush*, is how little Frum really knew about what was taking place inside the White House. His book does not purport to be an insider tell-all, yet his material suggests he could have written the same book without having worked at the White House and by merely having paid a few visits. This is not to say that Frum's book does not offer some unique insights, for it does. Unlike most of Bush's speechwriters, Frum enjoys financial independence and thus was unafraid, unlike many Bush staffers, to break the White House code of silence. Frum gives a few glimpses from the inside, and he was the first person to say anything remotely less than worshipful of his employer. Frum confirms the fact that leaks — which are not always recognizable from the outside — drive Card, Cheney, and Bush crazy, for they have not managed to completely shrink-wrap and seal the White House and have almost completely failed to stop the flow of information from the cabinet departments, particularly State and Defense.

Jack Nelson, a veteran Washington correspondent, studied the Bush administration's media policies and relations during his fellowship at the Shorenstein Center on the Press, Politics and Public Policy at Harvard's Kennedy School of Government. Nelson reported that "no president since Richard Nixon has been as secretive or as combative about leaks as George W. Bush."[21] Since Nelson completed his study and reported on it in January 2003, the situation has become only more severe. If he were to update the study, he would find that like the Nixon administration, this presidency is prepared to throw the book at low-level leakers of inconsequential, unclassified information, primarily for purposes of intimidation. Yet the administration will protect high-level leakers who disclose damaging classified information to attack a perceived enemy or make a policy point.

Suppressing Dissent and Leaks

As part of its image control, the Bush II administration has embraced a truly malevolent Nixonian tactic to deal with public dissent. Aside from selecting only venues that Bush and Cheney can control and manipulating the setting (potted plants here and floodlights there) and audience (please take off your neckties, gentlemen, and look casual standing behind the president), there is always the problem of getting to and from such protected venues. Bush and Cheney take extreme measures to avoid being confronted with public protest, just as Nixon did.

Nixon's intolerance became evident, for me, when traveling with him. All the antiwar demonstrators were removed from the route of his motorcade, and when on one occasion a few chanting protesters made their way to a location near his hotel, Nixon angrily ordered the Secret Service to remove them. Similarly, Nixon one day happened to look out a window of the White House second-floor residence and noticed a single silent demonstrator across Pennsylvania Avenue, carrying an END THE WAR sign in Lafayette Park. Nixon ordered the Secret Service to remove the man. By late 1972, I appreciated that these were not isolated incidents but rather part of a widespread use of illegal tactics and ploys by White House advance men and the Secret Service to keep demonstrators out of the president's sight (and the view of news cameras). These activities were fraught with civil rights and criminal implications, but the president simply did not care.[22] This systematic denial of First Amendment rights was about to explode into its own scandal, when the Watergate cover-up imploded, preempting and burying everything else. Still, civil lawsuits made very unpleasant headlines, and the practice was investigated, and reported on, by the U.S. Senate's Select Committee on Presidential Campaign Activities (the Senate

Watergate Committee), which expressed its dim views about White House operations blocking "undesirables" from attending Nixon rallies by using "cowboys" who "let things happen" if the Secret Service or local police failed to remove demonstrators.[23] As I recall, the civil suits were settled by paying off the complaining parties with campaign funds.

When traveling in the United States, Bush also uses his advance men and the Secret Service to remove demonstrators from his sight — notwithstanding the stink raised and lawsuits filed during Watergate, and its obvious illegality. Bush's White House has revived this unconstitutional practice by claiming, as did the Nixon White House, that it is necessary for presidential protection.* Bush has pushed it so far that the American Civil Liberties Union has filed a lawsuit (in late September 2003) alleging that the Secret Service has on not less than seventeen occasions, from California to New Mexico, Missouri, Connecticut, New Jersey, South Carolina, and Pennsylvania, forced groups and individuals into what are euphemistically called "free speech areas," which are always located blocks from a Bush or Cheney motorcade and speaking venue.[24] In addition, under the pretext of presidential protection, demonstrators are being arrested, and even prosecuted, by Bush under an arcane federal law adopted to hide demonstrators from Nixon.[25] This is the criminalization of dissent.

Nixon, of course, wanted to send leakers to jail but failed because of the government's misconduct in prosecuting Daniel Ellsberg for leaking the Pentagon Papers. In 1971, when Nixon's

---

*This was a bogus claim during the Nixon years, and it remains bogus. Those likely to create presidential-protection problems do everything they can to avoid drawing attention to themselves. Sign-carrying demonstrators are no more dangerous than brass bands that greet presidents, if not less so, because demonstrators typically must have a permit, requiring valid identification.

Justice Department charged Ellsberg (along with Tony Russo, who helped him), they relied on the 1917 Espionage Act and the general theft of government property law (even though the 1917 law did not deal with leaks but rather espionage, which neither Ellsberg nor Russo had engaged in, nor had they stolen anything, since Ellsberg had been given a copy of the papers). Dismissal of the Ellsberg and Russo cases left unresolved the question of whether these laws could actually be used to punish leaks. In 1986, Reagan's Justice Department put these laws to the test, making an example of Samuel Loring Morison, who had provided classified pictures of a Russian aircraft carrier to *Jane's Defence* magazine, for whom he worked. Even though no harm was caused to national security whatsoever, Morison was successfully prosecuted under the 1917 Espionage Act.

Morison's conviction sent a chilling message to government employees, editors, and publishers.[26] While no fan of leaks, President Clinton appreciated the hypocrisy of any government sending a low-level government employee to jail for leaking (based on a tortured ruling by the U.S. Court of Appeals for the Fourth Circuit, making the 1917 Espionage Act applicable, contrary to the express intent of Congress) when high-level officials regularly leak classified information to help them govern, so he pardoned Morison. Under the *Morison* v. *United States* precedent, several presidents and secretaries of state could have been prosecuted for information in their memoirs, for as President Kennedy once observed, the ship of state is unique in that it leaks most often from the top. Leaks can, and in fact occasionally do, cause damage.[27] Never, however, had anyone — before Morison (who worked part-time for U.K.-based *Jane's* as an American editor with the permission of his navy employer) — been prosecuted for publishing a leak. Indeed, this country has resisted adopting an "official secrets act," like that of Great

Britain, which makes it a crime to disclose both classified and unclassified government secrets. At the onset of World War I, Woodrow Wilson sought such a law as part of the 1917 Espionage Act, but Congress refused (a fact that the Fourth Circuit simply set aside). During the 1917 debate on criminalizing leaks, Senator William Borah, a Republican from Idaho, reminded his colleagues of the lesson of the infamous Sedition Act of 1789: "Once before in the history of this Government we undertook to establish something in the nature of an abridgment of speech and of the press. It was a complete and ignominious failure."[28] In 2000, President Clinton vetoed a proposed official secrets act (after almost letting it slip through), and Congress did not override that veto. Few doubt that the only reason the Bush administration has not sought such a law is that it does not want to spend the political capital necessary, for the American news media is unalterably opposed to such a statute, and rightly so.

There's also little need, since Bush, Cheney, and Attorney General John Ashcroft have cobbled together the equivalent of a new unofficial official secrets act more awesome than anything Congress might give them. They have used existing laws and the type of thinking employed by the Fourth Circuit in *Morison* v. *United States* (that if the language of the statute itself covers the situation, then the legislative history is irrelevant). This approach was employed to prosecute Jonathan C. Randel, a former intelligence analyst with a Ph.D. in history who worked in the Atlanta office of the Drug Enforcement Agency. Randel leaked *nonclassified* information to a British journalist.[29] The leak — which had nothing to do with national security — exposed the fact that the name of one of the richest men in the United Kingdom, Lord Michael Ashcroft (no relation to John), appeared in a number of DEA files relating to investigations into drug trafficking and money laundering in Belize. While law enforcement information is sensitive and agencies such as the DEA try to keep their files closed, such leaks are not uncommon and are typically ignored.

Wealthy Conservative lords living in the United States, however, are another matter with the Bush II administration. To criminalize Randel's leak, Ashcroft's Justice Department threw the book at him. The *twenty*-count indictment provides a sample of the administration's new unofficial official secrets law. It relies on the government's general theft statute,[30] a statute protecting information in government computers (where most all information is found today),[31] and the general mail/wire fraud statutes, making each of sixteen uses of the DEA computer to obtain information about his lordship a discrete scheme to defraud the government and claiming the same for the reimbursement Randel received from the *Times* (London) when he agreed to meet with them after they were sued by his lordship.[32] It is worth stressing again that none of these laws was written to criminalize leaks. Still, it is little wonder that Jon Randel pleaded guilty to the general theft statute (with only a ten-year sentence potential), for he was facing a staggering statutory maximum of 580 years — or life in prison for leaking information he believed needed to be known because Randel felt the DEA was giving his lordship a pass, when it should have been investigating him.*

Randel was given a year in jail, to be followed by three years of supervised probation, plus a $2,000 fine. Bush's U.S. attorney

---

*On August 7, 2002, the *New York Daily News* reported that New York City district attorney Robert Morgenthau had expanded his probe of Tyco, another major company with a record of executive high jinks, where Michael Ashcroft was a member of the board of directors. Morgenthau's expanded investigation is reportedly looking at racketeering, securities fraud, tax fraud, and falsification of records. The report noted that "at least three board members were being investigated, including Lord Michael Ashcroft."

in Atlanta, William Duffey (a former deputy independent counsel under Ken Starr), told the *New York Times* that he was pleased with the sentence and that the prosecution of Randel was "a warning to other government workers." Clearly this was a warning aimed at potential whistleblowers in the federal bureaucracy, advising them to keep quiet, or risk jail.

Other Controls of the News Media

"This administration is the most closed-mouthed, more closed-door than any in memory," Michael Duffy, a seasoned Washington bureau chief for *Time* magazine, told his former colleague John Stacks when Stacks was examining Bush's relationship with the news media. Stacks found such control of the news media disturbing: there is a "pernicious and damaging kind of secrecy being practiced by the administration of George W. Bush. Officials in Washington have largely stopped talking to the press except in set-piece briefings. Interviews are refused. Phone inquiries are left unanswered. The public is thus being denied access to the workings of the government it elected."[33] In fact, Bush and Cheney have pushed message and media control to new limits, but their operation is strikingly familiar to anyone who witnessed Richard Nixon's precedent-setting moves in controlling such information.

Nixon physically controlled the White House press crops by herding them into the small press room, which they still occupy. The room was created by covering the White House's indoor swimming pool. It was presented to the press as an "upgrading" of their facilities, when in truth it was designed to remove them from the West Wing Lobby and stop them from roaming around, by confining them to a small space. Bush held his first formal press conference in this cramped briefing room, and on the few occasions he has held a formal press conference in the spacious East Room, he has exercised very tight control of the journalists invited to attend, marching them into the East Room in pairs to their seats, like grade-schoolers, and then calling on only those reporters he had preselected.[34] He ignored the long tradition of giving the first question to the most senior member of the White House press corps, Helen Thomas, because she has said that Bush is the worst president in American history (and she has firsthand knowledge of many of them).[35] Another Nixon trick that Bush has used is bypassing the White House press corps by inviting out-of-town journalists to the White House to interview him, who his aides admit are "more hospitable and less judgmental" and thus a "better place to sell their wares."[36]

Bush, like Nixon until he was weakened by Watergate, uses sheer intimidation when dealing with the press. If a reporter does a story the White House doesn't like, his or her telephone calls are not returned. And if the president doesn't like a question, he'll openly take a shot at the reporter. Who can forget, on May 31, 2002, when Bush was in Paris, holding a joint press conference with French president Jacques Chirac, his exchange with NBC correspondent David Gregory? Gregory, at six foot five inches, seems to intimidate Bush before he even asks a question. Anyway, on that occasion Gregory asked why Bush thought there was such strong sentiment in Europe against him and, being fluent in French, then turned to Chirac and asked, *"Et vous, Monsieur le President Chirac, qu'en pensez-vous?"* [And you, Mr. President Chirac, what do you think about it?]

Bush, pursing his lips and barely able to contain his anger, responded with a stridently sardonic comment, not to Gregory but to the world: "Very good," he said, his head nodding with mock approval. "The guy memorizes four words, and he plays like he's intercontinental." Gregory, somewhat surprised, assured Bush he was playing no games. "I can go on —" but Bush cut him off. "I'm impressed — *que bueno* [that's good]. Now I'm literate in two languages." Bush, still steamed when the press conference ended, again turned to Gregory, in front of the others present, and added, "As soon as you get in front of a camera, you start showing off."[37] It was an absurd scolding, for Gregory is about as low-key a television journalist as can be found, a man who has no need to show off. But Bush let him and other American journalists know: Don't ask him tough questions and don't — even in subtle ways — exhibit the slightest bit of initiative, particularly at a press conference heavily covered by foreign news media.

Martha Brant, *Newsweek*'s White House correspondent, has said, "We're more dependent than ever on [Bush's] top aides because everything is so closely held." And she added, "Hopefully you're not just the tool of the administration."[38] But the very fact she stated her concern confirms that it is well founded.

Stagecrafting and Image Control

If any politician is better than Bush at hiding the truth through message control and concocted public images, I'm not aware of who it is. Bush's reliance on image and his continuous campaigning are reactions to his father's presidency and his father's failure to be elected to a second term. Bush senior was an experienced politician, with strong feelings about the presidency. He headed the Republican National Committee during Nixon's presidency and did not always approve of Nixon's political style, including extensive use of the latest communications techniques and stratagems. Later, Bush senior witnessed the next evolution of the image-crafted presidency, from even closer range, as Reagan's vice president. Michael Deaver made Nixon's team look like beginners (as they were, for television was still young). But this image business wasn't for Poppy, and though he used it to get elected in 1988, he ended it after he became president. Andy Card, recalling his time as Bush senior's deputy chief of staff, has said, "President [George H. W.] Bush clearly relished the role of governing and disdained the role of campaigning."[39] Therefore, Bush senior broke the tradition of the continuous campaign while governing, which Nixon had made part of his first term, setting a standard most of his successors would follow.[40] Bush senior refused to be stage-managed like Reagan. He did not even like highly crafted speeches, for he thought it less than manly to employ such techniques and that too much eloquence was slick, artificial, and phony.[41] Polls, for Bush senior, were "reflections of yesterday."[42]

When Bush senior headed toward reelection, after three years of some of the highest presidential approval ratings in modern times, his aides worried that he had failed to present a clear image of his presidency, not because he had none but rather because he refused to use the available tools to portray and project it. To some extent, they were correct. Bush senior's running mate and vice president, Dan Quayle, called their reelection effort "the most poorly planned and executed incumbent presidential campaign this century."[43] Not even Murphy Brown would disagree.

Bush witnessed his father's political demise firsthand, and reportedly the personal anguish of the loss may have been greater for the president's eldest son than for the president himself. Highly aware of his father's mistakes, Bush has proceeded during his presidency to do almost the exact opposite. He has run a continuous campaign, for he would rather campaign than govern. Unlike his father, Bush uses polls (although he denies it). Bush employs all the latest communications techniques and tricks. Bush has a White House that works constantly on projecting the image it wants to put out. At times his presidency is literally scripted. Before Bush took office, Karl Rove studied previous presidential debuts, looking for what had worked and what had failed. Working with the communications and policy staff, Rove developed and tested a detailed plan for the first seven days. Public relations, communications, and political operations from the campaign had been expanded, refined, and moved into the Bush II White House. The first-week launch went off like a successful Broadway opening. Andy Card later acknowledged that it was "like a screenplay, I had a script."[44]*

And they have scripted one event after another — often literally building sets for presidential appearances, with Bush needing only to show up in a well-tailored suit, or some other costume for the occasion, to read a speech that could be handled by a seventh-grader. The *New York Times* reported that Bush has gone "far beyond the foundations in stagecraft set by the Reagan White House." Not only are these efforts ambitious, they are expensive. For the first anniversary of 9/11, the White House rented Musco lights (the kind used in sports stadiums) and placed them on three rented barges "to illuminate all 305 feet of America's symbol of freedom" — the Statue of Liberty — to serve as a backdrop for Bush's speech.

---

*Paul O'Neill — who was a member of the National Security Council as well as being in charge of fiscal policy — made a shocking revelation to Ron Suskind that not only are public events scripted, but even cabinet (and other) meetings within the White House with this president are scripted, where everyone but Bush has speaking parts. Bush's role is merely to nod or listen expressionlessly, aside from his occasional cryptic (or cynical) comments. For example, at a meeting of Bush's war cabinet on Iraq, "each cabinet member spoke in an order and on a subject that had been designated in advance. At one point, Bush asked [Secretary of Defense] Rumsfeld to comment on something [Secretary of State] Powell had just said, but that was the extent of the interaction." O'Neill's wife told Suskind, "Paul just seemed to leave meetings with the President and shake his head. It was like, 'I'm not sure if this guy's got what it takes to pull this off.'" Suskind, *The Price of Loyalty*, 147, 160, 188.

At another speech, Bush's producers positioned his platform and the podium in such a fashion that when speaking at Mount Rushmore, "the cameras caught Mr. Bush in profile, his face perfectly aligned with the four presidents carved in stone."[45] Of course, there was the memorable staging of his *Top Gun* landing on the flight deck of the aircraft carrier *Abraham Lincoln*, with Bush dressed in a flight suit, greeting crew members. Bush did nothing to dispel the illusion that he had piloted the plane to the deck; in fact, he was a passenger in a pilot's costume. Then, after changing clothes and at a perfect moment of twilight (timed to the minute, with the great ship making lazy circles so the cameras would have an ideal setting), he delivered his speech announcing the end of hostilities in Iraq, a banner over his shoulder reading, MISSION ACCOMPLISHED (which, contrary to Bush's later claim, had been purchased and placed there by his staff, not the ship's crew). Later his producers came up with a better photo-op, sending the commander in chief to Baghdad for Thanksgiving with pictures of him carrying a large tray with a turkey (that turned out to be fake) to supposedly serve the troops (who had all been prescreened and transported to the airport site).*[46]

---

*Wondering how a real professional eye might judge Bush's staging skills, I asked eminent American playwright Arthur Miller, having earlier enjoyed his essay "On Politics and the Art of Acting," written shortly before the 9/11 attacks. In that essay, Miller finds Franklin Roosevelt, Ronald Reagan, and Bill Clinton the most skilled actors in the White House. When I asked him about Bush, he was less than impressed. "To me of course it is all puffery," Miller said. "He is strutting about like the bad actor that he is, but film and theatre are full of bad actors who find a public. The crowning moment of his pretension was his having emerged from an airplane that he did not land, in a pilot's get-up with the helmet gallantly under one arm, as if he had passed through heavy enemy fire. At long last some commentators caught on to this, but I'm afraid the yahoos may have fallen for it." E-mail response from Arthur Miller to the author, May 11, 2003.

Truth be told, 9/11 made Bush's image, and he has exploited it ever since. Ironically, his best image moment was an unscripted event, the day he visited Ground Zero. When he climbed up a mound of debris from the fallen Twin Towers to visit working firemen, an aide handed him a bullhorn, which malfunctioned when he spoke. Firemen standing atop another mound of rubble shouted that they could not hear him. Bush, standing with his arm draped around a fireman's shoulders, shouted back: "I can hear you. The rest of the world hears you. And the people who knocked down these buildings will hear all of us soon." With that there commenced a spontaneous chant of "USA! USA! USA!" This small rally, witnessed by millions on television, helped give Bush the highest and longest boost in approval ratings since polling has been conducted, better than FDR's after Pearl Harbor, better than JFK's after the Cuban missile crisis, and better than his father's after the 1991 Gulf War.[47]

That event at Ground Zero will be played and replayed during the 2004 presidential campaign. Doing so, of course, will be very expensive. Just as he did for 2000, Bush has raised unprecedented sums of campaign money. If you do not know it, let me tell you that it is not good citizenship or eleemosynary emotions that drive campaign contributors, particularly the big hitters, who require care and feeding — another area where Dick Cheney's expertise has proved invaluable to Bush. Major campaign contributors are investors, and Cheney's responsibilities have included managing that investment portfolio.

Cheney's Secret Energy Group

By any standard, the energy industry (oil companies, gas companies, energy-service companies, coal companies, nuclear power operators, electric utilities, etc.) has received one hell of a return on its campaign investments. For me, the line between bribes and contributions is only the label the parties place on the transaction. Big campaign money buys special access, the kind of access that provides a true opportunity to persuade, and obtain favorable policy. The energy industry "legally" bought Bush and Cheney, and it was a smart buy.

Only nine days into his new office at the White House, Bush created the National Energy Policy Development Group, chaired by his vice president.[48] The group was charged with developing "a national energy policy designed to help bring together business, government, local communities and citizens to promote dependable, affordable and environmentally sound energy for the future."[49] This project had actually started during the transition, so they were ready to go at full steam following the inauguration. By April 19, 2001, the buzz around the Capital City had it that Cheney's group was wheeling and dealing behind closed doors, with all signs indicating that the big hitters were going to get a nice return on their investment. In 2000, this was a staggering $25.3 million.[50] Of course, if energy was going to win, environmentalists would lose. Such rumblings troubled Congressman Henry Waxman (D.-Calif.), the ranking member of the Committee on Government Reform, and John Dingell (D.-Mich.), the ranking member of the Energy and Commerce Committee, two seasoned legislators — widely considered among the best of a vanishing breed of dedicated and knowledgeable public servants. Together they wrote both Cheney's energy group and the comptroller general, David Walker, the head of the General Accounting Office (GAO), the investigative and auditing arm of Congress. Waxman and Dingell made a simple request for information about the composition of Cheney's energy group and its activities in developing a national energy policy.

Counsel to the vice president David Addington responded to the congressmen, explaining that Cheney's group was not subject to the Federal Advisory Committee Act, so there was no legal requirement to provide information, but as a matter of comity, Addington provided a few vague answers to their questions. As for the General Accounting Office, Addington told it to get lost, that it was trying "to intrude into the heart of Executive deliberations, including deliberations among the President, the Vice President, members of the President's Cabinet, and the President's immediate assistants, which the law protects to ensure the candor in Executive deliberation necessary to effective government." Addington's response was surprising, not to mention a misstatement of the GAO's request. It was clear he was looking to pick a fight.

The GAO's general counsel advised Addington that as a matter of law, the GAO had statutory authority to "intrude into the heart of Executive deliberations," citing the relevant statutory law (chapter and verse), along with its legislative history, which was directly on point: "[The] mere fact that materials sought are subject to . . . [deliberative process] and therefore exempt from public disclosure does not justify withholding them from the Comptroller General." More to the point, however, the GAO advised Addington that it was "not inquiring into the deliberative process but [was] focused on gathering factual information regarding the process of developing President Bush's National Energy Policy." In a subsequent letter, the GAO even explicitly revised and narrowed the language of the request, to make the point that it did not seek information about the contents of conversations, or advice, only the names of those who had worked with the energy group and when.

But Cheney was playing hardball, and not by any preexisting rules. When this story became public, Cheney blatantly misstated the nature of the Waxman/Dingell and GAO requests. Time and again he made false statements asserting that the GAO was seeking to intrude into the deliberative process, even though this was not true.[51] With 9/11, the GAO backed off and did not resume pursuit of the information until operations of government had returned to normal. After nine months, with letters going back and forth and Cheney making one false statement after another, David Walker announced that he was ending the shilly-shallying. Cheney's bluff would be called. On January 30, 2002, the GAO informed Congress, the president, and the vice president that it had complied with all the statutory requirements, that the president had not exercised his statutory rights regarding the withholding of the requested information or invoked executive privilege, and that accordingly the GAO was going to court. For the first time since it was created in 1920, the GAO was required to "file suit to enforce [its] access rights against a federal official," because of Cheney's action.

This was, to say the least, a high-stakes lawsuit. It raised fundamental questions about the very nature of our system of checks and balances. If the GAO could not get the information it requested, then there was a black hole in the federal firmament — a no-man's-land where a president and vice president could go free from congressional oversight. This was not a political undertaking in the partisan sense. David Walker had been a member of the Reagan administration and the Bush I administration. President Clinton appointed him comptroller in 1998 to his fifteen-year term at the urging of top Republicans. Although the congressional request had emanated from two ranking Democratic members of committees in a House of Representatives controlled by a slight Republican majority, the GAO itself does not play politics. Regardless of which party controls Congress, the GAO undertakes such investigations whenever they are requested by either the chairman or the ranking minority member of any of the committees or subcommittees created by Congress.

The GAO hired a Washington law firm to file the historic federal lawsuit, *Walker* v. *Cheney*, in the U.S. District Court for the District of Columbia. The judge presiding over such a lawsuit can make a great difference (which is why Bush has devoted so much energy and effort to packing the federal judiciary with conservative judges). As fate would have it, Cheney got lucky, for the case was assigned (through a random-selection system by a computer) to U.S. District Court Judge John Bates, a career Justice Department lawyer who had worked for Independent Counsel Ken Starr, then gone into private practice, and had only recently been appointed to his new lifetime job by Bush. This was one of his first cases.

Normally, a lawsuit against the vice president would be handled by the Civil Division's attorneys at the Department of Justice. That is the standard operating procedure. But this lawsuit was one of a select few to be handled by a special unit operating under the immediate supervision of Deputy Solicitor General Paul Clement and the general supervision of Solicitor General Ted Olson (who had earlier, as a private lawyer, represented Bush in *Bush* v. *Gore*). Former associates from the Justice Department tell me that the creation of this special trial team, run by the Solicitor General's Office looking for cases they can take to the Supreme Court to rewrite existing law, has so offended career attorneys in the Civil Division (who view themselves as professionals, not partisans) that many have left (which is a great loss of legal talent for the government). When the solicitor general himself, Ted Olson, showed up at the government's trial table in Judge Bates's courtroom during the oral argument on a motion on Cheney's behalf to dismiss the case, Judge Bates, as a former Justice Department lawyer, got the message. As a rule, the solicitor general appears only before the U.S. Supreme Court.

Confounding both the law and logic, Judge Bates tossed the GAO's case out of federal court. Bates granted Cheney's motion to dismiss, claiming that David Walker, as comptroller general of the GAO, did not have "standing to sue" (meaning he did not have a sufficient legal stake in the controversy). In effect, Judge Bates was saying to Walker, Not only will I not let you step up to the plate, I want you off the playing field. The judge's reasoning, in essence, argued that the comptroller general is merely an agent of Congress; therefore, he had suffered no real injury by Cheney's refusal to produce information. In addition, the judge claimed that the GAO had provided no evidence to suggest that Congress itself had in any way been injured by the failure of Cheney to provide the requested information. Finally, the judge reminded the comptroller that Congress could have subpoenaed the requested information, but since this had not happened, the judge said he could not be sure that the GAO was truly representing Congress's interests in trying to get this information.

This was an absurd reading of the law. Comptroller Walker had filed his lawsuit pursuant to a 1980 statute that expressly authorized him to bring such an action. But Judge Bates effectively told Congress that it could not give the comptroller general standing (or authority) to act on its behalf, thereby gutting the enforcement authority of the General Accounting Office's statutory mandate. Although the judge did not rule that the statute was unconstitutional, as the Justice Department had requested, he relied on a Supreme Court ruling to drain the GAO's authorizing statute of its force.

Only more stunning than the ruling was the GAO's decision not to appeal it. In a formal statement, Walker stated he believed that Judge Bates's decision was wrong. Still, the GAO was not going to invest the time and resources in appealing. Since Judge Bates's "decision did not address the merits," placing a happy face on the calamity, the GAO took the position that the ruling "has no effect on GAO's statutory audit rights or the obligation of agencies to provide GAO with information." This position is wishful thinking at its best.

After reading a number of news stories stating that the Republican congressional leaders, who had regained full control of Congress after the midterm 2002 elections, told Walker to back off, I spoke with a high-level official at the GAO, who explained that the decision not to appeal had been based on discussions with the GAO's lawyers, plus conversations with Walker's two immediate predecessors (which added thirty years to his own four years of experience). All had agreed that Walker should not take further action, perhaps recognizing that if he did, the Supreme Court could do again what it did in *Bush* v. *Gore* and make *Walker* v. *Cheney* the landmark ruling ending virtually *all* congressional oversight.

Despite the GAO's extraordinarily cautious approach, lawyers at the Congressional Research Service (CRS) at the Library of Congress are concerned that *Walker* v. *Cheney* has serious implications for congressional oversight. It greatly diminishes the GAO's investigative powers, particularly against a president and vice president. The GAO has lost not only standing to file a lawsuit but the leverage of the threat of filing such a lawsuit, should an executive department or agency stonewall the way Cheney did. The GAO must now simply take what the White House (and its many appendages, such as the National Security Council, National Economic Council, Domestic Policy Council, Office of the Vice President, Office of the First Lady, White House Communications Agency, White House Transportation Agency,

White House Military Office, to mention a few) volunteers. This has never before been the case. Even if the GAO knows that a crucial document is missing or that the information provided is incomplete to the point of being inaccurate, it can do nothing. It will see only what Bush and Cheney want it to see and no more.

Not surprisingly, the CRS found that the ruling "not only severely hampers the main investigatory arm of Congress, but it also calls into question the ability of Congress to delegate investigative authority to its agents."[52] This, it appears, may be the true reason for the lawsuit and for Cheney's actions.

Cheney has taken an equally defiant "I'm above the law" position in a lawsuit filed by Judicial Watch, the conservative public interest group. That lawsuit, filed in July 2001, seeks, among other things, to determine if Cheney's energy group complied with the Federal Advisory Committee Act (a law that precludes secretly using nongovernment people to do government work). When ordered to comply by U.S. District Court Judge Emmett Sullivan to produce documents and information, Cheney refused and appealed to the U.S. Court of Appeals, which ordered him to comply. He refused and appealed to the U.S. Court of Appeals sitting en banc (rather than the three-judge panel that had ruled against him), but they turned him down and told him to comply with Judge Sullivan's order. He refused and has appealed to the U.S. Supreme Court. There, Cheney — being represented by Solicitor General Ted Olson — apparently hopes that the gang of five who put Bush in the White House will reverse their earlier holding that made President Bill Clinton subject to civil litigation while serving as president. In December 2003, the Court agreed to hear the case (somewhat extraordinarily), which will likely be decided in midsummer 2004.[53] But maybe Cheney knows something others do not, for shortly after the Court took the case, Justice Scalia joined his old friend Dick Cheney for a duck-hunting weekend.

So what is Cheney hiding, and why? And what kind of game was he playing with his hard-line refusal to provide basic, inoffensive information to the GAO and with his hardball tactics in a run-of-the-mill civil lawsuit? As with many Americans, my first reaction was that he wanted to conceal his meetings with Enron officials and other high-powered lobbyists who were getting their paybacks. But the more I thought about it, the less I believed that was his sole reason. After all, once his energy task force report was issued in May 2001, it was obvious that the national policy had been designed to assist big contributors to the Bush-Cheney campaign. Similarly, in seeking to convert Cheney's policies into law, congressional Republicans, operating largely behind closed doors, wrote a bill to please the energy folks. These are not hard-to-locate loopholes and tax breaks, as often is the case; the beneficiaries are clear, and — reading backward from who benefited — it is evident who Cheney and Bush, as well as lawmakers, had listened to. But Cheney's motives, while clearly designed to reward the energy industry and even possibly hide early discussions with the energy industry of exploiting Iraqi oil, suggest a still larger play. He was looking at a bigger picture, which — by connecting a few dots — begins to emerge, and Cheney's actions are part of the effort to weaken Congress, which is one of many building blocks in returning to a Nixonian imperial presidency.

Bush's Invoking Executive Privilege

Since the Nixon presidency, much has been written about the uses and abuses of the so-called executive privilege by presidents. It is one of the strongest tools of presidential secrecy, enabling a president to deny information to the other branches of government. Mark Rozell, a political scientist from Catholic University in Washington, D.C., keeps an eye on this doctrine from one presidency to the next. Professor Rozell is one of the few to correctly understand Nixon's feeling about this privilege, noticing that before Watergate, except for national security matters, Nixon was a remarkably open president. Rozell discovered that during the 1968 presidential campaign, Nixon had pledged to have "an open administration in which there would be a free flow of information from the executive branch to Congress, the media, and the public," and he repeated that pledge early in his presidency, with a formal declaration of his policy in a letter to the chairman of the House Subcommittee on Government Information.[54] Nixon actually started out in a far more open fashion than Bush and Cheney, who have been determined to close down the White House from the outset.

Professor Rozell views executive privilege as "a complex dilemma" for presidents: they need some secrecy to govern, yet other branches of government need information about executive activities to "fulfill their democratic responsibilities." Having worked at both ends of Pennsylvania Avenue, I view it a bit differently. It is no dilemma whatsoever for a president to keep secrets and use executive privilege, or the threat of it, to do so; rather, it is a political problem. A president seeking reelection does not want to appear dictatorial, but presidents (and vice presidents) can use their pulpit to make Congress look unreasonable in making a request (often by distorting the nature of the request). Few citizens care much about such esoteric matters. And when a president is not seeking reelection, there is no political check on his conduct. It was after Nixon was reelected that he truly abused executive privilege, invoking it to prevent both Congress and the courts from obtaining his incriminating tape-recorded conversations. It took the U.S. Supreme Court in *United States* v. *Nixon* to force him to produce the requested records, and even then many were still not sure if he would comply. But Nixon was facing the ultimate remedy of Congress should he refuse — impeachment and removal. But this, too, is a political remedy.

Bush has taken an extreme and radical position in invoking executive privilege, but for political reasons he has only staked out his ground, waiting for reelection to go all out in his assault. He went through an edifying drill with Dan Burton — an Indiana Republican who at the time chaired the House Government Reform Committee and sought more than twelve sets of internal Justice Department documents in early September 2001. Burton wanted Justice Department information on investigations of fund-raising abuses by Bill Clinton and Al Gore during their 1996 presidential campaign, as well as documents related to the FBI's use and handling of mob informants by its Boston office, where evidence indicated that the FBI had literally let informants get away with murder (with an innocent man going to prison, notwithstanding FBI information showing he was innocent).[55]

Burton's request was ticklish for Bush. His cabinet officers and agency heads had been told that they were to take a hard line on such requests, that Bush and Cheney were setting a powerful new presidential precedent. But earlier, when Burton had jumped on Clinton's midnight pardons during his final days in office, Bush had played partisan politics and provided truly unprecedented information about Clinton. By long presidential tradition, conversations between the president and foreign heads of state are recorded. Following the pardon of fugitive financier Marc Rich, Clinton had explained it was not Rich's ex-wife (a Clinton contributor who had asked for the pardon of her former husband) who persuaded him; rather, it had been his private conversations with then Israeli prime minister Ehud Barak, who had encouraged him to pardon Rich.[56] Burton thought this was baloney, and when he learned of the taping practice, he requested copies. Never before have such national security matters been released. Yet Bush, whose White House was quietly doing all it could to stir the controversy over the Rich pardon, provided Burton with select portions of the three relevant conversations. Burton, in turn, publicly released the transcripts.[57] Clinton was angry when he read them, for they were incomplete. When Clinton requested that all of the relevant passages in the conversations between himself and Barak be released, Bush's White House said no, claiming the material was classified.[58]

Burton packaged his requests for documents cleverly — combining another opportunity to dump on Clinton by turning over internal Justice Department materials related to former attorney general Janet Reno's decision not to call for independent counsel investigations of either Clinton or Gore with the truly serious matter of the Boston FBI office's misconduct. The high councils of the White House, however, realized that regardless of the political potential of further damaging Clinton, it was time to draw their line on executive privilege. On December 13, 2001, Bush sent a memorandum to the attorney general instructing him not to turn over the requested documents. The executive-privilege refusal was based on Bush's claim that it would violate the "national interest" to give Congress documents relating to "prosecutorial decision making."

Bush's position on the FBI material was baseless, and Burton — along with every member of his Government Reform Committee, both Republicans and Democrats — was outraged. Editorial writers jumped on Bush's misuse of executive privilege (not concerning Burton's endless pursuit of Clinton, which was dubious, but rather the very legitimate inquiry about the FBI).

Even more frustrating to the committee than the administration's refusal to talk about a compromise arrangement for the FBI material were its dissembling and misrepresentation. First the Justice Department, when asserting privilege at a hearing before the committee on December 13, 2001, falsely claimed that its action was consistent with long-standing Justice Department policy. This was followed by a January 10, 2002, letter from White House counsel Alberto Gonzales, making a similar bogus claim.[59] To put the lie to these fallacious assertions, the committee called University of Baltimore School of Law professor Charles Tiefer, who absolutely eviscerated the Justice Department and White House claims. Professor Tiefer told the committee his "testimony can be summarized as a survey showing that in the years from the 1920s through 1992, Congressional oversight committees were, indeed, provided with access to Justice Department deliberative documents — contrary to the Department's current executive privilege claim." And as for the Clinton years, from 1993 to 2001, Professor Tiefer reached the same conclusion.[60]

No press releases were issued, but quietly and privately Bush caved and provided the FBI information to the committee. Even most executive-privilege experts were unaware of this fact until the Government Reform Committee issued its disturbing report on its investigation, "Everything Secret Degenerates: The FBI's Use of Murderers as Informants." That lengthy report (about FBI corruption) ends with six pages devoted to the bogus, and misleading, claim by Bush of executive privilege. The committee, even though it got to look at what it wanted to see, obviously remained deeply disturbed. "The Committee's investigation was delayed for months by President Bush's assertion of executive privilege over a number of key documents," the report states. "While the Committee was ultimately able to obtain access to the documents it needed, the President's privilege claim was regrettable and unnecessary."[61]

Such chastisement, however, troubles neither Bush nor Cheney, for it has been ignored by the mainstream news media, so their actions cost no political capital whatsoever. "It is truly puzzling that President Bush took his first official executive privilege stand over materials concerning closed DOJ investigations," Mark Rozell has written, since there was so "little justification" — no national security implications, no clear public interest, and the claim fails to fall into the category of protecting ongoing criminal investigations.[62] But it makes absolute sense if the administration's aim is total information control. Accordingly, its policy remains to employ executive privilege aggressively, as long as the political price is not too high. If this administration is given a second term, there will be no price too high to expand this presidential privilege, enabling the executive branch to remain completely unaccountable. This is what Bush has done with presidential papers, where he pushed executive privilege beyond all prior limits by using an executive order (which is nothing more than the president directing those in the executive branch on what to do or how to do it) as a device to overturn existing law. Not unlike his whisking away his gubernatorial papers, Bush seeks to seal not only his own presidential papers but his father's as well. That his actions are contrary to the Presidential Records Act of 1978 appears to be of no concern to Bush or his counsel. This is not about the law. It is about power.

Sealing Presidential Papers

Nixon's efforts to take his papers and tapes with him when he resigned caused Congress to focus on an issue that had been largely ignored since the nation's founding — who owns presidential papers? By tradition, starting with George Washington, presidents had taken the records generated during their tenure, including those of their vice presidents and White House staff, as their own. Nixon was doing only what all those who had preceded him had done, but because his tapes and papers were potential evidence in pending, not to mention future, criminal investigations, the Watergate special prosecutor moved quickly to preserve them. When it became unclear whether Nixon would comply, Congress stepped in and passed a law making all his tapes, papers, and records the property of the people of the United States, whose taxes had paid for them.[63] After years of litigation, and because Nixon was being denied the prerogative his predecessors had been granted as part of the high office, Nixon was paid $9 million for the materials, which were all placed in the National Archives and Records Administration (NARA).

After dealing with Nixon's papers and records, Congress found itself looking at the larger question of other presidential papers, and in 1978 the Presidential Records Act was enacted. This law recognizes that because of its historical importance, this material truly belongs to the public and should be made publicly available within a sensible period of time.[64] Congress provided a reasonable opportunity for presidents to use their records first to prepare memoirs, but after twelve years the papers were to become open to the public, if not voluntarily made available sooner. The first president to whom the new law applied was Ronald Reagan (and his vice president, George H. W. Bush). The Reagan library in California, with holdings estimated at 40 million pages, had voluntarily released over 4 million pages, and was prepared to make available other portions of the remaining 36 million pages still being processed by archivists, but sought to withhold some 68,000 pages (which had been requested by researchers) for the full twelve-year limitation — January 21, 2001. Under the

1978 law, an incumbent president can double-check any release, making sure it falls within the law's provisions.

When Bush entered office, it was time to release the 68,000 Reagan pages. But Bush's White House lawyers asked for an extension so they could review the "many constitutional and legal questions" relating to these documents. Then they asked for another, and then another. (One can only presume Bush's wariness may have something to do with what those papers say about his father or members of his administration.) Finally, they released most of the pages but refused to release the rest. Bush then issued an executive order on November 1, 2001, virtually gutting the 1978 Presidential Records Act. Bush's in-your-face Executive Order No. 13223 created an entirely new set of procedures for handling presidential papers and imposed new access standards never fathomed by Congress for obtaining the information about former presidents. In essence, Bush was repealing an act of Congress and imposing a new law by executive fiat.

Congress, the news media, academics, public advocacy organizations, librarians, and archivists were infuriated by Bush's action. Congress held three sets of hearings, legislation was introduced to restore the law to its original intent and revoke Bush's executive order, and the American Historical Association, joined by several historians and other organizations, filed a lawsuit in February 2001.* The lawsuit has not resolved the consequences of

---

*Following the filing, the Department of Justice moved to dismiss the lawsuit on February 8, 2002, arguing that the case was moot because the White House had released 59,000 pages of the 68,000 Reagan pages that had provoked the lawsuit. On February 8, 2002, the plaintiffs filed a motion for summary judgment. On March 7, 2002, the White House filed a brief stating that Bush was authorizing release of all but 150 pages of these records "at the earliest practicable time." The case remains in legal limbo as of this writing, awaiting a ruling by the court. Bush has effectively stalled so he can keep presidential records closed until after the 2004 election.

Bush's action, and if his efforts are not overturned, Bush's expanded secrecy will make the following the law of the land:

- Former presidents can keep their papers sealed indefinitely.[65]
- Vice presidents have the authority to invoke executive privilege. (Since 1969, only the president himself, as the representative of the executive branch, has been able to invoke executive privilege.)[66]
- The burden shifts from former presidents seeking to withhold their papers to the person seeking presidential papers, to show justification why that person should have access to them.[67]
- Any request for access to a former president's papers must be approved by both the former president and the incumbent president, and if the former president objects to the release, the incumbent president — even if he disagrees — will authorize his Justice Department to protect the former president's objection. In short, taxpayer dollars will fight any effort to get a former president's papers.[68]
- "Representatives of former presidents" may invoke executive privilege after a former president is dead. Although there is no constitutional basis whatsoever for this, under Bush's order such a right can be passed from generation to generation, to friends, to anyone.

In short, presidential scholarship as it now exists will largely end. As the Association of American Libraries has noted, many of the best-known works about the American presidency would not have been possible had Bush's order been in effect.[69]

What to make of this action? Tom Connors of the Society of

American Archivists says, "What seems to be coming out of the [Bush-Cheney] administration is the idea that public information is a dangerous thing." And the late historian Hugh Davis Graham, who had joined in the lawsuit to overturn Bush's order, aptly observed: "George W. Bush has a fetish for secrecy. And unless this executive order is overturned, it will be a victory for secrecy in government — a victory so total that it would make Nixon jealous in his grave."[70] As I see it, controlling presidential documents is but one more undertaking in the Bush-Cheney effort at executive secrecy.[71] Recently, *U.S. News & World Report* discovered that on "Day 1" of this presidency, White House chief of staff Andy Card quietly issued a directive "to wall off records and information previously in the public domain."[72] National security had nothing to do with it. Bush and Cheney assumed office planning to take total and absolute control of executive branch information. The truth will be what they say it is. They will decide what the public should know and when, if ever.

I have not cataloged all the efforts of Bush and Cheney to control government information relating to their presidency (if not others); rather, I have selected a few examples relating largely to domestic and political matters to show the obsessive nature of their secrecy. It became only more obsessive after 9/11. This is not a strong presidency, but an insular and arrogant one, convinced of the wisdom of its messianic mission. And the strong man of this presidency, Dick Cheney, runs his own secret government operations that have aided him in foisting his dark worldview on this presidency, taking America to the most radical foreign policy in our history. We turn to that next.

Chapter Four

Secret Government

The voters aren't going to buy the sanctimonious argument that the Bush Administration has some sort of duty to protect the power of the presidency. . . . The American people do not and should not tolerate government by secrecy.

— Phyllis Schlafly, conservative commentator

Vice President Dick Cheney was in his West Wing office on the morning of September 11, 2001, talking with a speechwriter, when his secretary interrupted to tell him that an unidentified airplane had crashed into one of the Twin Towers of the World Trade Center. Cheney turned on his television in time to witness the second plane crash into the other tower. Cheney summoned his staff straightaway, and as they were discussing possible responses, Secret Service agents arrived at his office, telling Cheney that the White House appeared to be the target of another hijacked flight. They evacuated him by his armpits and belt (with toes barely touching ground) to the White House bunker under the East Wing. Condi Rice joined Cheney in the shelter. After being hijacked out of Dulles Airport, American Airlines flight 77 had initially headed west, then circled back east and headed directly for the White House (or the Capitol, both were in the flight pattern). Barbara Olson, wife of Solicitor General Ted Olson, was on the flight, talking on her cell phone with her husband, who in turn relayed information to a government command center; then at the last minute, the plane unexpectedly turned south and crashed into the Pentagon.

Cheney knew what to do and how to do it. This was why he had been placed on the ticket as Bush's running mate. In Cheney's nine months on the job, his role had evolved to something between that of superchief of staff and co-president, depending on the issue. For Cheney, the 9/11 attack was *not* a transforming event; rather, it was further confirmation of his long-held Hobbesian perception of the world's likely state of perpetual war. Those close to Cheney say of 9/11, "It wasn't an epiphany, it wasn't a sudden eureka moment; it was an evolution, but one that was primed by what he had done and seen at the end of the Cold War," back in 1991 and 1992, as secretary of defense.[1] Indeed, it was not only an evolution but an opportunity.

"One of the American people's most cherished notions about the presidency is that the office somehow ennobles the occupant and renders him fit to meet any crisis," George Reedy wrote many years ago in his "let me tell you how it really is at the White House" classic, *The Twilight of the Presidency*.[2] In fact, crisis doesn't make a president, it merely provides a chance to judge how a president responds to such an event. Bush's initial public responses, while shaky in the first hours, grew increasingly reassuring. He appeared measured, and within days it was evident he could actually read his teleprompter quite nicely when he tried. These were, without question, the finest days of his presidency. For a fleeting moment (and I was not alone), I thought we might have another Abraham Lincoln, whose formidable skills became more apparent because of the Civil War.

But presidential leadership scholar Michael Genovese says

that 9/11 also created something of an illusion. "The public needed to believe that [Bush] had grown," so "we chose to see him — because we need[ed] to see him — as bigger, better and different than he was."[3] In fact, Bush was in over his head, and soon it was obvious that the world was a far "more complex and nuanced" place than he seemed to understand and that true leadership required "a more sophisticated, complex and multi-dimensional view than he seemed capable of accepting."[4] Bush appeared unable to comprehend and envision the implications of many of his actions, a circumstance that his astute supporters appreciated and used to their advantage.[5]

Bush's initial responses to terrorism (appropriately and understandably) were developed behind closed doors. Information provided by Bush and others to *Washington Post* reporter and author Bob Woodward portray Bush as a decisive "I've got my act together" commander in chief. Yet as one looks beyond the spin and more closely at the furtive figures in the shadows, catching occasional glimpses of the players and picking up published and unpublished information here and there, it becomes obvious that it was Cheney (and Rumsfeld) who was more engaged in what military experts call "supreme command" than was the commander in chief himself. It was Cheney and his staff who began gathering and assimilating vast quantities of information they believed critical and who were asking the CIA and the intelligence community the tough questions about what they were doing and why. Yet Cheney's key role (and unusual power) is, as always, made to appear — both internally (to the degree possible) and externally — only incidental (and subsidiary) to Bush's command. When anyone asks about the vice president's level of influence, the official White House mantra is repeated: "The vice president has no personal or political agenda other than advising President Bush."[6] No doubt this is broadly true, for by advising Bush, Cheney understands that he can implement his vision for America and its role in the world.

For Cheney and his like-minded associates, 9/11 was a perfect storm, a moment they had even anticipated when looking earlier for a catalyst necessary to accomplish their broader goals. Cheney's persuasiveness behind closed doors, particularly one-on-one, is legendary, and with a rookie in national security matters like Bush, Cheney can be both a Svengali and a Rasputin. By way of comparison, Nixon and Kissinger had a partnership in national security, but Nixon was the senior partner. With Bush and Cheney, not only is Cheney the senior partner, he is prime minister *sub silentio.* Cheney's enveloping influence on Bush and national security policy has been noted within the Beltway, even if it is largely unnoticed beyond. For example, by the end of the third year of the Bush-Cheney administration, the *American Conservative* (Feb. 2, 2004) declared Cheney the American Richelieu, "the hand behind the throne." In describing the Bush II White House, Washington-based journalist Georgie Anne Geyer has written that Cheney is "the most important vice president in history — some say the most influential man in America." She reported that "George W. [Bush] most resembles the many French dauphins come suddenly to the throne — the young, inexperienced prince, with a defense chief who has definite Napoleonic tendencies, and a flowing group of courtiers with their own agendas and loyalties, some to foreign countries and some to secret societies outside the realm. With this court, Dick Cheney has become George Bush's Cardinal Richelieu."* The comparison is, indeed, fitting.

During the 2000 campaign, Cheney kept his dogs of war

---

*The *American Conservative* also provided a brief history refresher to make its point: "You do remember Cardinal Richelieu? It was the time of the religious

caged, and not until 9/11 did he set them free. However, the policies Cheney has now put into practice have been quietly in the making for over a decade. Only the tip of the iceberg is presently visible.

Cheney/Wolfowitz World Dominance Philosophy

As secretary of defense (1989–93), Cheney accepted the decision not to march to Baghdad in 1991 and remove Saddam. Yet before he left the government, he'd had serious second thoughts. Iraq became a part of a far larger picture and vision. In late 1991, recognizing that the United States' military needs had changed with the end of the Cold War, Cheney formed a group at the Department of Defense to develop "forward leaning" military plans for the future. No secretary of defense had ever done more for the care and feeding of the military-industrial complex than Cheney, and his forward-looking plans would follow that pattern. Paul Wolfowitz, a mathematician-turned-political-scientist (Ph.D., University of Chicago, 1972), then serving as Cheney's undersecretary of defense for policy (with some seven hundred policy wonks at his command), took charge of the study.* Cheney and Wolfowitz decided to use the department's Defense

---

wars in Europe in the 16th century and the era of a weak king, Louis XIII. In 1585, Armand-Jean du Plessis, Cardinal and Duke de Richelieu, was born to a minor noble family and became a priest, a bishop, a cardinal, then France's Secretary of State for foreign affairs in 1616, and, finally, the prime minister of France in 1624. He would go down in history as a man obsessed with bringing order to France under royal authority, and he believed in the divine right of the king and the obedience of the people. Yet, even as he believed in the 'light of natural reason,' still he remained always the pessimist with regard to human nature and believed fully that the ends justify the means." The magazine further noted Richelieu's "horrible overspending for France on war he fostered" as he "committed war expenditure with little regard for the difficulties of raising revenue and he was given to economic improvisation that was often unsound."
*Today, Paul Wolfowitz is undersecretary of defense.

Policy Guidance report, a top-secret internal document to assist when preparing long-term budgets and plans, as the vehicle to rethink foreign and military policy. Wolfowitz gathered his brightest stars to "think out of the box," with Cheney often joining the group on Saturdays, as they looked for answers to questions about America's appropriate post–Cold War position. It was at this time that Dick Cheney's radical strategic thinking took shape.

When the new Defense Policy Guidance plan was being circulated for comment in the spring of 1992, it was leaked to the *New York Times* by a Pentagon "official who believe[d] this . . . strategy debate should be carried out in the public domain."[7] Public debate, however, quickly killed Cheney's plans for the United States' "ruling the world," as one commentator described it.[8] The plans, which were "conspicuously devoid of references to collective action through the United Nations" or other multinational organizations, anticipated "future coalitions to be ad hoc assemblies, often not lasting beyond the crisis being confronted." Even then, the United States would "act independently when collective action cannot be orchestrated," or if necessary to respond quickly. The proposed plans further contemplated the need "to take military steps to prevent the development of weapons of mass destruction" by "pre-empting [such] an impending attack."[9]

President George H. W. Bush's Democratic and Republican opponents, seeking the 1992 presidential nomination, went after the far-reaching new plans. Democratic presidential candidate Senator Paul Tsongas (from the left) opposed the Pax Americana nature of the plan and called for continued collective security; Democratic governor Bill Clinton (from the center) was appalled at the expense of the plans; and Republican Patrick

Buchanan (from the right) lashed out at not only the expense but the concept of America serving as the ultimate guarantor of world security.[10] As a result, "Cheney was forced to revise the document, sanding down its edges considerably."[11] But this did not change Cheney's thinking one scrap, nor did it result in the plans being shelved. On the contrary, these concepts became the basic tenets of neoconservative foreign policy. Cheney's departure from the government with Bush senior's defeat was not the end of this radical planning, only just the beginning.

To encourage continuing debate on the Cheney/Wolfowitz ideas, William Kristol (who had been Vice President Dan Quayle's chief of staff and then founder of the *Weekly Standard*, the voice of the neocons) and Robert Kagan (a senior associate at the Carnegie Endowment for Peace, a columnist for the *Washington Post*, and a contributing editor at the *Weekly Standard*)* wrote about these policy plans in the July/August 1996 issue of *Foreign Affairs*, explaining them as America's opportunity to exercise a "benevolent hegemony" of the world while promoting democracy and free markets abroad (nice Orwellian doublespeak for American world domination). By the spring of 1997, Kristol and Kagan had created the Project for the New American Century, a well-funded, "non-profit, educational organization" to promote the Cheney/Wolfowitz plans. Joining this effort were Wolfowitz and a who's who of a growing neoconservative establishment.[12] In 1998, eighteen prominent associates of the New American Century wrote President Clinton urging him to remove Saddam Hussein. Although Cheney did

---

*Robert Kagan's wife, Victoria, a former U.S. deputy chief of mission at NATO, is Cheney's deputy national security advisor; she replaced Eric Edelman, who is serving in Turkey as U.S. ambassador.

not sign the letter, his former mentor Don Rumsfeld did, as well as many of his close associates.* (Maybe Cheney refrained from signing because Halliburton was doing such a nice business with Saddam.)

By September 2000, the Project for the New American Century had published a report further refining and expanding on the Cheney/Wolfowitz ideas, titled *Rebuilding America's Defenses: Strategy, Forces and Resources for a New Century*. The study lamented the lack of effort to "preserve American military preeminence in the coming decades" and acknowledged that to do so was going to be difficult. The study criticized Clinton for squandering his opportunity and explained that what was needed was a transformation strategy. Such a transformation process was "likely to be a long one, *absent some catastrophic and catalyzing event — like a new Pearl Harbor*." (Emphasis added.)[13]

Before the actual catalyzing event occurred, Kagan and Kristol, in their ongoing advocacy, sought to create such a compelling event. Accordingly, they edited and wrote the introduction to a collection of essays published in early 2001 — *Present Danger: Crisis and Opportunity in American Foreign and Defense Policy* — making the case for the latest iteration of the Cheney/Wolfowitz concepts.[14] Their provocative "present danger" title — a term presumably taken from a landmark U.S. Supreme Court ruling *(Schenck* v. *United States)* discussing the type of grave and immediate danger necessary to justify setting aside the First Amendment, which the Court called "a clear and present danger" — referred to their concern that "the United States,

---

*The signators were Elliott Abrams, Richard L. Armitage, William J. Bennett, Jeffrey Bergner, John Bolton, Paula Dobriansky, Francis Fukuyama, Robert Kagan, Zalmay Khalilzad, William Kristol, Richard Perle, Peter W. Rodman, Donald Rumsfeld, William Schneider Jr., Vin Weber, Paul Wolfowitz, R. James Woolsey, and Robert B. Zoellick.

the world's dominant power on whom the maintenance of international peace and the support of liberal democratic principles depends, will shirk its responsibilities and . . . allow the international order that it created and sustains to collapse."[15] (It is worth noting that *Present Danger* hardly deals with the threat of terrorism and concludes that Iraq would "be able to reconstitute viable WMD and missile capabilities within six months" but only after "it emerges from the current sanctions.") They offered neither a "clear" nor "present" danger, but with 9/11 the neoconservatives had their catalyzing event, and they were positioned at the top of the Bush II administration to make the most of the opportunity.[16]

Cheney's Shadow National Security Council

From the outset of the administration, Cheney focused on national security. Look, for example, at I. Lewis "Scooter" Libby, an attorney who served at the Pentagon (1989–93) while Cheney was in charge.* Scooter Libby not only carries the designation of Cheney's chief of staff but also has the title national security advisor to the vice president, and he is an assistant to the president (the highest title on the White House staff). Libby's foreign-policy background (and title) clearly reflects Cheney's perception of, if not his preoccupation with, his war role in the Bush II administration. But Libby was just the beginning. To support his national security work, rather than relying on the National Security Council (NSC) — a statutory

---

*Ironically, Scooter Libby represented fugitive financier Marc Rich and told Congress, after he had become Cheney's chief of staff, that he believed the prosecutors from the U.S. Attorney's Office had "misconstrued the facts and the law" when they went after Rich on tax-evasion charges. This, of course, was one of the principal reasons Clinton pardoned Rich.

creation, which is part of the Executive Office of the President (and where Condi Rice as national security advisor to Bush was cutting back on staff) — Cheney formed what is, in effect, a shadow NSC. Indeed, it was actually Bush's NSC staff who first called Cheney's operation a "shadow" government.[17] This shadow operation, while informally integrated, actually has its own agenda as well as the power to realize it through the vice president's clout. It is a secret government — beyond the reach of Congress, and everyone else as well.

Cheney has under him some fifteen experienced national security experts — aides such as Eric Edelman, a foreign service officer and former ambassador to Finland who was with Cheney at the Defense Department (and who he later sent to Turkey as ambassador, not to mention the eyes and ears for the vice president), and John Hannah, who had been at Bush senior's State Department and is an expert on the Middle East. To serve as Hannah's top assistant, William Luti, a former adviser to House Speaker Newt Gingrich, was hired (and later dispatched to the Defense Department when Cheney's shadow operation increased its outsourcing).*[18] Cheney's academic and scholarly bent (he holds a master's degree in political science from the University

---

*Investigative journalist Sy Hersh has reported at some length in the *New Yorker* — for example, "Who Lied to Whom" (Mar. 3, 2003) and "The Stovepipe" (Oct. 27, 2003) — about Cheney's out-of-channels intelligence-gathering operations. In addition, the information about Cheney's hidden intelligence-collection operations has been further puzzled together by Robert Dreyfuss and Jason Vest for *Mother Jones* (in "The Lie Factory," Jan./Feb. 2004). Dreyfuss and Vest reported that dubious and untested intelligence was assembled by the Office of Special Plans, set up in the Pentagon (a "shadow agency within an agency") and composed largely of neoconservative ideologues, assembled to make the case for war in Iraq, and did so when others in the government's intelligence community had no information justifying the case that Cheney and Bush wanted to make.

of Wyoming) explains his reliance on others with advanced degrees. Not only is Cheney's staff smart, they know how Washington works. And running through this staff is the common thread of a shared neoconservative political philosophy. As the *New Republic* noted, "Cheney's office came to be viewed as the administration's neocons sanctuary."[19]

A Cliffs Notes–level analysis of neoconservatism is found in a widely circulated floor speech by Congressman Ron Paul (R-Tex.), a libertarian (thus no fan of neoconservatism).[20] "Modern neoconservatives are not necessarily monolithic in their views," the congressman says, "but they generally can be described as follows":

- They agree with Trotsky's idea of a permanent revolution.
- They identify strongly with the writings of Leo Strauss.
- They express no opposition to the welfare state and will expand it to win votes and power.
- They believe in a powerful federal government.
- They believe the ends justify the means in politics — that hardball [in] politics is a moral necessity.
- They believe lying is necessary for the state to survive.
- They believe certain facts should be known only by the political elite, and withheld from the general public.
- They believe in preemptive war and the naked use of military force to achieve any desired ends.
- They openly endorse the idea of an American empire, and hence unapologetically call for imperialism.
- They are very willing to use force to impose American ideals.
- They scoff at the Founding Fathers' belief in neutrality in foreign affairs.

- They believe 9/11 resulted from a lack of foreign entanglements, not from too many.
- They are willing to redraw the map of the Middle East by force, while unconditionally supporting Israel and the Likud Party.*
- They view civil liberties with suspicion, as unnecessary restrictions on the federal government.
- They despise libertarians, and dismiss any arguments based on constitutional grounds.[21]

Also revealing is how neocons see themselves. Irving Kristol, putative godfather of the "persuasion" (he says it is not a "movement"), explained their thinking broadly in "The Neoconservative Persuasion: What It Was and What It Is." He wrote that the "disillusioned liberal intellectuals" of the 1970s, who became the initial neoconservatives, sought to convert the Republican Party — and American conservatives — to their thinking. That, however, did not occur; neoconservatism has not become mainstream American conservatism. "It is hopeful, not lugubrious; forward-looking, not nostalgic; and its general tone is cheerful, not grim or dyspeptic. Its 20th-century heroes tend to be TR, FDR, and Ronald Reagan (but not Calvin Coolidge, Herbert Hoover, Dwight Eisenhower, or Barry Goldwater)." As for foreign policy, Irving Kristol has been surprised by the recent attention to neocons, "since there is no set of neoconservative beliefs concerning foreign policy, only a set of attitudes derived from historical experience." Neoconservatives' favored "text on foreign affairs . . . is Thucydides on the Peloponnesian

---

*Israeli prime minister Ariel Sharon is the leader of the Likud Party, which is considered right of center in Israeli politics.

War."* And Kristol said that what unites them with traditional conservatives is a shared concern about the "steady decline in our democratic culture, sinking to new levels of vulgarity."[22] Apparently beside the point is the vulgarity of sleazy business deals, bullying demeanor, and utter disregard for norms of behavior honoring international laws respecting the sanctity of human life.

Neoconservative Vulcanization of Bush

Bush does not spend a lot of time reading *Foreign Affairs*. In fact, he does not spend a lot of time reading anything. "Nobody needs to tell me what to believe. But I *do* need somebody to tell me where Kosovo is," Bush said as he prepared to run for president. For those national security experts working as tutors to the candidate, it was an opportunity to mold the thinking of a man who had a good chance to become president, a man who knew virtually nothing about the subject and had thought little about the world beyond the United States. He was, for all practical purposes, a blank slate to be written on.

The group of tutors was headed by Condoleezza Rice, and she named her team "the Vulcans" (after the Roman blacksmith god of fire and metalworking) to honor her hometown, Birmingham, Alabama, where she had first seen a Vulcan statue — a symbol of the city's steel industry. Perhaps there was an attempt at humor, too: tutors in the mold of *Star Trek*'s Mr. Spock, they

---

*An ironic foreign-policy favorite, given that the democratic superpower Athens, whose expanding powers and influence provoked a war with the despotic Spartans, who ultimately defeated the Athenians in the Peloponnesian War, as recorded by Thucydides.

hoped to be pleasant but utterly without emotion — coldly viewing the universe without sympathy or empathy.

Condi Rice and Bush had become close friends earlier, particularly over their mutual love of sports, and she would become his closest aide on both a personal and professional level at the White House. The Vulcan tutors represented two of three Republican philosophies in national security: those of the "realists" and those of the "hard-liners." Realists look to the policies of the Bush I administration as exemplars for foreign policy, such as not marching into Baghdad in 1991 or not roaming the planet looking for fights. The hard-liners seek to remake American policy and want an aggressive, militarily muscular (if diplomacy fails) American global hegemony (read: domination). The excluded "isolationists" reject all foreign entanglements. The Vulcans were predominately neocons, or hard-liners.[23]

Foreign policy was a nonissue in the 2000 campaign, yet to those who paid attention, the signs of war were apparent. Nicolas Lemann, a Washington correspondent for the *New Yorker*, had interviewed and profiled Cheney during the campaign. Speaking at the Massachusetts Institute of Technology, Lemann told his audience (less than fifty days into the new administration), given Cheney's rapid rise to that of co-president, to "look for swashbuckling adventures, hawkish foreign policy and an active, interventionist military."[24] So it would be, but much more.

Not unlike Nixon's decision decades earlier to depend on Kissinger and take a hard line on almost everything after the leak of the Pentagon Papers, Bush has relied on his trusted vice president and taken his hard line. It is not likely that Rice — who does not consider herself a hard-liner — would have encouraged Bush to embrace the neoconservative philosophy. But it is not difficult to understand the appeal to Bush of this kick-ass approach, for he likes bold moves, has no hesitation to gamble with his policies (and American lives), and has his manhood tied up with his job as president. Former secretary of the treasury Paul O'Neill said war with Iraq was on the agenda at the very first NSC meeting; the *New Republic* reported that Cheney got the commander in chief marching toward Baghdad in early January 2002.[25] Obviously, the success in Afghanistan (if it can truly be called that, given Bush's subsequent near abandonment of the reconstruction efforts there, the return of the Taliban, and the inability to shut down al Qaeda) emboldened the president. But it is entirely possible that even had 9/11 not occurred, Cheney still would have convinced Bush of the wisdom of his philosophy. In fact, the delay by Cheney and his national security team in addressing terrorism suggests that they might well have been busy constructing plans (or Cheney, who keeps his thoughts to himself, may have privately been mulling them) to be implemented when a disaster like 9/11 occurred. Cheney knew that terrorism was the perfect excuse, an ideal raison d'être, for his "let's rule the world" philosophy. Politically, it would be much easier to be seen as shooting back instead of shooting first, given the caliber of weapon Cheney sought to wield. But he and his team did far worse than simply waiting for an attack that would kill a sufficient number of Americans.

Cheney's Stall on Terrorism

The threat of terrorism, even of terrorists striking in the United States, was understood by both Bush and Cheney long before they arrived in the White House. In his 1999 speech to the cadets at The Citadel, Bush had warned of such domestic terrorism. In May 2000, Bush's speech on national security opened on this note: "The emerging security threats to the United States, its friends and allies and even to Russia now come from rogue states, terrorist groups and other adversaries seeking weapons of mass destruction [WMD] and the means to deliver them."[26] Later in the 2000 campaign, following the terrorist attack on the USS *Cole*, Bush was vague about the proper response, saying only, "It must have consequences."[27] Bush similarly told Fox News, who asked if there should be a military response to the *Cole* bombing, that he wanted to study the matter but thought the United States should send a "swift, sure and a clear signal to terrorists around the world that we are not going to tolerate terrorism."[28]

During the transition period, Bush and Cheney learned more about the terrorism problem. Bill Clinton told Bush, when he visited the White House as president-elect on December 19, 2000, that his "biggest [national] security problem" would be "Osama bin Laden" and terrorism.[29] Bush and Cheney were told in CIA briefings before assuming office that the CIA "had been warn[ed] about bin Laden and al Qaeda."[30] Clinton's national security advisor, Sandy Berger, set up ten briefings for his successor, Condoleezza Rice, and her top deputy, Stephen Hadley, with Berger personally attending the session on terrorism, which was presented by "terrorism czar" Richard Clarke (who would remain on Bush's National Security Council staff). Berger attended the terrorism session to underscore the importance of the subject. Berger told Rice, "I believe that the Bush Administration will spend more time on terrorism generally, and on al Qaeda specifically, than any other subject."[31] Bush and Cheney also learned that after the 1998 bombing incidents at U.S. embassies in Africa, CIA director George Tenet had "declared war" (at least for the CIA) on Osama bin Laden and al Qaeda.[32]

In January 2001, after their inauguration, Bush and Cheney received the report of a multiyear study of national security problems likely to confront the United States during the next quarter century. Clinton's secretary of defense, William Cohen (a Republican), initiated this blue-ribbon, bipartisan study by experts, co-chaired by two Washington insiders familiar with military and foreign policy, former senator Warren Rudman (R-N.H.) and former senator Gary Hart (D-Col.). The fourteen-member commission and its professional staff, with a $10 million budget, sought answers and found them.[33] The final report was issued on January 31, 2001, and the highest recommendation and first priority urged the president to focus on terrorism: "A direct attack against American citizens on American soil is likely over the next quarter century," and "even excellent intelligence will not prevent all surprises."[34]

Cheney, however, decided to put terrorism on a back burner and closed down the Rudman-Hart commission.[35] Rather than relying on the bipartisan judgment of this uniquely qualified group, Cheney told Bush to turn the matter over to him (since he was already looking at everything else). Accordingly, on May 8, 2001, Bush issued a statement: "Some non-state terrorist groups have . . . demonstrated an interest in acquiring weapons of mass destruction. . . . It is clear that the threat of chemical, biological, or nuclear weapons being used against the United States — *while not immediate* — is very real." (Emphasis added.) He said that he had asked Cheney "to oversee the development of a coordinated national effort so that we may do the very best possible job of protecting our people from catastrophic harm." In addition, Bush would "create an Office of National Preparedness" in the Federal Emergency Management Agency to implement Cheney's recommendations.[36] This announcement killed the Rudman-Hart commission proposal to create a homeland security department with cabinet rank (a plan the White House would soon claim as its own). Later that morning (May 8), Secretary of State Colin Powell all but conceded that terrorism was a problem without solution. After explaining what the State Department was (and had been) doing, which was not insubstantial, Powell rhetorically asked, "Does that mean we are going to thwart or successfully defend against every terrorist act possible? Of course not."[37]

Only days before the 9/11 attack, on September 4, 2001, plans for dealing with al Qaeda arrived in the vice president's office. Why had it taken so long to address what Cheney had to know was a very serious threat? To a great extent, the delay was due to Bush and Cheney's blanket rejection of any idea — however good — that had come out of the Clinton administration. Indeed, Richard Clarke — who had served in high-level positions for three Republican presidents as well as Clinton — would soon resign in frustration regarding Bush and Cheney's discarding of numerous antiterror programs. But not all of the Bush administration's actions were about politics of the past, for 9/11 created its own political predicament for this presidency. Given the effort to prevent others from learning what they knew about such a threat, when they knew, and what they were planning to do about it, it is reasonable to believe that they planned to exploit terrorism before 9/11 handed them the issue ready-made for exploitation — a fact they obviously want to keep buried.

Blocking 9/11 Investigations

Understandably, Americans (particularly the families of those who lost loved ones on 9/11) want to know how nineteen foreign-born hijackers with box cutters could elude security, commandeer four fully fueled jumbo airliners, and, with remarkable synchronism and accuracy, fly three of them as human-guided missiles into designated and highly symbolic targets in

New York and Washington. The fourth airliner, which crashed in a Pennsylvania field, is believed to have been headed for the White House or the Capitol. If the plot were part of a movie or novel, it might well be dismissed as wildly unrealistic. And yet it happened.

Given the dimensions of the government's failure, it was inevitable that several congressional committees, in both the House and Senate, quickly expressed plans to investigate. But this was exactly what Cheney wanted to avoid. With the Democrats in control of the Senate and the Republicans in control of the House, the White House had only partial control over Congress. Working behind the scenes, however, Cheney was able to do what a White House does when it does not want to be investigated — stop the process by jamming the gears of government.

Both Bush and Cheney spoke with Senate Majority Leader Tom Daschle in late January 2002 about the probes. The *Washington Post* reported that the "president said the inquiry should be limited to the House and Senate intelligence committees, whose proceedings are generally secret" and that Cheney told Daschle, "A review of what happened on September 11 would take resources and personnel away from the effort in the war on terrorism."[38] It was not a viable excuse to forestall an investigation. When they failed to block the congressional inquiry, Bush and Cheney next used their political influence to control it.

Cheney employed well-proven tactics — in fact, we used a variation of them during Watergate. First Daschle and then the House Republican leadership agreed (out of concern for "national security") to permit only the intelligence committees to investigate 9/11. Then, to further limit those inquiries and prevent separate investigations by the House and Senate intelligence committees, an "unprecedented" (only because Democrats controlled one house of Congress, Republicans the other) joint committee was formed by combining the two committees. With thirty-seven members constituting the joint inquiry, the impact of the investigation was immediately weakened. Cheney understood that all members of such a high-profile undertaking would jealously seek to be involved, which dilutes the effort. For example, the time allotted to any single member for questioning witnesses must be limited, so everyone gets his turn, and the staff cannot assist three dozen-plus members as well as it can a few. And reaching agreement on anything is difficult with such expanded membership, not to mention mixing the House and Senate together. In short, such large joint committees are remarkably cumbersome and poor at investigations, and for that reason they are rarely used. Second, to keep the focus off the Bush-Cheney White House, it was agreed that the congressional inquiry would investigate the roots of the terrorism problem, thus going back into the Clinton administration, where Republicans hoped to dump the blame for 9/11. Finally, since all the information was controlled by the executive branch (i.e., the White House) and much of it subject to national security classification, Bush and Cheney could — and did — control what would be provided to the joint inquiry. The committee would get only what Bush and Cheney wanted it to get.

Although the joint inquiry held a few public hearings for show (members of Congress like to be seen on television), the real work took place behind closed doors. Running this investigation was no easy task, because the Bush administration was determined to foil the effort — and succeeded. The staff director, who is important to any such inquiry, was an able former federal prosecutor from Tampa, Eleanor Hill, who spent over a decade as a Senate investigator before serving as inspector general at the Department of Defense. Whatever her political affiliation, she has worked with, and for, both Democrats and Republicans for years, appearing more interested in doing the job well than in the politics of it.

The White House took an unprecedented stance in refusing to permit either Don Rumsfeld, as secretary of defense, or Colin Powell, as secretary of state, from testifying about matters relating to pre-9/11 counterterrorism activities.[39] Republican senator Richard Shelby, a member of the joint committee, explained to the *New York Times* that while the White House had taken one position publicly, privately it was working to kill the investigation. "You know, we were told that there would be cooperation in this investigation, and I question that," Senator Shelby said, noting, "I think that most of the information that our staff has been able to get that is real meaningful has had to be extracted piece by piece."[40] As Ms. Hill testified at the first public hearings, she had been through "a long and arduous process" to obtain classified information from the intelligence community. Senator John McCain summed it all up when he told *Time* (on February 3, 2003) that the administration had "slow-walked and stonewalled" the joint inquiry.

If Bush and Cheney and their aides had acted reasonably and responsibly before 9/11, why the endless efforts to block the investigation? A logical inference can be drawn from their behavior (for example, classifying previously unclassified information, launching an FBI investigation of leaks from the congressional inquiry, publicly trying to discredit it) that Bush and Cheney want to hide what they were doing. Because of the lack of White House cooperation with the joint inquiry, the families of 9/11 victims began lobbying Congress to create an independent commission, with subpoena power, to investigate 9/11, even before the congressional effort had been completed. Bush and Cheney, of course, objected. When they claimed that such an investigation would hamper the war on terror, *USA Today* editorially spoke for many when it said, "Nonsense," pointing out that a number of blue-ribbon commissions had investigated the attack on Pearl Harbor by Japan *during* World War II, so "why isn't it logical, ethical and necessary to get to the bottom of how [the] Sept. 11 attacks could have happened?"[41] Both Republicans and Democrats demanded an investigation. Even neocons Bill Kristol and Robert Kagan joined the chorus (in their May 27, 2002, *Weekly Standard* editorial) because the White House position was not only arrogant but stupid. Still, Bush and Cheney resisted. "This President responds, once again" to the request for a true investigation, the *Nation* observed (in a June 10, 2002, editorial), "by calling for more secrecy in government, more silence from his critics."

But the political pressure was growing, and unable to block this additional inquiry, Cheney again moved to control it. Bush and Cheney dropped their objections "after winning the power to appoint the chairman, who also has the power to block subpoenas."[42] And the White House had a chairman in mind: Henry Kissinger, a selection described by the *Nation* (on December 23, 2002) as "a sick, black-is-white, war-is-peace joke — a cruel insult to the memory of those killed on 9/11." Given Kissinger's record of "coddl[ing] state-sponsored terrorists" and standing as "a proven liar, . . . Bush has rendered the independent commission a sham."

Kissinger didn't last long, for he was unwilling to disclose his clients in his international consulting business to avoid any conflicts of interest, profit trumping his patriotism. Next the White House selected former New Jersey governor Thomas Kean, a fine man with absolutely no experience in national security matters, which made him a perfect selection. But the real reason the White House wanted authority to select the chairman was that it wanted the ability to control the selection of the key staff, for this is where the investigation would be conducted. Co-chairman Kean, not by coincidence, selected as executive director for the commission Phillip D. Zelikow, who might as well have come directly from the Bush-Cheney White House. Zelikow had co-authored a book with Condi Rice (*Germany Unified and Europe Transformed: A Study in Statecraft, 1995*) and had served with Rice on Bush senior's NSC. In addition, Zelikow had worked with Cheney on the transition. Understandably, the 9/11 families felt the fix was in when they learned this, and requested his removal.[43] But Zelikow remained. Those who know Zelikow, a highly ambitious fellow, say they would be amazed if he has not provided a back channel to and from the White House regarding the work of the commission — and if he has not, it is simply because he is taking good care of everything for them. With Zelikow in such a vital post, any report by the 9/11 commission is suspect. Regardless of the good intentions of the commission members, the staff can have a tremendous influence on their knowledge and focus, and thus their report. The White House successfully managed to reach inside the 9/11 commission to protect itself.

Even with that protection, the White House has been less than cooperative with the 9/11 commission, stalling, negotiating everything, distracting its focus. The co-chairmen are both rather independent-thinking men. Kean, a Republican, has not been hesitant to lean openly on the White House and threaten subpoenas.[44] Privately, he tells friends the White House is doing its best to make it impossible to meet the deadline of May 2004. Even publicly, Kean has expressed frustration. "It makes it inconvenient when you can't take things back to the office with you to study, when you've got to refresh your memory by going across town to a little room in the White House to read your notes," he told the *New York Times.*[45] Co-chairman Lee Hamilton, the former Democratic congressman who was responsible for the legislation that opened all the JFK files to end the secrecy of the Warren Commission, understands the highly negative impact such secrecy can have on public trust in government. But the co-chairmen, and their commission, have been outfoxed — notwithstanding their honest efforts.

Tragically, Bush and Cheney are not merely doing a disservice to the families of 9/11 victims. Their failure to cooperate with this investigation (if not putting in the fix) can reverberate through history. Aside from their unwillingness to hold themselves accountable, their arrogance ignores the long-term problem they have created. They need only look at the painful lessons from the mishandling of the Warren Commission investigation of JFK's assassination. When important information is withheld, or the work is less than complete, the public will believe the worst. Not unlike the shallow Warren Commission inquiry (which most recently has resulted in the father of Bush's press secretary, Scott McClellan, publishing a book claiming that Lyndon Johnson was responsible for Kennedy's assassination), Bush and Cheney's secrecy about 9/11 has already fostered a cottage industry on 9/11 conspiracy theories. Just as happened with the Kennedy assassination because of the secrecy surrounding the Warren Commission investigation, rumors and speculation about 9/11 have become rampant, if not accepted fact, which will spawn only more mistrust in government. Among the absurd is the French book *L'Effroyable Imposture* (The Horrifying Fraud), which contends that it was not a hijacked American Airlines jet that crashed into the Pentagon but rather a missile fired by the American military itself. CNN reported that by the summer of 2002, more than 200,000 books had sold, making it a runaway bestseller. Along the same absurd lines, and also a big seller, is the work of German author Mathias Broecker, *Conspiracies, Conspiracy Theories and the Secrets of September 11*, which has sold more than 100,000 copies, arguing that all the unanswered questions point to a massive cover-up by the United States. In a story on the growing number of conspiracy theories, ABC News added one I'd not heard: "The reason the tapes from the cockpit recorders of the four hijacked planes have not been released is because the voices they recorded are not humans, but the voices of aliens." (Probably true, but not the extraterrestrial kind.) Large numbers of Europeans and growing numbers of Americans find themselves drawn to these simplistic conspiratorial answers because no legitimate, unbiased independent official body has provided answers to the many questions emerging from that fateful day. To mention but a few that should be addressed:

- Is it true that many governments (Germany, Israel, Morocco, Russia, Jordan, Egypt, and France among them) had advance knowledge and warned the United States that the 9/11 attack was imminent?
- Is it true that Bush personally intervened to block an investigation of the bin Laden family's investments and activities in the United States before 9/11?
- Why were no military fighter jets scrambled until over an hour and a quarter after the FAA became aware of the first hijacking (whereas the FAA had fighters alongside golfer — a stalwart Republican and friend of Bush — Payne Stewart's private jet within twenty minutes of loss of radio contact)?
- Who purchased (and made all that money on) put options (betting that the stock price would go down) for companies that would be most affected by 9/11 attacks,

such as United Airlines, American Airlines, and tenants at the World Trade Center Merrill Lynch and Morgan Stanley?

- Why were so many of these put options traded through an investment firm with executives who have ties to the CIA? Why did the president of the firm abruptly resign after 9/11?

- Is there any basis to the many stories in the British press about the financial rewards from 9/11 accruing to the Carlyle Group (for whom Bush once worked and his father worked until recently)?

- Who authorized Saudi businessmen (and their families) to be picked up throughout the United States by a private airplane right after the 9/11 attacks, when all other private and commercial aircraft were grounded in the United States, and then fly off to Europe? Who was on the airplane? And why were they so anxious to get out of the United States?

- Is it true that two senior intelligence and terror experts from Israel's Mossad visited Washington in August 2001 to warn the CIA and FBI that a cell of two hundred terrorists (including four who would be among the 9/11 teams) was planning a major operation?

These are but a few of the unanswered questions.[46] Bush and Cheney have stonewalled all of them. As a result, the conspiracy theories continue. Among the uglier ones are those that have been invented for anti-Semitic purposes and are so offensive that the Anti-Defamation League commissioned a full report addressing them. For example, some Arab, Islamic, and neo-Nazi groups claim that Mossad is the true villain, for it purportedly is "sufficiently cunning, resourceful, and wicked . . . to have carried out the attacks and blamed them on [its] enemies." Another related theory claims that a group of Israeli spies, posing as art students studying in the United States, had been tracking the 9/11 terrorists but did nothing to stop them. Other theories have Israeli companies involved in 9/11, or the Jewish ownership of the Twin Towers as the explanation (since only the owners might gain from the destruction of the buildings). At least one of these theories is purportedly corroborated by the claim that some four thousand Jews who worked at the World Trade Center were all warned to stay home on 9/11.[47]

All these contentions and questions need to be disposed of with facts. The irresponsible secrecy of Bush and Cheney and their efforts to keep the truth of 9/11 from being revealed are enabling, if not encouraging, such conspiracy theories to flourish. History teaches that it is the secret keepers who ultimately become the subject of such baseless theories. But Bush and Cheney clearly assume that history will be as they want it to be written — thus, their restrictions on the press, on access to government documents and presidential papers, and the truth about 9/11.

Bush and Cheney have politicized and concealed so much connected with 9/11 and their war on terror that even such fundamental matters as the government's plans for continuity of government, should a catastrophe occur in the nation's capital, are suspect. Not only the public is being kept in the dark; so is Congress. Yet these are matters of public business. The public has a right to know what Bush and Cheney are doing with their government, for contingency planning is an area fraught with problems and potential for political mischief, not to mention mistakes that could have long-lasting effects.

Hiding and Politicizing Contingent Government

Bush is the first president to truly employ a secret government, and I'm not referring to Cheney's shadow operations. Cold War veterans on the morning of September 11, 2001, remembered the highly classified contingency plans, first adopted during the Eisenhower administration (about the same time the first White House subterranean shelter was constructed). Known as the continuity of government plans, or COG, they had remained in effect until the early 1990s, when they were largely shelved with the end of the threat of mutually assured destruction and the Cold War. The plans had not been repealed, nor had they been updated since 1985, when President Reagan issued a couple of directives.*

Within hours of the 9/11 attack, Bush and Cheney activitated those long-dormant COG plans. It was the first time they had ever been used. Television network news and newspapers mentioned that the government had invoked "continuity of government" plans, and even though a few experts vaguely explained them, no one understood what this really meant. Typical was the *Washington Post* report in its final edition on September 11, which stated that "Bush flew immediately to Barksdale Air Force Base in Louisiana where he was expected to consult with top advisers, who had already begun outlining backup plans that go by the grim name of 'continuity of government.'" No further

---

*I learned of these plans when serving as the associate deputy attorney general: I was taken to the helicopter pad at the Defense Department, flown to a site not far from Washington, and then taken to an underground facility, where I spent the day in an orientation program, deep under the earth in a government office/hotel/survival complex, nothing fancy but certainly comfortable; from this location, in the event of nuclear attack, the federal government could operate almost indefinitely.

explanation. Most people thought this activity really meant keeping the president and vice president at separate locations. It did, but it involved much more, too.

With little notice, and no announcement, men and women throughout the federal government in Washington — principally career people, plus a few select political appointees — were told shortly after the 9/11 attacks to pack up for a trip. They were forbidden — under the threat of criminal prosecution — from revealing where they were going or why. They were transported by Military District of Washington helicopters and buses to one of the two East Coast underground facilities. (The MDW is a unique command that protects the Capital City and provides a ceremonial military presence at countless events.)[48] This action was undertaken as a precautionary move, for the White House had no intelligence indicating the terrorists possessed nuclear capabilities. But no chances were being taken; it was the president's responsibility to be sure the executive branch could continue to function after such an attack. What started as a precaution soon became permanent.*

The COG plans were in operation for six months before enterprising reporters from the *Washington Post* figured out what was occurring, and on March 1, 2002, with a startling front-page headline, SHADOW GOVERNMENT IS AT WORK IN SECRET; AFTER ATTACKS, BUSH ORDERED 100 OFFICIALS TO BUNKERS AWAY FROM CAPITAL TO ENSURE FEDERAL SURVIVAL, the COG came to light.[49] Many in Washington were stunned to learn that literally

---

*Was this, in truth, a legitimate effort to continue the government, or were the rumors I picked up true, that those being selected for COG duty thought in the mold of Bush and Cheney? Dispatch of 70 to 150 government executives to one of the two COG locations (for a period of ninety days, after which they are rotated and replaced by other executives) is ripe for political abuse. But by keeping it all secret, no one will know until it is too late.

hundreds of federal employees had been involved. No one doubted the wisdom of this move, but the way Bush and Cheney have undertaken it has raised as many concerns as any comfort it has provided. While it is good to know that the executive branch will remain in operation, what kind of executive branch? Congress had not been advised of the extent of the COG operations, yet the Speaker of the House, Representative Denny Hastert (R-Ill.), and then president pro tempore of the Senate, Senator Robert Byrd (D-W. Va.), are in line ahead of members of a president's cabinet under the very dated presidential succession law.[50] The other two branches of government have long had their own continuity plans, but they rely on the executive branch to tell them when to duck and cover. Had they known that Bush and Cheney had implemented the COG and were operating a contingent government, it might have given Congress and the Supreme Court reason to consider their own activities. Or did Bush and Cheney want only the executive branch and the presidency to survive? Or maybe they wanted succession to jump over Hastert and Byrd to Colin Powell, who is next in line — or merely get around Byrd, since Denny Hastert's son works for Cheney and may have been told about the COG efforts? Though this is good material for late-night comedians, should a catastrophe occur, it would not be very funny if a cabal of right-wing zealots were all that was left of the U.S. government.

After all, unlike during the Cold War, when there would have been at least some warning of incoming nuclear missiles, and time to go underground, with terrorists there will likely be no warning before a briefcase-size nuclear weapon (ten kiloton, the equivalent of the bomb that wiped out Hiroshima) is detonated on Pennsylvania Avenue midway between the White House and Capitol, killing and leveling all within a one-mile radius. Such an action, of course, would take out the White House and the Capitol. Unfortunately, such a possibility is not far-fetched, given the available information (although much of it is conflicting). According to published reports, since 1997 it has been known that almost one hundred Russian-made suitcase-size nuclear weapons are unaccounted for, and shortly after 9/11, Uzbekistan's president, Islam Karimov, reportedly advised Secretary of Defense Rumsfeld that "Osama bin Laden has bought two and possibly three ex-Soviet nuclear warheads from Russian organized crime."[51] United Press International reported that Congressman Curt Weldon (R-Pa.) was told by the Pentagon's Defense Intelligence Agency that there is "reason to believe" that "two Soviet-manufactured suitcase nukes may have fallen into bin Laden's hands." The *Political Science Quarterly* reported that "former CIA Director James Woolsey and former United Nations weapons inspector Richard Butler, as well as Russian sources, have estimated that there are a dozen or more suitcase bombs unaccounted for."[52] Whatever the reality, it may explain why Bush has kept the COG in operation. But, of course, the COG program serves another purpose for Bush and Cheney. Operating in secret bunkers, they can hide "right thinking" people not just from terrorist attacks but from a curious public and an inquisitive press. And come an attack, that they could find no room in their shelters for any who disagree with them would be a moot issue — for decades.

The COG plans were not conceived in secrecy but rather through open dialogue, discussion, and debate. A shadow, or contingent, executive government should not be created by secret presidential order. The current effort to bury these plans in a bunker not only is undemocratic but hides the serious problems that exist in the presidential and government succession laws. Bush and Cheney, rather than hiding these problems, should be openly and aggressively engaging in public discussion about them. Their failure to do so shows that their uncalled-for secrecy is precluding effective leadership. And since they are ignoring the problems, other concerned citizens have to take up the slack. Not waiting for Bush and Cheney, the bipartisan Commission on Continuity of Government has been created, a joint undertaking by the Brookings Institute and the American Enterprise Institute, and is co-chaired by former White House counsel (for Carter and Clinton) Lloyd Cutler and former Republican U.S. senator Alan Simpson. Former presidents Carter and Ford are serving as honorary co-chairmen. It has completed its first phase: recommendations for the continuity of Congress. Next it will turn to the executive branch and the presidency, and then the judiciary and the Supreme Court.[53] But it will take open presidential leadership, not more secrecy, to implement the needed changes. Not all the planning for the war on terrorism can, or should, be designed behind closed doors, as the Bush II administration has done, for example, in concocting new repressive techniques to track terrorists in the United States, civil rights and liberties be damned. Or by demanding that Congress move so fast, neither they nor anyone else knows what is being done, as occurred with the USA Patriot Act — which was lawmaking at its worst.

Secret and Repressive Law Enforcement

Attorney General John Ashcroft, who had been saved from political oblivion by Bush (or Karl Rove, who had worked on previous Ashcroft campaigns) after losing his seat in the Senate, is a politician who sees himself as presidential timber. He is a divisive and strange man, with a sensibility so prudish that he requested $8,000 for curtains to cover a partially nude statue of

Lady Justice in the Justice Department's auditorium. The last attorney general with presidential ambitions was A. Mitchell Palmer, Woodrow Wilson's third and final attorney general — best known for his infamous raids to round up Bolsheviks, arresting and deporting thousands of them while totally ignoring the Constitution. Ashcroft's plans for fighting terrorism bear a striking resemblance to Palmer's work. To address terrorism, Ashcroft first aggressively utilized existing laws to round up purported potential terrorists who might be part of sleeper cells already in the country and then sought new law enforcement powers from Congress. These new laws were needed as quickly as possible, Ashcroft insisted, to preclude further attacks. His religious fundamentalism, his less-than-exemplary record in public service on civil rights, his less-than-compassionate brand of conservatism was (and remains) reason for apprehension. It was predictable that Ashcroft would go over the top, and he has not disappointed.

Newsweek noted after 9/11 that "Americans seem more willing to sacrifice civil liberties on the altar of security than we have been at any time since President Lincoln suspended the right of habeas corpus during the Civil War or President Roosevelt rounded up 110,000 Japanese-Americans for preventive detention after Pearl Harbor. The United States, vowed Attorney General John Ashcroft, will 'use every legal means at our disposal to prevent further terrorist activity.'"[54] Strong leaders would have reminded Americans that the United States did not prevail in World War I because it enacted the intolerant Alien and Sedition Act of 1917; World War II was not won because our government locked up Japanese Americans, German Americans, and Italian Americans in "relocation" camps; and Cold War victory was not the result of the demagoguery of Joe Mc-

Carthy with his lists of fellow travelers and demands for loyalty boards. Similarly, a war on terrorism will not be won by reviving any, let alone all, of these repressive tactics and stratagems. Yet that is what has occurred.[55]

Very few Americans worry about their rights and liberties; rather, they take them for granted. Americans are even less concerned about the rights of others, particularly foreigners, for they foolishly believe they have no reason for concern.* Still, as Georgetown University law professor David Cole has pointed out, Americans are tolerating conduct they would find unacceptable for people who may not be guilty of anything more than not being an American. Everyone wants terrorists brought to justice. But dragnets are notoriously ineffective.

Some five thousand Arab American and Muslim men have been secretly detained under the various antiterrorism initiatives, with only five of this initial roundup having been charged, one convicted of a crime, and the rest being ever so slowly released — even when not a shred of evidence suggests they have ties to terrorism. Those apprehended are not being treated well, as we know from a study of the inspector general of the Justice Department, who has reported (as required by law) numerous beatings and episodes of mistreatment. Some 650 men, ranging

---

*Bush has sought to test his power with a few Americans, however. The U.S. Court of Appeals for the Second Circuit ruled that the president cannot detain an American citizen seized on U.S. soil as an alleged "enemy combatant" indefinitely, without charges or counsel, as Bush sought to do with Jose Padilla from Brooklyn, New York. That Padilla may be a bad guy does not strip him of his rights as a citizen. According to a Reuters report (of the ruling on December 18, 2003), Mark Graber, a government professor at the University of Maryland, said, "There is growing evidence that even conservatives on the bench are uncomfortable with the powers that the president has appropriated." Let us all hope the professor is correct. At this writing, the matter is before the U.S. Supreme Court.

from teenagers to seniors, are imprisoned in metal cages in
Guantánamo Bay, Cuba — without convictions, without charges,
and without access to lawyers.

Think about it: of the more than five thousand detained (that
we know about), Ashcroft has found sufficient evidence to con-
vict only a handful (as of this writing) in the two-plus years after
the 9/11 attacks. This is evidence of either massive incompetence on the part of the Bush administration or massive overkill
in seizing the innocent, or both. And much, if not all, of this activity is patently unconstitutional since our Bill of Rights applies
to all "persons" in the United States, regardless of whether they
are American citizens or not. Corralling or deporting aliens, or
imprisoning them indefinitely without charges or evidence of
criminal activity, in the belief that it provides security is an illusion, not to mention a vile undertaking. History has shown that
what our government does to others today, it will do to Americans tomorrow. When our government denies basic human
rights to citizens of other nations, it has no standing to demand
that other nations afford such basic rights to Americans. Simply
stated, by treating others as we would want to be treated, we not
only realize our humanity and follow our Constitution but protect ourselves in the long run. If there is a flaw in this logic (argued by David Cole), it escapes me.

Congress did little it can be proud of in passing repressive
new laws in a bill that was reviewed by no congressional committee, a new law too massive and complex for any representative or senator to read, yet was rushed through both chambers
to become the USA Patriot Act. And no provision of that law
has been found more offensive than the one giving Ashcroft
power to send FBI agents into libraries and bookstores to find
out what patrons read (section 215).[56] With this authority

granted by a secret court proceeding (requiring almost nothing more than suspicion of terror activities or some relationship to such activities, or merely the search for such a potential), FBI agents are empowered to demand that librarians and bookstores provide names of readers of books in which they are interested. In addition, the new law makes it unlawful for the librarians and bookstores to inform anyone that such a search has taken place. The University of Illinois conducted a survey and learned that within sixty days of this new law being enacted, some eighty-five libraries had already been approached by the FBI[57] — although Ashcroft refuses to give hard numbers and actually belittles librarians and others for their concern. Bush in his 2004 State of the Union address asked that the Patriot Act be further extended, notwithstanding widespread public opposition to this controversial law.

So offensive are these activities that a nationwide citizens' movement has blossomed to resist the efforts of Bush-Cheney-Ashcroft to shred the fabric of our Constitution. Towns, cities, counties, state legislatures, and other representative organizations have spontaneously signed petitions telling the president and his attorney general that they want their communities to have nothing to do with the USA Patriot Act's violations of civil rights and liberties. So far, more than 250 petitions have been filed, representing thirty-five states and almost 30 million people.[58] Opposition to this extraordinary legislation (and overreaction by Bush and company) has come from every point of view along the political spectrum. But given the conservative orientation of the Bush-Cheney-Ashcroft mind-set, none is more important than the reactions of their conservative peers. The American Civil Liberties Union has been collecting such reactions, and a small but representative sampling shows the extreme nature of these policies, given their rejection by such people as:

NEWT GINGRICH, the former Republican Speaker of the House, and no moderate, said, "I strongly believe Congress must act now to rein in the Patriot Act, limit its use to national security concerns and prevent it from developing 'mission creep' into areas outside of national security."

SENATOR LARRY CRAIG, a Republican from Nebraska, on joining as a sponsor of legislation to roll back the USA Patriot Act, said, "It's time we adjusted this law to assure civil liberties are not being trampled."

GROVER NORQUIST, president of Americans for Tax Reform, board member of the National Rifle Association and American Conservative Union, stated, "It's been two years since 9/11, and for the administration to still answer the public's questions about how these powers are being used with 'Just trust us' is insulting."

RON YOUNG, a Republican congressman from Arkansas, said, "I'm very concerned that, in our desire for security and our enthusiasm for pursuing supposed terrorists, that sometimes we might be on the verge of giving up the freedoms which we're trying to protect."

BOB BARR, a former U.S. attorney and former Republican member of Congress, said, "There are a lot of people who say, 'I don't have anything to hide.' But every one of us is subject to being criminalized."

DICK ARMEY, at the time a Republican member of the House of Representatives from Texas, the House majority leader and chairman of the House Select Committee on

Homeland Security, said, "I told the President I thought his Justice Department was out of control. . . . Are we going to save ourselves from international terrorism in order to deny the fundamental liberties we protect to ourselves? . . . It doesn't make sense to me."[59]

With conservative Republicans feeling this way, imagine what moderates and liberals think. If Bush and Cheney have pushed their secret and repressive law enforcement measures beyond appropriate limits — and they have — they have reached further with their even more radical, not to mention illegal, national security measures. Their war has many fronts — a few publicly known, more unknown. They have launched unprecedented covert activities around the world, where borders, states, and foreign sovereignty of other nations mean nothing to them. But because these operations are covert, they are never discussed, only hinted at. Yet distilling the underlying and hidden agendas of this presidency, as intelligence agencies throughout the world are surely doing, is not particularly difficult. Even those who get their news from Comedy Central (actually, not a bad source) knew that Bush and Cheney planned to take out Saddam Hussein, long before it became their publicly declared policy. But the way they sold this war to Americans and to Congress would cause even a gauntlet thrower like Richard Nixon to blanch, for he never played the world — or his government — for fools.

Chapter Five

Hidden Agenda

There is scant evidence to tie Saddam to terrorist organizations, and even less to the September 11 attacks. Indeed Saddam's goals have little in common with the terrorists who threaten us, and there is little incentive for him to make common cause with them. He is unlikely to risk his investment in weapons of mass destruction, much less his country, by handing such weapons to terrorists who would use them for their own purposes and leave Baghdad as the return address.

— Brent Scowcroft, chairman,
Foreign Intelligence Advisory Board

George W. Bush has not chosen to deal honestly with the American people regarding his true agenda, where he is taking this nation and why. Or how. In matters of war and peace, his hidden agenda could not be more troubling. Nor could the manner in which he (once again, not unlike Nixon — only worse) has chosen to take care of friends on an unmatched scale, at the expense of the health and safety of Americans. In addition, Bush — in another example of being worse than Nixon — is openly attacking enemies through dirty tricks that are breathtaking in their audacity (with the news media remaining mostly silent, if not complicit).

Most Americans have no awareness of Bush and Cheney's radical national security policies, and not even experts fully un-

derstand what this administration is doing. Have we returned to
Nixon's madman theory, in which he wanted the Russians to
think he was crazy and might nuke them if they supported the
North Vietnamese? Are we trying to terrorize the terrorist? Do
Americans not have a right to know if they have a warmongering presidency? Is international law now irrelevant to the
United States? How long do Bush and Cheney believe America
should rule the world under their new doctrines? Is their secrecy
hiding a high level of incompetence? All these questions are im-
plicitly raised by their actions and words. But neither Bush nor
Cheney is providing any answers.

Preemptive and Preventive Military Policy

No secretly developed policy has startled Americans, and the
rest of the world, more than the Bush-Cheney decision to make
the nation's response to terrorism a policy of warmongering.
The Congressional Research Service (CRS), the nonpartisan
think tank within the Library of Congress, has more blandly described this new Bush-Cheney policy as calling for "military action . . . against another nation so as to prevent or mitigate a
presumed military attack or use of force by that nation against
the United States." Yet the CRS found this policy unprecedented in our history. The United States had "never" (as of the
time of the CRS study, which was before going to war in Iraq)
undertaken such a preemptive attack on another nation. All so-
called precedents to the contrary are shown to be pure spin.
With the exception of the Spanish-American War in 1898 (which
the CRS pointed out was not truly "preemptive"), the United
States had never (before Iraq) "attacked another nation militarily prior to its first having been attacked."[1]

In his January 2002 State of the Union address, Bush identified Iraq, Iran, and North Korea as America's enemies. He did not lay out his doctrine of preemptive war at that time, only hinted at it: "Time is not on our side. I will not wait on events while dangers gather. I will not stand by as peril draws closer and closer. The United States of America will not permit the world's most dangerous regimes to threaten us with the world's most destructive weapons."[2] Not until June 2002, when addressing the graduating class at the U.S. Military Academy at West Point, did he explain where he was headed. "Containment is not possible when unbalanced dictators with weapons of mass destruction can deliver those weapons on missiles or secretly provide them to terrorist allies," he told the cadets, rejecting the policy of containment and deterrence that had existed for half a century. "If we wait for threats to fully materialize, we will have waited too long," he explained. For that reason, he said, "we must take the battle to the enemy, disrupt his plans, and confront his worst threats before they emerge." Because of the world situation, our "only path to safety is the path of action, and this nation will act," he said. "We are in a conflict between good and evil, and America will call evil by its name," he proclaimed in announcing his less than fully articulated policy.[3]

By design, Bush does not distinguish between "preemptive" and "preventive" war. There is a difference. Those who launch "preventive" wars are aggressors — notwithstanding efforts to claim, as all such aggressors do, that they are acting in self-defense. On the other hand, those who engage in "preemptive" wars are viewed as acting in self-defense, with the preemptive action being akin to a quick-draw response to an obvious threat. International law has long accepted preemptive actions and rejected preventive wars.

On September 17, 2002, Bush and Cheney publicly set forth a bit more of their policy. They had no choice. Under the

Goldwater-Nichols Department of Defense Reorganization Act of 1986, all presidents are legally required to report regularly to Congress and the American people on their national security strategy. Bush and Cheney were fifteen months late in filing their report, which had been due since June 15, 2001.[4] But the timing of their report, titled *The National Security Strategy of the United States of America*, was no accident; rather, the release opened a national campaign — just before the midterm congressional elections — in which the president would make war and terrorism the issue as he traveled the country to help Republican candidates. Attention has focused on the fifth goal of their stated policies: "Prevent Our Enemies from Threatening Us, Our Allies, and Our Friends with Weapons of Mass Destruction."[5] The call for action was premised on Bush's West Point speech, which was quoted at the top of this section: "The gravest danger to freedom lies at the crossroads of radicalism and technology. When the spread of chemical and biological and nuclear weapons, along with ballistic missile technology — when that occurs, even weak states and small groups could attain a catastrophic power to strike great nations. Our enemies have declared this very intention . . . and we will oppose them with all our power."

Citing international law, the report says that "the legitimacy of preemption" rests "on the existence of an imminent threat — most often a visible mobilization of armies, navies, and air forces preparing to attack." But with terrorists who might have weapons of mass destruction, the policy statement claims that principle will not work. "We must adapt the concept of imminent threat to the capabilities and objectives of today's adversaries." Accordingly, "the greater the threat, the greater is the risk of inaction — and the more compelling the case for taking anticipatory action to defend ourselves, even if uncertainty remains as to the time and place of the enemy's attack. To *forestall or prevent* such hostile acts by our adversaries, the United States will, if necessary, act preemptively." (Emphasis added.)

Lawyers who worked on this policy statement intentionally fudged it, talking in terms of traditional preemption (quick-draw self-defense) but also in terms of preventive war — acting as the aggressor. In fact, experienced policy analysts doubt that preventive war is viable. For example, James J. Wirtz, a professor in the Department of National Security Affairs at the Naval Postgraduate School, and James A. Russell, a fellow at the Naval Postgraduate School, believe this formal declaration of policy is more rhetoric than reality, for there are too many obstacles to implement such a policy on any sort of sustained basis, everything from the logistical problems of trying to go it alone to "political costs of abrogating international law."[6] But the history of this presidency and the evolution of this strategy suggest that Bush and Cheney fully intend to implement this appropriately described muscular Wilsonism. International law is only a problem if you respect it and are not a sole superpower so strong that you can act with impunity.

Proof of the Bush team's hidden intentions to push their will on the world is found in the extremes to which they went to fabricate a justification for the war against Iraq. Their actions speak clearly. Rather than simply making it a war because Saddam failed to comply with the terms of his 1991 surrender after Gulf War I, or even an action to arrest a known war criminal and inhumane dictator, they made going after Saddam part of their war against terrorism, and their war against terrorism justifies their grander plans. They tie their action to terrorism for both political and legal reasons. Clearly, they are proceeding one step at a time, one war at a time. But to make it work, they must lie to the American people and mislead Congress and continue their extraordinary abuse of power. In short, this presidency has adopted a pure Nixonian end-justifies-the-means mentality. But Nixon was trying to end a war, not start one.

Misleading the American People

With the Bush-Cheney presidency, it appears that mendacity has become policy. Their lying relates to matters large and small. Lies are told to hide, to mislead, and to gain political advantage. Their pervasive lying is remarkably well documented, and that documentation has been ongoing.[7] One of the more carefully assembled collections of Bush's dissembling, from the 2000 campaign to late summer of 2003, is the work of Washington journalist David Corn.[8] He is not the only journalist to explore the dishonesty of this presidency, however, for the activity is so extensive and the evidence of falsity in case after case so clear that it cannot be simply dismissed as the wishful thinking of Bush-bashers. While all presidential lies may be considered morally bad, not all presidential lies are equal. James Pfiffner, a professor of political science at George Mason University who has written widely on the modern American presidency, examined presidential lying in a 1999 essay for the *Presidential Studies Quarterly*, in which he set forth a hierarchy of presidential lies. For example, he believes that some lies are justified; for example, "lying to foreign governments is often considered a necessary element of diplomacy." But "presidential lying to citizens in a democracy should entail exceptional justification" — which typically would relate to national security.[9] When I went through the Bush II administration's deceptions, lies, and falsehoods — literally several hundred — I could find none that appear even *potentially* justifiable by reason of national security or some other greater good. While lying regarding national security may on occasion be justifiable (such as President Eisenhower's having his staff lie about U-2 flights over the Soviet Union), lies made about national security matters are usually the most egregious. They are what Pfiffner has labeled "lies of policy deception," which occur when "a president says that the government is doing one thing when in fact it is doing another." These lies are inexcusable because they mislead "the public about the direction of government policy" and therefore deny the electorate the ability "to make an informed choice [which] undermines the premise of the democratic process."

Pfiffner gave three examples of such inexcusable presidential lying: (1) "Lyndon Johnson's [misleading] the American public and conceal[ing] his policy of escalation in Vietnam in 1964 and 1965," which was accomplished by his "far-reaching deceptions" in orchestrating congressional approval of the Gulf of Tonkin Resolution; (2) Nixon's secret bombing of Cambodia for fourteen months, which was accompanied by lies and deceptions that "deprived the American people of the information necessary to make informed political decisions"; and (3) Reagan's lies about sending arms to Iran and aid to the Nicaraguan Contras. Pfiffner noted that "Reagan changed his story at least three times during the [Tower Commission] investigation," and to attribute this to the president's lack of interest in details, self-deception, or incipient Alzheimer's, as his admirers have done, invites "condescension." Bush and Cheney, who have been untruthful with the American people and Congress, have incorporated nothing less than LBJ's, Nixon's, and Reagan's most reprehensible deceptions — as raised in Pfiffner's analytical grading of presidential lying — in their action regarding the war with Iraq.

Without beginning to exhaust the body of bogus information that Bush and Cheney have provided the American people,

Congress, the United Nations, and the world to take the country to war in Iraq, a sampling of their central contentions will make the point. Their core case for war with Saddam was based on the allegations that he had weapons of mass destruction (chemical, biological, and nuclear in progress) and that Iraq had ties to al Qaeda, and thus directly or indirectly to the 9/11 attack. Typical false and misleading statements given to the American people include:

- On September 7, 2002, Bush spoke of an International Atomic Energy Agency report indicating that Saddam was just "six months away from developing [a nuclear] weapon." No such report existed.[10]
- Bush (and other administration officials) often repeated as fact (with no qualification whatsoever) the claim that Mohamed Atta, the leader of the 9/11 attacks, had met with Iraqi intelligence officials in Prague in April 2001. However, Czech president Vaclav Havel found — based on information available to Czech intelligence — that there was no evidence such a meeting had ever occurred, and CIA director George Tenet told Congress that the United States had no such information.[11]
- Dick Cheney gave two speeches in late August 2002 in which he "predicted that Iraqi President Saddam Hussein will obtain a nuclear weapon, *fairly soon.*"[12] (Emphasis added.) This fact was broadly disputed by military experts, and Cheney provided no basis for his unequivocal statement.[13] Time has shown the experts to be correct.
- On October 7, 2002, Bush gave a nationally televised speech in Cincinnati, Ohio, riddled with false and misleading statements, none more so than a claim that Iraq

"has trained [al Qaeda]* members in bomb making and poisons and deadly gases." His own intelligence officials disputed this information.[14] He also claimed that satellite photos showed that "Iraq is rebuilding facilities at sites that have been part of [Saddam's] nuclear program in the past," but when some two hundred reporters visited the site, no sign of the nuclear weapons program was found.[15]

Sadly, one could literally fill a fair-size book with nothing but Bush and Cheney's false statements about Saddam's purported nuclear capabilities and ties to al Qaeda. In fact, the nonpartisan Carnegie Endowment for International Peace has, in effect, done just that with its January 2004 study, *WMD in Iraq: Evidence and Implications.* The study's findings are devastating and, in point of fact, make liars of Bush and Cheney. All of their key assertions are examined in detail and shown to be wanting. Established evidence is lined up in charts beside the assertions of Bush-Cheney, making the administration's dishonesty obvious. The Carnegie study asserts that "administration officials systematically misrepresented the threat from Iraq's WMD and ballistic missile program," explaining that conflating nuclear, chemical, and biological weapons as a single "WMD threat" was a distortion; "insisting without evidence — yet treating as a given truth — that Saddam Hussein would give whatever WMD he possessed to terrorists"; the distortions — by "routinely dropping caveats, probabilities, and expressions of uncertainty" — of intelligence assessments when making public statements; and

---

*Note: The White House uses *Al Qaida* while most news organizations use the term *al Qaeda*. To use a consistent spelling, I have used *al Qaeda* throughout, and inserted "[al Qaeda]" for other spellings.

"misrepresenting [U.N.] inspectors' findings in ways that turned threats from minor to dire."[16] In the end, even greater deceptions were employed to get Congress to provide legal authority for war with Iraq.

Had Bush, Cheney, and their administration been honest, they would have explained what they did, and did not know. The reason they did not is obvious. They wanted war and felt that without their distortions, they would be unable to muster public and congressional support.

Deceiving Congress — An Impeachable Offense

When it came to the war against Iraq, Congress was deceived, just as the American people were, only what happened with Congress deserves a very close look because it reveals that Congress did not give the administration a blank-check authorization. In fact, Bush deliberately violated the very authorization that he sought from Congress, which was not merely a serious breach of faith with a trusting Congress but a statutory and constitutional crime.

When Bush met with congressional leaders in early September 2002, he told them he would seek a resolution to authorize military action in Iraq and needed them to move quickly. He did not explain why it was necessary to move quickly. After meeting with Bush, congressional leaders passed the word that the president had suggested new intelligence about Saddam's nuclear capabilities would be forthcoming.[17] It wasn't. Rather, as the congressional debate matured, the British released a report saying that Saddam was two to five years from having a nuclear device, which the *New York Times* pointed out meant that "attacking Iraq [did not] fit under the classic definition of pre-emptive self-defense."[18]

To further nudge lawmakers, on October 3, 2002, Bush called

another leadership meeting at which he provided a briefing, claiming, among other things, that Saddam's "regime has the scientists and facilities to build nuclear weapons and is seeking the materials needed to do so."[19] He hinted that he would have even more to say soon. But he never did so. Florida senator Bill Nelson later reported that at another classified briefing, about seventy-five senators were told that not only did Saddam have biological and chemical weapons, he had the ability to use them against the East Coast of the United States via unmanned drone aircraft.[20] It was a frightening prospect for legislators whose offices had been closed down with less than half a thimble of anthrax spores. It was also totally false.

With his October 7 speech in Cincinnati, delivered just before the first key vote on a war resolution, Bush aimed his remarks at both Congress and the public, giving it his best shot in laying out the case against Saddam. An early draft of that speech contained a remarkable bit of new intelligence they had just acquired, no doubt the information Bush had hinted at with the congressional leaders, which indicated that Saddam was trying to acquire uranium from the African nation of Niger, a sure sign of his nuclear intentions. But when CIA director George Tenet reviewed the draft of the speech, he recommended removing the Niger-connection intelligence because his agency was still investigating it. His advice was followed, so on the question of nukes, Bush had nothing more he could add. As for a pre-9/11 connection to al Qaeda, he said, "We know that Iraq and the [al Qaeda] terrorist network share a common enemy — the United States of America. We know that Iraq and [al Qaeda] have had high-level contacts that go back a decade. Some [al Qaeda] leaders who fled Afghanistan went to Iraq. These include one very senior [al Qaeda] leader who received medical treatment in Baghdad this year, and who has been associated with planning for chemical and biological attacks. We've learned that Iraq has trained [al Qaeda] members in bomb making and poisons and deadly gases," he said. Then he tied it to 9/11. "And we know that after September the 11th, Saddam Hussein's regime glee-fully celebrated the terrorist attacks on America."[21]

It was anything but persuasive evidence of an al Qaeda con-nection. But as propaganda, this stuff worked wonderfully. After Bush had traveled throughout the country, dropping his hints, he managed to convince Americans — without ever saying it — that Saddam was responsible for 9/11. By the fall, a stagger-ing 69 percent of Americans believed this to be true, with no supporting hard evidence whatsoever — other than Bush and Cheney's hinting at it.[22] And on October 10, Congress over-whelmingly approved a resolution authorizing a war with Iraq.[23] But there was a kicker in the authorization: Congress condi-tioned its grant of authority on a formal *determination* by the president of the United States that there continued to be a threat that could not be dealt with through diplomacy and that his actions were consistent with the war against those involved in 9/11 — a detail unreported by the news media. It was because of this agreed-upon language that the Democratic leadership was willing to support the resolution. Still, congressional sup-port was not wholehearted, many Americans also had serious doubts, and the rest of the world was strongly opposed to the proposed action.

To convince the doubters, Bush and his advisers decided to present their best case with a one-two punch, beginning with his State of the Union address on January 28, 2003, followed by Secretary of State Colin Powell, who would provide the down and dirty details to the United Nations on February 5. The State of the Union message is a highly focused media event, where presidents draw an audience of a large cross-section of the American public (in the image-rich setting of the House chamber with the Supreme Court justices, the diplomatic corps, the president's cabinet, and the membership of both houses in attendance). But it is also much more than a media event, for it is a solemn constitutional occasion, whereby the president meets his responsibility, required by Article II, section 3, of the Constitution, to give "the Congress Information on the State of the Union."

The heart of Bush's second State of the Union address was his case for going to war against Saddam Hussein. Regrettably, it proved a moment of high deception, an endeavor to mislead Congress and the American people. Using declarative, unequivocal, and unqualified statements, Bush presented what appeared to be hard facts, the sort of information to which the commander in chief of a national security apparatus spending $400-plus billion annually was uniquely privy. But so egregious were Bush's misrepresentations that one can only conclude they were a calculated and deliberate effort to mislead Congress. APPENDIX I is a summary of these misrepresentations.

Colin Powell gave a dazzling but shocking performance a week later. It was shocking because Powell, knowingly or otherwise, also presented one false and misleading statement after another to the United Nations. Among the falsehoods: Powell's satellite photos of "decontamination vehicles" — they were merely water trucks; Powell's three damning audiotaped conversations — two not verifiable and the third incorrectly translated; his "classified" documents found at a nuclear scientist's home — they turned out to be old, going back to the 1980s; the purported rocket launchers with biological warheads hidden in palm groves — they weren't there and have never been found; Powell's claim that no U-2 flights were possible and Iraqi scientists were too frightened to talk — two weeks after his speech U-2s were flying, and by early March 2003 twelve scientists had

spoken freely with inspectors; his estimated 25,000 liters of anthrax — never found, and three weeks before the invasion, U.N.
inspectors were given soil samples indicating the Iraqis had
destroyed their stock, and were provided a list of verifying witnesses; Powell's showing an Iraqi F-1 Mirage jet spraying "sim-
ulated anthrax" and saying that four such tanks were missing —
U.N. inspectors say Powell's video predated the 1991 Gulf War,
and the Mirage and tanks were destroyed; Powell's statement
that Iraq had produced four tons of VX nerve gas (with a single
drop capable of killing) — he forgot to mention most of it was
destroyed under the supervision of the United Nations, which
had also made a good-faith effort to find it all, but since British
officials report it would have degraded by 2002, it was no threat;
Powell's claim that illicit weapons had been embedded in legitimate civilian industries — none have been found; Powell's claim
that Iraq had 500 tons of chemical agents (not identifying any
source) — the Defense Intelligence Agency has reported there
is "no reliable information" of such stockpiles and none have
been found; Powell's contention that the 122mm chemical war-
head found by U.N. inspectors shortly before his speech might
be the tip of the iceberg — he failed to mention that the war-
head was empty, and to date none have been found; the flat
statement that Saddam has chemical weapons and that "sources"
had told the United States he had authorized their use — it
never happened, and such weapons have not been found at any
military base; there being no evidence Saddam has "ever aban-
doned" his nuke program — U.N. inspectors found no evidence
of a nuclear program, and even countries doing business with
Iraq prewar said no such program existed, and no evidence of
one has been found postwar; Powell's claim that "most U.S. experts" believed the aluminum tubes sought by Iraq were for enriching uranium — both the U.S. Energy Department and his

own State Department had already rejected that claim; Powell's statement that multiple intelligence sources had said Iraq sought "magnets" for uranium processing — U.N. inspectors traced the magnets to a legitimate use and established that their weight was not suitable for a uranium centrifuge; and Powell's saying that Iraq had Scud missiles with a six-hundred-mile range — not a single such missile has been found.[24]

Truth was slow in getting its boots on, but soon it was marching. Leading one brigade was former U.S. ambassador Joseph Wilson, who as the head of the American mission in Baghdad had stood up to Saddam to make certain all American personnel were safely out of harm's way when the 1991 Gulf War was launched. Wilson had been a regular television commentator during the buildup to the invasion of Iraq, and he was clearly unsettled by the invasion plans. Unknown, until he wrote about it on July 6, 2003, in the *New York Times*, was that he had undertaken a secret mission to Niger at the request of the CIA (for he had been an ambassador in Africa and knew the players) to determine if Saddam had indeed acquired uranium there. Notwithstanding earlier warnings not to, Bush had obliquely used the claim that Saddam had acquired uranium in Africa in his State of the Union address; Powell had blatantly made the claim. Wilson put the lie to the story. The White House conceded that the statement should not have been in Bush's State of the Union but later backed off, claiming it had relied on unidentified British intelligence. The White House has simply ignored Bush's other distortions in his January 28, 2003, constitutionally mandated message to Congress. Powell has never explained any of his false statements.

After Ambassador Wilson's editorial in the *New York Times*, Washington became rampant with stories of Bush's false statements. For the first time the mainstream news began catching up with the Internet and taking a much closer look at what Bush and Cheney were selling, or had sold. Curious myself, I decided to parse Bush's argument for war in Iraq. With only a few hours of research online, reading source documents that the president himself had cited, which were publicly posted by the International Atomic Energy Agency, the U.S. Department of State, the CIA, and the United Nations, I was amazed at the patently misleading use of the material Bush had presented to Congress. Did he believe no one would check? The falsification was not merely self-evident, it was feeble and disturbing.* The president was playing Congress and the public for fools. By August 2003, Charles J. Handley of the Associated Press had completed a detailed analysis of Colin Powell's United Nations speech with the hindsight of six months — and eviscerated it. Every key contention Powell had made was shown to be without basis, but because of Powell's high standing and stature, very few newspapers prominently featured or even carried the devastating report by the Associated Press. Nor was there any real concern other than by a few commentators that the administration's case for war was completely bogus.

After the war's launch in March 2003, with its embedded reporting of bombs over Baghdad and its Fourth of July shock-and-awe theater, even less notice was given the actual war-making authority granted by Congress back in October 2002.[25] This joint resolution (Public Law 107-243) begins with twenty-three (unnumbered) "whereas" clauses, which are not uncommon but are a bit excessive in this instance. These clauses are introductory or prefatory statements meaning "considering that" or "that being the case." They are, however, only legalese win-

---

*See Appendix I.

dow dressing, opinions at best, and not a part of the operative provisions. For example, some of these clauses no one would dispute, such as the eighth: "Whereas the current Iraqi regime has demonstrated its capability and willingness to use weapons of mass destruction against other nations and its own people." Other of the clauses, though, are highly questionable, such as the thirteenth, which takes the existence of Iraq's weapons of mass destruction (WMD) as fact and states that "the risk that the current Iraqi regime will either employ those weapons [of mass destruction] to launch a surprise attack against the United States or its Armed Forces or provide them to international terrorists who would do so, and the extreme magnitude of harm that would result to the United States and its citizens from such an attack, combine to justify action by the United States to defend itself." At the time, there was anything but agreement in Congress that Iraq possessed WMD or that Saddam would give WMD to others if he had them, for Bush had failed to provide such evidence; obviously, he did not have it. But these seemly declaratory statements have no real meaning, so they are not debated — and are seldom discussed — by Congress. They are part of the joint resolution, which when approved by both the House and Senate and signed by the president, as occurred with the Iraq war resolution, becomes law. But that does not make the whereas clauses either fact or findings of fact by Congress. Legal scholars call these clauses "precatory" — words of entreaty, desire, wish — and here, hope, with no other meaning.[26] Understanding the nature of these clauses is necessary to appreciate the absurd game Bush played with Congress.

To avoid having to return to Congress for more debate on Iraq, Bush had pushed for and received authority to launch a war without further advance notice to Congress. Never before had Congress so trusted a president with this authority.[27] But in granting this unprecedented authorization, Congress insisted that certain conditions be established as existing and that the president submit a formal determination, assuring the Congress that, in fact, these conditions were present. Specifically (and here I am summarizing technical wording; the actual language may be found in the endnotes), Congress wanted a formal determination submitted to it either before using force or within forty-eight hours of having done so, stating that the president had found that (1) further diplomatic means alone would not resolve the "continuing threat" (meaning WMD) *and* (2) the military action was part of the overall response to terrorism, *including* dealing with those involved in "the terrorist attacks that occurred on September 11, 2001."[28] In short, Congress insisted that there be evidence of two points that were the centerpiece of Bush's argument for the war.

On March 18, 2003, Bush sent his formal "determination" to Congress (as a letter to the Speaker of the House and the president of the Senate). His letter merely tracked the exact language of the statute, making that language his determination.[29] Accompanying his letter was the "Report in Connection with Presidential Determination under Public Law 107-243."[30] It is an extraordinary document. Its content can be accurately analogized to male bovine droppings; H. L. Mencken might have described it (to paraphrase him) as "the topmost pinnacle of slosh, for it is rumble and bumble, it is flap and doodle, it is balder and dash." For certain, it is not material befitting a "determination" by the commander in chief to undertake the grave responsibility of expending the nation's blood and treasure in an act of war. It is closer to a blatant fraud than to a fulfillment of the president's constitutional responsibility to faithfully execute the law.

With one pathetic (yet false) exception, this report explains that the president made his determination by inexplicably relying on alleged congressional findings of fact, which did not exist. Congress made no such findings, and if it had done so, it surely would not have required the president make *his* determinations.[31] Bush, like a dog chasing his tail who gets ahold of it, relied on information the White House provided Congress for its draft resolution; then he turned around and claimed that this information (*his* information) came from Congress. From this bit of sophistry, he next stated that these congressional findings were the basis of his "determination."

Bush's report on his determination speaks for itself. On the first page, he claims that "Congress found" that Iraq was continuing to aid and harbor international terror organizations, including organizations that threaten the lives and safety of American citizens. This statement of what Congress purportedly found is a recitation of the eleventh "whereas" clause. It appears an effort to have the reader accept that the whereas clauses (which are never mentioned by Bush) are congressional findings. A few pages later he adopts additional whereas clauses as his determination. By page six, he makes the determination that Iraq possessed WMD by relying on the sixth whereas clause (which among other claims says that Iraq continues to possess and develop a significant chemical and biological weapons capability and is actively seeking a nuclear weapons capability). This, of course, is at best only one of the two preconditions Congress demanded for use of the armed forces in Iraq.

In a separate section of his report — Part 4, "Use of Force Against Iraq Is Consistent with the War on Terror" — Bush explains his "determination" of Iraqi ties with 9/11, the other condition that Congress called for in the resolution, by once again using circumlocutory logic and explanations. Bush states that

In Public Law 107-243, Congress made a number of findings concerning Iraq's support of international terrorism. Among other things, Congress determined that:

- Members of [al Qaeda], an organization bearing responsibility for attacks on the United States, its citizens, and interests, including the attacks that occurred on September 11, 2001, are known to be in Iraq. [This is the tenth of the whereas clauses.]
- Iraq continues to aid and harbor other international terrorist organizations, including organizations that threaten the lives and safety of United States citizens. [This is the eleventh whereas, for the second time.]
- It is in the national security interests of the United States and in furtherance of the war on terrorism that all relevant United Nations Security Council resolutions be enforced, including through the use of force if necessary. [This is the last part of the nineteenth whereas.]

In fact, Bush's report shows that he made only *one* determination (if it can be called that), and the report totally fails to comply with the requirements of the Iraq war resolution. Bush, in essence, gave Congress only one purported fact to meet the requirement of making a congressional determination. He cited the information offered by Secretary of State Colin Powell to the United Nations. Bush merely reminded Congress that Powell's report "revealed a terrorist training area in northeastern Iraq with ties to Iraqi intelligence and activities of [al Qaeda] affiliates in Baghdad." Bush added that "public reports indicate that Iraq is currently harboring senior members of a terrorist network led by Abu Musab al-Zarqawi, a close [al Qaeda] associate," and that in the past Iraq had "provided training in document forgery and explosives to [al Qaeda]."[32] He offered no governmental confirmation of this "public report."

Federal laws are filled with requirements for "presidential determinations" — trade laws, labor laws, environmental laws, telecommunications laws, military laws, and on and on. Congress relies on presidential determinations (and often seeks reports on them) because he, as chief executive and the person who carries out the laws, is in a unique position to make such determinations. If there is a precedent for Bush's slick trick to involve America in a bloody commitment, where the Congress requires as a condition for action that the president make a determination, and the president in turn relies on a whereas clause (which he provided to Congress as suggested introductory language) and a dubious public report (which fails to address the substance of the conditions for war set by Congress), I am not aware of it and could not find anything even close.

Bush's reliance on Secretary Powell's statement about Abu Musab al-Zarqawi is similarly flawed. As anyone who has followed this intelligence knows, Zarqawi's role, if any, and connection to al Qaeda, if any, are highly disputed. Zarqawi is described as a one-legged fellow and said to be an expert with poisons, but his connection to al Qaeda is weak at best, for he is thought to belong to a subgroup that may be loosely associated with al Qaeda. Contested intelligence information leaked to the *Weekly Standard* claims that Zarqawi had connections with Iraqi intelligence officials and that he was setting up a sleeper cell in Baghdad in the event Americans took control of the city.[33] Other reports say that U.S. intelligence officials know that Zarqawi operated outside al Qaeda control.[34] Further intelligence reports indicate that Zarqawi was in Baghdad only for medical treatment, hospitalized after being injured by the Americans in Afghanistan.[35] According to *Newsweek*, Zarqawi is closer to Iran than to Iraq.[36] Neverthe-less, President George W. Bush made his determination that the United States, in effect, should go to war against Iraq because Zarqawi may have trained a few members of al Qaeda.

Not since Lyndon Johnson hoodwinked Congress into issuing the Gulf of Tonkin Resolution, which authorized sending American troops to Vietnam, has a president so deceived Congress about a matter of such grave national importance. And not since the Reagan administration's disregard of the Boland Amendment has a president shown less regard for congressional authorization in matters relating to war and peace.* After the Iraqi invasion ended and during the occupation, Bush conceded that Saddam had no connection with 9/11, notwithstanding public opinion to the contrary, which he and Cheney facilitated.[37] Cheney and Bush are still looking for weapons of mass destruction, which have not been found, and ties to al Qaeda remain to be verified. Whether WMD are found or not, and regardless of whether better information is located linking Iraq and al Qaeda, the facts are clear — however they are sliced, diced, or spun — that Bush and Cheney took this nation to war on *their* hunches, *their* unreliable beliefs, and *their* unsubstantiated intelligence — and used deception with Congress both before and after launching the war.

---

*The Boland Amendment, adopted by Congress in 1984, placed legal restrictions on the use of appropriated funds by the CIA to support the Nicaraguan Contra movement. It was introduced by Representative Edward P. Boland of Massachusetts and became central to the Iran-Contra scandal when it was learned that the restrictions were being ignored and skirted. Dick Cheney, at the time a member of Congress and the joint committee investigating Iran-Contra, said Reagan "should have vetoed the so-called Boland amendment." There are no reports that Cheney called for the president to veto the provisions of the Iraq war resolution placing conditions on going to war and requiring a presidential determination that such conditions had been met. See Bush remarks on signing the resolution on October 16, 2002, at www.whitehouse.gov/news/releases/2002/10/20021016-1.html.

Both the Senate and House intelligence committee have on-going investigations of the faulty intelligence about Iraq weapons of mass destruction and the failure to find any WMD whatsoever in Iraq after American troops took control of the country. The intelligence committees have similarly been looking at the lack of verifiable information about connections between Iraq and al Qaeda. Cheney and Bush, not unlike with the 9/11 investigations, have done their best to block these inquiries, and with the Republicans controlling both the House and Senate, there has been little incentive to look too closely. Whether Bush and Cheney get a second term or not, an independent bipartisan commission should be created to look at the prewar Iraqi war intelligence, not to mention the abuses and misuses that have been made of it in taking the nation to war. No one can, or should, have confidence in the Bush/Cheney-controlled investigation set up in early February 2004.

Bush's defense against the charge that he exaggerated (or misled with) his evidence to go to war in Iraq is as telling as his case for war. It came up during an interview with Diane Sawyer of ABC News, some eight months after he had declared the mission accomplished. Bush said, "The intelligence I operated on was good sound intelligence, the same intelligence that my predecessor operated on."[38] His predecessor, however, never claimed that Saddam had imminent (or "very soon [available]" in Cheney's words) nuclear capacity, nor did his predecessor say that Iraq had ties to al Qaeda. "Saddam was a danger and the world is better off 'cause we got rid of him," Bush told Sawyer. When she pressed the issue that his administration has insisted there were hard facts of "weapons of mass destruction as opposed to the possibility that [Saddam] could move to acquire those weapons still," Bush cut her off. "So what's the difference?" he asked; he had toppled Saddam. Not only does he consider the reasons he went to war to have become irrelevant, he apparently cannot recognize his own deceit and hypocrisy and that he has adopted precisely the sort of ends-justify-the-means thinking that Nixon belatedly admitted adopting. Famed sociologist and student of politics Max Weber's take on such thinking is as valid today as when he wrote it many years ago: "From no ethics in the world can it be concluded when and to what extent the ethically good purpose 'justifies' the ethically dangerous means and ramifications."[39]

During the Nixon impeachment debates, a remarkably bipartisan House Judiciary Committee realized the implications of its actions for future presidents. At one point, after the committee had largely concluded its work, the question arose of whether Nixon should be impeached because of his secret bombing in Cambodia. It was not an afterthought; rather, there had been so much for the committee to consider that the issue had been pushed aside. As the debate about the Cambodian bombing progressed, it was revealed that, on the contrary, Nixon had not kept this activity secret from Congress. In fact, the chairmen and ranking members of the key committees of the House and Senate, as well as the congressional leadership, had been informed. Yet the debate itself set an important precedent for later presidents.

Congresswoman Elizabeth Holtzman, a Democrat, raised a point with which colleagues on both sides of the political divide agreed. She said, "We must give notice to this President and other Presidents that deceit and deception over issues as grave as going to war and waging war cannot be tolerated in a constitutional democracy."[40] Similarly, Congressman Henry Smith, a Republican, agreed, saying, "The debate here will offer guidelines to future Presidents."[41] Congressman Robert W. Kastenmeier, a Democrat, had been sufficiently troubled by Nixon's actions to look to the Founders for guidance. He reported:

The question is really a constitutional one. If, in fact, the President did issue false and misleading statements, engage in deception and concealment concerning a matter of such great importance to the country as the conduct of war in which thousands and thousands of Americans were killed, irrespective of how Americans now view that war, and then, in fact, he has committed an offense for which he is accountable. I would only say that going back to the earliest times, one James Iredell, one of the Framers of the Constitution, stated the proposition that the President, and I paraphrase, must certainly be punishable for giving false information to the Senate. He is to regulate all intercourse with foreign powers, and it is his duty to impart to the Senate every material intelligence he receives. If it should appear that he has not given them full information, but has concealed important intelligence which he ought to have communicated, and by that means induced them to enter into measures injurious to their country in which they would not have consented to had the true state of things been disclosed to them, in this case I ask whether an impeachment for a misdemeanor would lie.*[42]

It is doubtful that Bush and Cheney secretly advised key members of Congress that they were going to lie about Iraq. And the evidence is overwhelming, certainly sufficient for a prima facie case, that George W. Bush and Richard B. Cheney have engaged in deceit and deception over going to war in Iraq. This is an impeachable offense. It is also evidence of the men-

---

*The statement by James Iredell, reported in J. Elliot, *Debates in the Several State Conventions on Adoption of the Constitution, As Recommended by the General Convention at Philadelphia in 1787* (Washington: 1836), vol. 4 at p. 127, was unequivocal during the ratification debates in North Carolina, when he said: "The President must certainly be punishable for giving false information to the Senate." Iredell was later appointed to the U.S. Supreme Court by President George Washington.

tality that characterizes the Bush-Cheney presidency, which has led to other abuses of presidential power, not unlike those underlying Watergate — only worse.

Worse than Watergate

Nixon's infamous enemies list, and his use of incumbency to hurt those who were against him and help those who were friends, is one of the distinguishing features of Watergate and its related abuse of presidential power. The Nixon White House set up an operation under Nixon aide Fred Malek, euphemistically called "the responsiveness program," to take care of friends and enemies and help with Nixon's reelection. The Senate Watergate Committee, which investigated these activities, described them in considerable detail: how political considerations were employed in the "letting of Government grants, contracts, and loans; the prosecution of legal and regulatory action; the making of administration personnel decisions; the determination of issues and programs to be stressed by the administration; [and] the communications of administration activities to the voting public."[43] The contention of several witnesses that prior presidents' having engaged in such activities justified Nixon's actions was rejected by the Senate, which pointed out that in several instances it appeared that the administration's conduct involved a criminal conspiracy to defraud the government of the faithful execution of its laws.*

Because of Watergate, no president has been so foolhardy as to openly initiate a program like Nixon's to screw those with

---

*The committee cited Title 18 of the United States Code, section 371, which makes it a crime to conspire to cheat the government by improperly carrying out federal programs and laws or by denying it of the proper work by its employees.

whom he or his top aides are unhappy and to blatantly help friends — that is, until the Bush II administration. Although I was not looking for this type of Watergate behavior with Bush and Cheney, it jumped out at me when surveying their secrecy — and soon it jumped out at everyone else when they attacked Ambassador Joe Wilson's wife, a covert CIA agent, blowing her cover in an effort to seek revenge against him — every bit as stupid an action as the Watergate break-in that was the beginning of the end of a presidency, except the Bush-Cheney attack was worse because it was immediately life-threatening and damaging to national security and thus a far more serious crime than foolishly planting a bug in an opponent's office. Before examining the Wilson case, a passing glance at the Bush and Cheney "responsiveness" program is fitting.

Cheney's energy group, and its recommendations, was about as "responsive" as a White House can be to big contributors without using the words *quid pro quo* — which is the essence of bribery. Actually, those words may, in fact, be applicable, but the Cheney group's work has been kept so hidden by the vice president that no one truly knows whether there was misconduct, or improper influence by contributors on the nation's energy policy. Nor is the energy task force an isolated example of this hidden "responsiveness." Throughout this administration's tenure other such activities have taken place whereby federal programs have been adjusted for the benefit of Bush-Cheney political friends and contributors. In December 2003, *U.S. News & World Report* completed a five-month study by two reporters who interviewed more than one hundred people about the Bush and Cheney secrecy. This was the first mainstream news organization — other than Bill Moyers at PBS (who has run two specials on Bush and Cheney secrecy) and Dana Milbank (who keeps a close eye on excessive secrecy for the *Washington Post*) — to explore the Bush-Cheney shadowlands.[44] Highlights from the *U.S. News* special report:

- The Bush-Cheney actions are "a reversal of a decades-long trend of openness in government," and the administration is "making increasing amounts of information unavailable to taxpayers who pay for its collection."
- The Bush-Cheney administration's "efforts to shield the actions of, and the information obtained by, the executive branch are far more extensive than has been previously documented," and its actions have effectively "place[d] large amounts of information out of the reach of ordinary citizens."
- Among the areas of Bush and Cheney's secrecy are "important business and consumer information" and "critical health and safety information potentially affecting millions of Americans."*
- "New administration policies have thwarted the ability of Congress to exercise its constitutional authority to monitor the executive branch, and, in some cases, even to obtain basic information about its actions."

U.S. News further reported that those with knowledge of these activities at the White House refused to comment, and the one person who did employed the standard Bush White House

---

*One of the most appalling examples, arising after the *U.S. News* report, has been the efforts of United Press International and other news organizations to obtain information about the threat of "mad cow" disease in the United States: UPI reporters spending six months filing FOIA requests, being promised information by the Department of Agriculture, but never being provided the information. On December 24, 2003, mad cow was discovered in the United States, and the Bush II administration's efforts to protect the beef industry collapsed, but relevant information continues to be withheld.

line denying there was any secrecy in the Bush II administration. If Dan Bartlett, White House communications director, had told *U.S. News* that pigs can fly, it would have been more believable than his assertion that "the administration is open, and the process in which this administration conducts its business is as transparent as possible." (That, Mr. Bartlett, either is an unmitigated lie, or you don't have a clue about your administration.)

Not only does this secrecy far exceed anything at the Nixon White House, but much of the Bush-Cheney secrecy deals with activities similar to Nixon's "responsiveness program." In other words, their secrecy helps corporations and industries that are major contributors. But with a *deadly* difference. Bush and Cheney have, from the outset of their presidency, shown utter disregard for the human consequences of their actions, both at home and abroad. Their pay-no-heed corporate favoritism now places literally thousands of blameless Americans at risk (no doubt, many of their supporters included) by pandering to their big contributors by withholding vital business, consumer, health, and safety information. While there are many instances, I have selected just a few horrifying situations to make the point.

Well before Bush became president, a high-profile scandal involving Firestone tires failing on Ford SUVs resulted in Congress's creating a system to prevent such problems (and scandal) from ever happening again. The early-warning system was carefully designed to make the safety information from the manufacturers publicly available. Before returning to government service, Andy Card, White House chief of staff, was General Motors' top lobbyist and head of a trade group for domestic automakers. Consequently, he is quite aware that the auto industry was unhappy in making this safety information available, given its negative nature and potential impact on car sales. Notwithstanding the congressional action, the early-warning reporting system has been made secret, denying public access to the information. Bush's "transportation officials," *U.S. News* reported, "decided to make vital information such as warranty claims, field reports from dealers, and consumer complaints — all potentially valuable sources of safety information — secret." To no avail, public interest consumer groups have tried to get this safety information reported.[45] This is what Nixon would have called "responsiveness." It has other names as well. But what Bush and Cheney are doing to the environment to curry favor with their contributors is far worse than anything Nixon's "responsiveness program" ever did. The Bush-Cheney presidency is engaged in crimes against nature, not to mention failing to faithfully execute the laws of the land.

Making Nixon Look Good

No aspect of the Bush-Cheney hidden agenda is more disturbing than the stealth mistreatment of the environment. Bush makes Nixon seem an appropriate icon for Rachel Carson, who revived the conservation movement in the 1960s. Robert F. Kennedy Jr., an environmental attorney representing a number of public interest groups, has made a career of pursuing polluters. He recently noted that "the Bush administration has initiated more than 200 major rollbacks of America's environmental laws, weakening the protection of our country's air, water, public lands and wildlife." Kennedy said that the Bush administration has "deceive[d] the public" about its plans "to eliminate the nation's most important environmental laws" and that "the Bush White House has actively hidden its anti-environmental program behind deceptive rhetoric, telegenic spokespeople, secrecy and the intimidation of scientists and bureaucrats."[46] To better understand how Bush is demolishing three decades of environmental law and policy, a bit of background is essential.

Congress, either on its own or at the request of prior presidents, has created our national environmental policy. Ironically, the two presidents who have done most of the heavy lifting are Richard Nixon and George H. W. Bush. Nixon signed into law the Magna Carta (as described by the *New York Times*) of environmental protection laws — the National Environmental Protection Act — as well as several of its progeny.[47] Bush senior added to and updated Nixon's laws in 1990. It is the Environmental Protection Agency (EPA) that has virtually all of the enforcement responsibility. The EPA issues rules and regulations to implement the various laws, doing so through rule-making proceedings that are highly public. When the EPA seeks to make its rules and regulations, it issues a public notice and the public has an opportunity to be heard. And those unhappy with the proposed rules and regulations, or the way the process was conducted, can contest them in federal court.

Bush has largely avoided public proceedings to roll back the laws. To get around the open government procedures, Bush's people rely on closed-door activities and a number of sneaky ploys. For example, his White House (1) simply tells the EPA what to do or what not do by telephone, e-mail, and memoranda or in private meetings — all of which can be discovered only by a Freedom of Information Act (FOIA) request that the EPA or the White House may or may not honor; (2) issues directives instructing the EPA as to how a given law is to be implemented, or not implemented (although this type of unilateral action is ultimately published in the *Federal Register*); (3) reverses enforcement based on a new legal opinion (by a Bush administration lawyer), overruling the prior legal basis — and these rulings are seldom published and may or may not be flushed out by a FOIA request; and (4) refuses to enforce the laws and regulations — including not seeking funding from Congress for enforcement. A few potentially *fatal* examples, where Bush has opted to help a special interest at the expense of the general public, show how each of these bureaucratic tactics is used to accomplish the Bush agenda. Let's look briefly at each area.

White House Instructions to the EPA

In early September 2001, the EPA administrator Christie Todd Whitman traveled to the little town of Libby, Montana, which had a big problem. Libby is where they long mined vermiculite, a material used in soil conditioners and insulation, which they had been digging from Zonolite Mountain since 1924. They stopped mining in 1990 because a substance in the vermiculite — called tremolite — contains lethal levels of asbestos fiber and has killed or seriously injured thousands of Libby miners and their families. Ms. Whitman was not only concerned about the residents of Libby, however. The EPA's records show that almost 16 *billion* tons of this deadly ore have been shipped from Libby to some 750 fertilizer and insulation manufacturers throughout the United States, and the EPA estimates that between 15 million and 35 million homes have been insulated with this toxic material. Never before had the EPA had such a dire situation, or one calling for a public declaration of a public health emergency.

Unbelievably (I wish I had an even stronger adjective to express the shocking political arrogance of the action; the only word in my thesaurus even close, but still not potent enough, is *astonishingly*), the Bush-Cheney White House killed the EPA's planned (and much needed) emergency announcement. Fortunately, the story leaked and the *St. Louis Post-Dispatch* broke it in late 2002 after obtaining documents confirming that the White House had done the dirty deed just days before the planned announcement. Former EPA administrator William Ruckelshaus (who worked for Nixon and Reagan) told the *Post-Dispatch* that the actions of the Bush White House were "wrong, unconscionable."[48] What transpired within the White House remains hidden. Dick Cheney has been working to get Congress to pass legislation removing liability for companies with asbestos problems (such as Halliburton, and no doubt those who were involved with lethal Libby ore). After the *Post-Dispatch* broke the story, Bush had no choice but to back down and let the EPA issue its warning. Noticeably, Congress has said nothing officially about this lack of concern at the White House for public health and safety. Similarly, the Republican-controlled Congress was prepared to remain silent about the equally troublesome failure of the EPA, acting at the direction of the Bush White House, regarding the foul air at Ground Zero until New York senator Hillary Clinton forced disclosure of the true situation.

Who can forget the images of the imploding Twin Towers, with clouds of dust and debris literally chasing people down the streets of New York City? Who could not worry about the quality of the air around Ground Zero once the dust and silt had settled everywhere within blocks of the tragedy? Families with children, who are always more vulnerable, wanted to know if it was safe to return. Like others, Senator Clinton relied on the EPA for advice, which her office imparted to her constituents: Yes, the EPA said it was safe.

This, however, was bad advice — incautious, unverifiable, if not incorrect. The EPA's top internal watchdog, Inspector General Nikki Tinsley, issued a report, two years after the 9/11 tragedy, stating that the EPA's post-9/11 assurances had been given without any facts to support them and that the EPA had done so based on instructions from the White House. For example, the initial draft of the EPA news release after 9/11 warned that the air around Ground Zero contained higher levels of asbestos than was considered safe. After the White House reworked the press release, everything was hunky-dory. The White House wanted to get Wall Street (home of Bush-Cheney contributors) up and running, so it decided that the asbestos levels in lower Manhattan met government standards and were "not a cause for public concern." This information was the White House speaking ex cathedra — no science, no solid data, just politics guiding its decision. It took two years — and no one knows how many injured lungs — to discover the truth.

Senator Clinton was livid upon learning of the inspector general's report. "I know a bit about how the White House works," she said. "Somebody picked up the phone, somebody got on a computer, somebody sent an email, somebody called for a meeting, somebody in that White House probably under instructions from somebody further up the chain told the EPA, 'Don't tell the people of New York the truth.' And I want to know who that is!" To force the issue, Senator Clinton placed a "hold" (a right of every senator under Senate procedures to stop a confirmation) on Bush's nominee to replace Christie Todd Whitman (who'd had enough and resigned months earlier). Purportedly, the White House provided the Senate the information it sought and the Senate issued a report exonerating the White House. Senator Clinton, who had removed her hold, remains unsatisfied. Yet she understands with the Republicans controlling the Senate, she will not get any further information, only excuses and denials from the White House.[49] Still, she has made her point. This White House cannot — and should not — be trusted in times of emergency, since it has its own agenda.

Presidential Directives

Unable to totally interpret the law into oblivion, Bush has sought to amend (and weaken) the Clean Air Act of 1970. Obviously, this can't be accomplished in secret. But he can and is using misleading information to sell his program, and he has unilaterally taken such action as he can, which has enabled him to drop fifty investigations that the Clinton administration had initiated into the failure of coal-burning electric power plants to comply with the Clear Air Act. To sell his program (and wave to his contributors), Bush traveled to the "dirtiest power plant in Michigan" (not his assessment but that of others, and not a fact that would have been overlooked by the industry). On the site of this old coal-burning, smoke-and-soot-belching behemoth operation run by Detroit Edison, a plant suspected of giving children asthma and other respiratory ailments and causing or aggravating heart disease in adults, Bush promoted his euphemistically (and cynically) titled "Clean Skies" initiative, with all the conviction of a snake oil salesman.

His new initiative proposes to permit those who are willing to invest in the equipment necessary for clean air emissions to sell their legal rights to pollute to others. This would authorize a startling number — 17,700 — older coal-burning electric power plants throughout the United States (Texas has almost 2,000, California has over 1,200, and New York has over 500) to become even worse polluters. They could purchase the right to further foul the air from others, which would enable them to expand their present facilities without purchasing expensive new equipment that scrubs their toxic emissions.[50] The basis of Bush's decision is rather simple: this is what the special-interest campaign contributors want. When Bush's rule changes were published in the *Federal Register* as a fait accompli, attorneys general from several states responded by saying they will enforce their own state laws even if Bush will not enforce the federal law. But Bush seeks to prevent this as well. For example, when California's South Coast Air Quality Management District sought to enforce its own clean air requirements, Bush's Justice Department filed a brief with the U.S. Supreme Court, claiming the district could not do so, since federal law controlled (even if it was not being enforced.)[51] Many Republicans are upset and disgusted at what a *New York Times* editorial called a "transparent giveaway" of clean air enforcement by Bush for his corporate allies.[52]

New EPA Legal Opinions

Carbon dioxide is almost universally considered the principal cause of global warming. The United States is the world's greatest producer of carbon dioxide (which traps the earth's heat, causing harmful environmental and climatic changes). Bush's lawyers at the EPA have disposed of this as a regulatory problem with a new legal opinion that carbon dioxide "isn't a pollutant that the EPA can cite to regulate emissions from cars and power plants."[53] Sadly, you can find a lawyer to give a contrary opinion of anything from the time of day to the meaning of a law. Bush's people used the same ploy, for example, to avoid regulating "ballast water" in ships under the Clean Water Act. When foreign vessels arrive in American ports carrying hundreds of gallons of ballast seawater filled with strange fish, plants, and weird species that scientists have determined are a serious threat to marine life in American waters, well, that's okay by Bush, because it makes maritime interests (contributors) happy.[54]

Doing Nothing

Bush has chosen to ignore what is one of the most challenging problems confronting this planet and the well-being of not only its people but wildlife and plant life, if not mankind's way of life everywhere — global warming. The reality of global warming is accepted by overwhelming scientific opinion. (Just as Bush can find "lawyers" for his purposes, he has found "scientists" who reject the contention that global warming is caused by human pollution or that it is a real problem.) Because global warming is an expensive problem to fix (and fixing it could put the energy industry as currently constituted out of business), Bush wants to study the problem further — for a decade (more compassionate conservatism for his contributors).

Meanwhile, the rest of the world has recognized the problem and agreed to reduce carbon dioxide emissions. In 1997, President Clinton, along with 175 other countries, signed a U.N. agreement — at ceremonies in Kyoto, Japan — to place limits on carbon dioxide emissions. American polluters went ballistic over Clinton's action, sending their top lobbyists to Congress to make sure the Kyoto treaty would be dead on arrival in the Senate. Rather than have it rejected, Clinton held it, hoping that if Al Gore were elected, he could turn the Senate around. Bush, however, has openly repudiated the Kyoto accord, to the dismay of the entire world, and claims that the United States will voluntarily reduce its greenhouse gases. But given his policies, his words are meaningless. Michael Oppenheimer, a climate expert, geoscientist, and professor of international affairs at Princeton, said that with Bush's posture, "we have a situation where the most significant environmental problem of this century the United States has essentially no plan for dealing with. . . . That will have the effect of significantly diluting global efforts to deal with the problem, and that inevitably means more global warming."[55]

The United States may still be able to address this problem, notwithstanding Bush's unenlightened position. In fact, Bush may even be embarrassed into action. So far, six Republican governors and a total of ten eastern states are currently working together on a regional basis to tackle the issue. When Bush refused to lead, New York governor George Pataki (a Republican) called his fellow governors. "Climate change is beginning to affect our natural resources," said Massachusetts governor Mitt Romney (a Republican) when joining the effort, explaining that "now is the time to take action toward climate protection."[56] Sir David King, Prime Minister Tony Blair's chief scientist, has said that the Bush failure to tackle global warming "is more serious than terrorism." Writing as a scientist, not a politician, in the journal *Science*, King demolished Bush's excuses for inaction, pointing out that any delaying action, even for a few years, "is not a serious option." Sir David also addresses the future consequences of Bush's actions and how he is exposing the entire world to "the risk of hunger, drought, flooding, and debilitating diseases."[57]

In addition to quietly telling the EPA what to do, issuing directives, rewriting legal opinions, and doing nothing, there are other stealth tactics being employed by Bush. He is using two techniques (discussed in general terms previously) to control public outrage at his pillage of the environment: press control and intimidation of federal employees. To implement his hidden environmental agenda,* his administration releases environ-

---

*Probably the term *unspoken* is better than *hidden*, since Bush's actions after three years have become apparent to those who study the field. Still, he pretends he is actually solving environmental problems. But his rhetoric and the consequences of his policies are totally incompatible. So, to that extent, it remains his hidden agenda.

mental information in a manner designed to minimize the public's awareness. "The administration routinely times its major environmental announcements to make it as difficult as possible for the news media to report on them, usually releasing information late on Friday afternoons. Especially important pronouncements are saved for big holidays when most reporters are unavailable. For example, the EPA announcement of its . . . changes in clean air regulations [were announced] on the afternoon before Thanksgiving and on New Years Eve."[58] Because few federal employees want to go to jail for speaking their mind about his environmental policies, I offer a bizarre example of the current fear within their ranks. This telling episode was played out recently at the National Press Club in Washington, D.C. "Two longtime National Park Service workers, disguised by dark glasses, hats and scarves, arrived . . . in a sedan with tinted windows," reported Elizabeth Shogren, a Washington correspondent for the *Los Angeles Times*. "Then, with their voices modified by a 'voice disguiser' from a counterespionage store, they denounced the Bush administration for 'enacting policies and laws that will destroy the grand legacy of our national parks,' as one put it." Shogren offered nothing more to protect her deep throats.[59] If this story had come from a reporter less savvy than Elizabeth Shogren, I would have said the reporter had been had by a stunt, a prank. But given her credentials and what I know about the mentality of this presidency, I believe she has accurately reported what it has come to for those who disagree with Bush and Cheney and wish to speak out. For this White House plays even rougher with its enemies than Nixon's.

Just as the mentality of the Nixon White House surfaced publicly with the Watergate break-in, the mind-set of the Bush-Cheney White House showed itself with the attack on Ambassador Joe Wilson and his wife. The methodology — that of

planting a nasty leak — is not new, but enlisting the news media
as criminal co-conspirators is a breathtaking bit of bravado. Like
their stagecrafting and image control, they have pushed dirty
tricks into a new dimension. Using those in the news media willing to be complicit, the Bush White House is attacking enemies
by planting hurtful information. It has made old-fashioned gossip-
mongering into high-powered smart bombs, firing explosive information by publicly releasing it and using the reporter's code
of confidentiality to protect itself from blowback. This, of course,
is akin to what Nixon aide Chuck Colson went to jail for. The
best example of this activity, but not the only one, unfortunately,
is the Valerie Plame Wilson situation.

Dirtiest of Dirty Tricks

On July 14, in his syndicated column, conservative *Chicago Sun-
Times* journalist Robert Novak reported that Valerie Plame Wilson — the wife of former ambassador Joseph C. Wilson IV —
was a covert CIA agent. (She had been known to her friends as
an "energy analyst at a private firm.") Novak reported that he
learned this top-secret information from "two senior Administration officials." Usually, the term *senior official* refers to a vice
president, cabinet officer, or top White House aide. On July 17,
Time published the same story, attributing it to "government officials," and in a later story the *Washington Post* confirmed that
two officials had called around trying to stir greater interest in
the planted story. Reportedly, some six different reporters were
told of Plame's CIA work, but only Novak and *Time* reported it.
(It is unclear whether *Time* has the same information as Novak
or obtained it later.) On July 22, *Newsday*'s Washington Bureau
confirmed that "Valerie Plame . . . works at the agency [CIA] on
weapons of mass destruction issues in an undercover capacity."

More specifically, according to a "senior intelligence official," *Newsday* reported, she worked in the "Directorate of Operations [as an] undercover officer." In other words, Valerie is/was a spy involved in the clandestine collection of foreign intelligence, covert operations, and espionage, part of an elite corps of those willing to take great personal risk for their country. Revealing her identity damaged both national security and her career, and resulted in the loss of a valuable government asset (for much time and training go into such work).

Planting (or leaking) this story about Valerie Plame Wilson is one of the dirtiest tricks I've seen in lowball/hardball politics. When the *American Prospect* wrote that "we are very much into Nixon territory here," it was an understatement. I thought they played dirty at the Nixon White House, but this is worse for two reasons. Nixon never went after his enemies' wives, and he never employed a dirty trick that was literally life-threatening. Anyone in the White House with sufficient access to this information had to be sophisticated enough to realize that revealing the identity of a covert agent placed not only her life in danger but also the lives of those with whom she had worked in foreign countries. In fact, covert agents' names are seldom provided even to the president, not to mention his staff. It was clear from the timing of Novak's first article that the leak was an act of revenge against Wilson for speaking the truth about the Bush administration's bogus claim that Niger provided uranium to Iraq. Novak ran his story only days after Wilson had set the record straight. And it was leaked to suggest the ambassador's wife was behind his fact-finding mission — which was not true. It also sent a message to the intelligence community that if you mess with this White House, we will mess with you, which they did by attacking Wilson's wife.

On July 24, 2003, Senator Charles Schumer (D-N.Y.) requested an FBI investigation of the planted leak. Schumer's letter states: "If the facts that have been reported publicly are true, it is clear that a crime was committed. The only questions remaining to be answered are who committed the crime and why?" The crime Senator Schumer was referring to is the criminal provision prohibiting the revelation of the identity of a covert CIA agent, an action that Bush senior, a former CIA director, had told his former associates in Langley, Virginia (when they named their headquarters building after him in 1999), was tantamount to the work of the "most insidious of traitors." The leak of Valerie Wilson's identity was a clear breach of national security and an obvious misuse of government information, making it potentially subject to several criminal laws, particularly given Ashcroft's aggressive use of existing laws against leaks.

Given his father's strong and well-founded feelings about such leaks, one would have thought that Bush would have gone after the leaker with a vengeance, starting with his own White House, which is almost universally believed to be the source of the information. For a president as sensitive to leaks as he is, who has jumped all over Congress for leaking information, it would have been expected that he would tell his attorney general to get cracking. Bush could have taken the initiative with his own staff and demanded that they provide sworn affidavits, one of the more effective tools for dealing with such matters. Having everyone who might possibly have had access to information about Valerie Wilson's covert work sign a sworn statement that he or she was not involved would also have shown that the president was serious. (Most people think twice before signing a false statement and subjecting themselves to perjury charges.) On the contrary, Bush has given every signal that his White House is covering up this incident, hoping it will go away. Indeed, Bush told reporters he did not think the leaker would be found once the Justice Department commenced an investigation, effectively saying in advance that the whole effort would be a waste of time — so why bother?

The matter was referred to the Department of Justice by the CIA, which meant that based on a preliminary examination of the law and facts by the attorneys at the CIA, there appeared to be a violation of federal law. The Justice Department investigation is ongoing, and slow going. After months of dillydallying, Ashcroft recused himself* and had his deputy — Jim Comey — assign the case to the U.S. attorney from Chicago, Patrick J. Fitzgerald. Fitzgerald is an old friend of Comey's, and the godfather of one of his children. Comey said that he has delegated his authority to investigate (which is the authority of the attorney general, since Ashcroft's withdrawal) to Fitzgerald, but the Justice Department is unwilling to release the formal delegation of authority.

Unlike Watergate, which the *Washington Post* kept alive on its front page with the smallest increments of information, this story, after its initial splash, has largely disappeared. To some extent this is because news cycles move faster today than three decades ago. But the Bush-Cheney-Ashcroft team also pushed the story out of the thinking of Washington journalists by making certain they had nothing new to consider. At first blush, the appointment of Fitzgerald in late December 2003 suggested that any action would be delayed until after November 2004 — that is, after the election. But the sudden recusal of Ashcroft and the

---

*A much-rumored source of the leak has been Karl Rove, who was a consultant to Ashcroft during one or more of his political campaigns and the person many believe secured Ashcroft his post as attorney general. For this reason, as soon as the investigation commenced, there were demands that Ashcroft either appoint a special counsel or recuse himself. He stalled as long as possible before finally giving way, sending more signals that he did not want this investigation to get out of hand.

selection of Fitzgerald, who will remain in his post in Chicago, suggests that a cooperative witness may have surfaced over the Christmas holiday (a time when a White House staff member could quietly engage a criminal lawyer, who would immediately try to make a deal with the Justice Department). At this writing, it is too early to know the outcome — with one exception. Any investigation of the White House in a post-Watergate world will be incomplete and suspect, absent a sworn statement by the president as to what he knew and when he knew it. In this case, that applies to the vice president as well.

Valerie Plame has several potential civil causes of action. If she files a civil lawsuit and starts taking depositions, the dynamics of unraveling the matter will also change, for this is no mystery, with over half a dozen newspeople privy. In Washington, D.C., the law protecting newspeople and giving them a qualified privilege to keep secret their news sources is tenuous at best when criminal activity is involved. In civil lawsuits, when a party has exhausted all other sources to locate such information, the courts also require reporters to reveal their sources.*

There is no question that Fitzgerald, who has empaneled a grand jury, can force members of the news media to testify about a criminal activity. They could, in fact, potentially be charged with criminal conspiracy. Hard-nosed prosecutors think noth-

---

*The *New York Times* (December 18, 2003) reported that two of its reporters had been ordered to testify in a civil lawsuit filed by former Los Alamos scientist Wen Ho Lee against the government for leaking his employment records to the *Times*, although the reporters had stated in court papers that they were prepared to go to jail rather than reveal their sources. In ordering the two reporters to testify, Judge Thomas Penfield Jackson said, "The court has some doubt that a truly worthy First Amendment interest resides in protecting the identity of government personnel who disclose to the press information that the Privacy Act says they may not reveal." Add to the Privacy Act national security, as is the case with Valerie Plame Wilson, and the justification for protecting a source is even less compelling.

ing of putting journalists before grand juries and forcing them to reveal their sources relevant to a criminal investigation, and the Supreme Court has said they can do so. Thus, it will not take too long to determine how serious Mr. Fitzgerald is pursuing his investigations, for hauling journalists before a grand jury is the quick way to get the answer of whodunit.

Inevitably, I believe, the source of this leak is going to surface. And the government will be hard-pressed not to prosecute. While some leaks are never uncovered — as Bob Woodward and his friend Deep Throat can attest — that occurs only when the information is known by only two parties (I have always entertained doubts that Woodward shared this information with his reporting partner and editor) and the source is not involved in criminal behavior (a point Woodward goes to some length to make about Throat). In this instance, with no fewer than six journalists and two senior officials reportedly privy to the source who planted the story with Novak, it will be difficult to keep the identity of the source bottled up. There are several ways the truth is likely to get out: (1) the FBI/Justice Department may get lucky and find the guilty person(s) — but no one should hold his breath waiting, unless a witness comes forward or journalists start appearing before the grand jury; (2) one of the journalists who is privy to the truth may leak it to another journalist for an election-year scoop of no small proportion; (3) one or more journalists who know the source of the leak may find their conscience and reject being a tool of a White House–engineered crime; (4) one or more journalists may leak the information to help one or more of their professional colleagues who they know will refuse to testify and thus be sent to jail for contempt; (5) if Valerie Wilson files a lawsuit and subpoenas the key players to testify in depositions; or (6) if Congress decides to investigate.

The known facts — that the activities involved two (or more) senior officials — indicate there is evidence of a criminal conspiracy. That criminal conspiracy is ongoing, and now involved with covering up the initial crime, thus creating secondary transgressions. (Sound familiar?) The federal law of conspiracy, along with the federal laws dealing with obstruction of justice, are among the most far-reaching of the federal criminal laws. Whether they know it or not, the Bush II White House — given this active and ongoing criminal activity — has dangers it has never dreamed possible by not ending this matter itself. It is only going to get worse before it gets better. And if Patrick Fitzgerald fails to investigate this aspect of the situation, he has only a fraction of the prosecutorial talents and integrity of his advance billing.

To look closely at only a few key activities of Bush and Cheney explains why they hide their real agenda. Thus, because there was no solid evidence to justify a preemptive war, they lied. At least Nixon and Kissinger, with their secret bombing of Cambodia, whispered the truth to Congress. Even when defending himself during Watergate, Nixon never sent Congress a document as spurious as Bush's formal determination to go to war with Iraq. While Nixon thought environmentalists were "clowns" and their programs "crap," by the standard of Bush and Cheney on environmental issues, Nixon could have run for reelection on the Green Party ticket, given his panoply of environmental initiatives that Bush and Cheney now seek to eradicate. I find no evidence that with his "responsiveness program" to handle the needs of his supporters, Nixon ever opted for a potentially *fatal* alternative to help his contributors, nor am I aware of his ever having denied Americans vital health and safety information. Nixon did not order "hits" of those on his enemies list, either.

Watergate, of course, initially appeared an effort by Nixon to win reelection by any means, fair or foul. It was that. But it was also the manifestation and culmination of Nixon's highly political governing style to win reelection — which had been the overriding purpose of his first term, as it has been for Bush and Cheney. It is too early to know how Bush and Cheney will play their 2004 reelection, but given the pattern of their presidency, watch for them to pretend to be on the high road, busy running the country — as Nixon played it — while Rove dispatches surrogates and activates his sleeper cells of loyalists to savage their political opponents. Watch this devil's brew of obsessive secrecy, hidden agendas, and hard-nosed presidential politics to be stirred by the 2004 presidential campaign, but hopefully this mess will not be tested by another terror attack in the United States, given that Bush and Cheney have made themselves — and thus the nation — unnecessarily vulnerable. Subjects to which I turn next.

Chapter Six

Scandals, Or Worse

Principle is okay up to a certain point, but principle doesn't do any good if you lose.

— Dick Cheney, White House chief of staff,
campaign advice to associates, 1976

Secrecy has consequences, and not always those that are desired. That certainly was the case with Watergate. It will, I believe, be the case for George Bush and Dick Cheney's co-presidency. If they do not pay the price while in office, they will when historians one day penetrate their obsessive secrecy, for the truth has a way of getting out. I can find no legitimate justification for their pervasive secrecy, only rationalizations and weak excuses. There can be no justification for lying, misleading, obfuscation, deceit, and other such secrecy-protecting ploys and tactics. Controlling the news media, avoiding press conferences, sealing the White House — these are obvious efforts to avoid being held accountable and, given their aim, cannot be justified, either. Bush and Cheney have provided no explanation of why they have reversed the trend of prior presidents to declassify national security information; rather, they have used 9/11 to vastly increase the amount of information to be so classified. Instead, Bush and Cheney stonewall their stonewalling, dissemble over their dissembling, and offer boilerplate defenses that fail to address their secret presidency or the needs of American citizens.

Bush and Cheney's Excuses for Secrecy

Both men have frequently spoken of their need to strengthen the presidency and prevent further erosion of presidential powers.* Such talk is claptrap. If they actually believe it, Americans (and others) have only more reason to worry about them, for it shows that their reliance on secrecy is truly evidence of their weakness as leaders who cannot be trusted. Another favorite rationalization is to claim that they need to protect the president's "deliberative process" — his right to receive advice without the chilling, or inhibiting, impact of revealing those with whom he deals, thus assuring unfettered counsel. Show me a person who does not want his advice to a president made public and I will show you someone who is giving that president information that is not in the public interest. Maybe Bush and Cheney can sell their excuses to those who do not have a clue about such matters or to blind loyalists who will tolerate anything, but none of their secrecy rationalizations can withstand scrutiny.

When refusing to permit the new director of homeland security, Tom Ridge, who was on the White House staff before a department for homeland security was created, to appear before Congress to answer questions, Bush told White House report-

---

*White House counsel Alberto Gonzales told the *New York Times* (May 22, 2002) that "the framers of the Constitution, I think, intended there to be a strong presidency in order to carry out certain functions, and [President Bush] feels an obligation to leave the office in better shape than when he came in." In fact, the framers intended the exact opposite, and the president did not even have a staff until 1857, and what has become the modern presidency (beyond anything contemplated by the founders) occurred during the presidency of Franklin Roosevelt, with the creation of the Executive Office of the President.

ers: "First of all, I'm not going to let Congress erode the power of the Executive Branch. I have a duty to protect the Executive Branch from legislative encroachment. I mean, for example, when the GAO demands documents from us, we're not going to give them to them. These were privileged conversations. These were conversations when people come into our offices and brief us. Can you imagine having to give up every single transcript of what is — advised me or the Vice President? Our advice wouldn't be good and honest and open. And so I viewed that as an encroachment on the power of the Executive Branch. I have an obligation to make sure that the presidency remains robust and the Legislative Branch doesn't end up running the Executive Branch."[1] When Bush invoked executive privilege (refusing to turn over FBI and Justice Department information to Congress on the Boston FBI office's handling of informants), in his formal memorandum to Attorney General Ashcroft, he claimed that his action was necessary to protect presidential powers, specifically, the so-called deliberative process.[2] This was also the reason Cheney refused to give the GAO any information, claiming that it was intruding into the deliberative process. So their explanations come down to protecting the presidency from Congress and protecting the deliberative process. (The other explanatory approach, of course, is to simply deny they are being secretive, as was done with *U.S. News & World Report*, which is the equivalent of Nixon's claiming he had not committed an impeachable offense, after he resigned.)

Bush's claims that he cannot let Congress "erode" the power of the executive branch and that he has a "duty to protect the Executive Branch from legislative encroachment" are utter nonsense. Today Congress must struggle to impose any checks whatsoever on presidents, and when there is no divided government (i.e., when one or both houses of Congress are not controlled by a party different from that of the president), Congress in effect becomes an ally of the president (with the opposition party serving as nothing more than irritating gnats that a president swats away if they bother him). In fact, Bush is merely repeating what Cheney says about "eroding" presidential powers, for Cheney has long believed that Congress has no business telling presidents what to do, particularly in national security matters.

Cheney's thinking was formed during his years in the White House as Ford's chief of staff, in the wake of Vietnam and Watergate, when Congress set about dismantling the imperial presidency.* Cheney still seems to resent these moves by Congress to bring the presidency back within the Constitution. Later, when serving as a member of Congress, Cheney was unhappy with his colleagues' exercising their constitutional powers (and responsibilities) during the Reagan presidency, culminating in the congressional investigation of the Iran-Contra scandal, which Cheney participated in from his seat in Congress, as a member of the Republican leadership and a ranking member of the joint investigating committee.

---

*Writing recently for the *Washington Post* (June 28, 2003), Arthur Schlesinger Jr., historian and adviser to President John F. Kennedy, discussed (and described the parameters of) the imperial presidency in the context of the Bush administration by quoting President Lincoln's concern about preemptive war: On February 15, 1848, Lincoln denounced the proposition "that if it shall become *necessary to repel invasion*, the President may, without violation of the Constitution, cross the line, and *invade* the territory of another country; and that whether such *necessity* exists in given case, the President is to be the *sole* judge." Lincoln continued: "Allow the President to invade a neighboring nation, whenever *he* shall deem it necessary to repel an invasion . . . and you allow him to make war at pleasure. . . . If to-day, he should choose to say he thinks it necessary to invade Canada, to prevent the British from invading us, how could you stop him? You may say to him, 'I see no probability of the British invading us' but he will say to you 'be silent; I see it, if you don't.'"

"The Founding Fathers," Lincoln said, "resolved to so frame the Constitution that *no one man* should hold the power of bringing this oppression upon us."

Cheney rejected the majority report of the Iran-Contra committee's investigation, which said that the common elements of both "the Iran and Contra policies were secrecy, deception and disdain for the law" and that the entire affair "was characterized by pervasive dishonesty and inordinate secrecy."[3] Cheney was not the least bit concerned by either the secrecy or lawbreaking, and said so when filing a minority report. He called the failures of the Reagan White House to comply with the laws "mistakes" and said they "were just that — mistakes in judgment and nothing more."* After scolding Congress for "abusing its power" by adopting laws restricting the president's spending money to aid the Nicaraguan Contras, Cheney said, "Congress must recognize that effective foreign policy requires, and the Constitution mandates, the President to be the country's foreign policy leader."[4] Cheney's attitude about the Congress vis-à-vis the president has changed little since 1987.

Contrary to Cheney's assertion, the Constitution has no such mandate. Since the time the Constitution was adopted, there has been an unresolved (and irresolvable) debate over the allocation of foreign policy powers between Congress and the president.** Mighty tomes written by highly respected authorities

---

*These so-called mistakes in judgment were called criminal offenses by Independent Counsel Lawrence Walsh, who successfully prosecuted some eight Reagan officials, all of whom either had their cases reversed on technicalities or were pardoned by President George H. W. Bush. The Bush II administration hired many of these people.

**Because Article II of the Constitution creating the presidency is so vague, there has been debate from the beginning about most all presidential powers. Not even those involved in framing the Constitution agreed about Article II powers, as the debates in the First Congress (with a number of framers serving) show. Earlier, James Madison made the point in Federalist No. 37, "that no skill in the science of government has yet been able to discriminate and define, with sufficient certainty, its three great provinces — the legislative, executive, and judiciary; or even the privileges and powers of the different leg-

support both sides of the question. Harvard professor and constitutional scholar Edwin S. Corwin years ago explained that the Constitution itself "is an invitation to struggle for the privilege of directing American foreign policy." Corwin says, "The verdict of history . . . is that the power to determine the substantive content of American foreign policy is a *divided* power, with the lion's share falling usually, though by no means always, to the President." (Emphasis in original.)[5] If there is a more accurate assessment of these powers, I have never found it.

Cheney's concern that presidential powers have been diluted over the past three decades seems even more misplaced when looking at recent legislative impotence. Law professor Phillip Trimble (who has both legislative and executive experience, having worked for both the Senate Foreign Relations Committee and the Department of State) examined this issue of dilution of executive powers and found that Congress's actions in the 1970s and 1980s "did not in practice constrain executive power." Rather, "the President is still the dominant force in foreign policy."[6] With its 535 members, Congress has no head and often 535 ideas on any given issue; it has become increasingly a reactive body, with most of its members spending more time seeking reelection than governing. Presidents literally overwhelm Congress. Preventing encroachment on the institution of the presidency by Congress, Bush and Cheney's excuse, is about as weak

islative branches." And he suggested the meaning of laws would "be liquidated and ascertained by a series of particular discussions and adjudications." Garry Wills, ed., *The Federalist Papers by Alexander Hamilton, James Madison and John Jay* (New York: Bantam Books, 1982), 179. Donald Rumsfeld — Cheney's onetime mentor — is a man of rules. He makes lists of them and has for years. One of his rules: "The legislative branch is in Article I of the Constitution; the executive branch in Article II. That is not an accident." Midge Decter, *Rumsfeld: A Personal Portrait* (New York: Regan Books, 2003), 154. Unfortunately, Cheney has rejected this Rumsfeld rule — which was obviously established by our founders.

an explanation as any modern president, or vice president, has ever offered for secrecy.

Their other excuse, the need to protect the deliberative process, is even weaker. This canard, which has become new presidential canon, deserves a burial. The so-called deliberative privilege was invented — out of whole cloth — by the U.S. Court of Claims and has slowly spread to other courts.* At the presidential level, it borders on being a hoax when invoked. *New York Times* columnist Bill Safire, a former White House insider, has written (with regard to this Bush-Cheney excuse for secrecy) that "when it comes to federal officials, the argument that only secrecy ensures candor is specious. Presidents record and blab; speechwriters remember and tell all; most advisers want their 'private' advice to become known. When, in a memoir, I protected a colleague by not mentioning his unpopular advice in an Oval Office meeting, he objected furiously to having been left out of history."[7]

Law professor Gerald Wetlaufer looked at the contention that the privilege was necessary to prevent chilling or inhibiting advice given to decision makers. He found exactly the opposite to be the case. It chills neither advisers nor decision makers. "So far as I have been able to determine," he wrote, those who claim such chilling effects "have never offered any kind of formal

---

*"This privilege] has come . . . from two quite different places. One was the British House of Lords and the other was Dwight Eisenhower and the ideas about command and 'organizational leadership' that he brought with him to the White House from a lifetime in the military. These two tributaries joined at the Court of Claims where the privilege was adopted as a compromise. . . . The privilege is a product of historical contingencies and of its being in the right place at the right time. Moreover, it has managed, in all the cases in which it has been applied, to escape full and careful scrutiny." Gerald Wetlaufer, "Justifying Secrecy: An Objection to the General Deliberative Privilege," *Indiana Law Journal* 65 (Fall 1990), 845, 882.

empirical evidence in support of its assertion." This is because there is none.

Evils of Excessive Secrecy

Lame excuses aside, excessive secrecy in any democratic government is inherently a problem. Because it is so prevalent in the Bush-Cheney presidency, it is a serious matter that is being widely ignored at the nation's (if not the world's) peril. Such secrecy is antithetical to democratic government and unworthy of any modern presidency. Though they have been mentioned in passing, it is appropriate to recap and summarize the innate evils of such government secrecy:

Secrecy Is Undemocratic

Our system is premised on citizens' having information about their leaders, including their actions and their intentions, so they can express consent or dissent. For the president and vice president of the world's greatest democracy to deny such basic information to Americans, merely to satisfy their own political whims and aims, is unconscionable and inexcusable and should be unacceptable. "Democracies die behind closed doors," Judge Damon J. Keith of the U.S. Court of Appeals for the Sixth Circuit recently reminded the Bush administration.[8] So does liberty.

Secrecy Threatens Liberty

Patrick Henry presciently warned, "The liberties of the people never were nor ever will be secure when the transactions of their rulers may be concealed from them." This sentiment was echoed a century and a half later when Woodrow Wilson advised that "the only truly self-governing people is that people which discusses and interrogates its administration."[9] People without information cannot question, influence, or even understand secret government policy, and when they do, they no longer have any choice or voice. Lack of government information worries many Americans; government secrecy frightens them. Thomas Jefferson famously admonished: "When the government fears the people, there is liberty; when the people fear the government, there is tyranny."[10]

Secrecy Precludes Public Accountability

In 1980, political scientist John Orman concluded his study *Presidential Secrecy and Deception* by expressing his concern about accountability. "If an individual controls the facts . . . , then that person negates any system of accountability." In 1990, Orman returned to this subject in *Presidential Accountability: New and Recurring Problems*, explaining the difficulty in holding presidents accountable: "Presidents can lie, withhold information, and systematically try to manipulate public opinion."[11] When Congress fails to hold presidents accountable, as so easily occurs without divided government, the only institution that can do so is the news media. If they give a president a pass and secrecy prevails, we have unaccountable leadership, and nothing is more dangerous.

Secrecy Alienates

Noted Gerald Wetlaufer: "Secrecy operates to alienate — to create subjective distance between — the secret keepers and one from whom the secret is kept. In the public sphere, such alienation between the governed and the governors tends toward hierarchy and away from democracy and citizen sovereignty."[12] Public opinion polls show that the secrecy surrounding the Kennedy assassination, followed by the secrecy surrounding

Vietnam, and then Nixon's secrecy alienated much of the American public from its government, and regaining trust has been slow. The extreme secrecy of Bush and Cheney will eventually be noticed by the public and will further reduce trust in government, which is vital to democracy.

Secrecy Negatively Affects Character

Philosopher Sissela Bok has found that secrecy "allows people to maintain facades and conceal traits such as callousness or vindictiveness — traits which can, in the absence of criticism or challenge from without, prove debilitating." She said, "As secrecy debilitates character and judgment, it can also lower resistance to the irrational and the pathological. . . . We know all the stifling rigidity that hampers those who become obsessed with secrecy."[13] That she wrote this more than a decade before the Bush-Cheney presidency seems not only correct but prophetic.

Secrecy Is Dangerous

There is cause to fear secrecy. Bok has further found that "secrecy is central to planning of every form of injury to human beings." In addition, "while not all that is secret is meant to deceive . . . all deceit does rely on keeping something secret. And while not all secrets are discreditable, all that is discreditable and all wrongdoing seek out secrecy," except in the case of open coercion.[14] In a word, little good comes from secrecy.

Secrecy Encourages Incompetence

When mistakes are easily concealed, there is no reason to take care. Sissela Bok has explained how secrecy also hampers "the exercise of rational choice at every step: by preventing people from adequately understanding a threatening situation, from seeing relevant alternatives clearly, from assessing the consequences of each, and from arriving at preferences with respect to them."[15] It also encourages (and hides) "groupthink," a collective bad judgment that can easily occur behind closed doors, when outside input and critical analysis is missing because decision making is being hidden.[16] Based on Bob Woodward's reporting in *Bush at War* and Ron Suskind's *The Price of Loyalty: George W. Bush, the White House, and the Education of Paul O'Neill,* there is ample evidence of groupthink at work in the Bush-Cheney presidency. The problems with the American occupation of Iraq have all the markings of classic groupthink decision making.

Bush and Cheney's Potential Scandals

Secrecy is also an indispensable element of scandal, fostering it and, for a time, hiding the wrongdoing that will become scandalous. Had there been no secrecy, it would not have been possible to accomplish the misconduct. Having experienced Watergate firsthand and having studied virtually every presidential scandal (out of personal curiosity), I have some understanding of the dynamics. But amazingly, although there has been no shortage of historical, legal, and political examinations of political scandals, there has been almost no analysis of their mechanics and dynamics, no "scandalology." For that reason, I found the work of sociology professor John B. Thompson from the University of Cambridge and his book *Political Scandal: Power and Visibility in the Media Age* fascinating. For me, his work confirms what I have learned from my own observation about the biology, or anatomy, of modern scandals.

Concisely stated: For a scandal, there must be "transgressions . . . sufficiently serious to elicit the disapproval of others" but falling short of "heinous crimes." The misconduct must be concealed and then revealed, with today's political-scandal revelations coming from the news media, making the media central players and actually part of the mechanics of a political scandal. The media must also express their disapproval of the misconduct, doing so in a scornful, contemptuous, and critical fashion that "reproaches and rebukes" or "scolds and condemns," not to mention often shaming or stigmatizing those involved. If the media learn of a transgression and fail to so react, there is no scandal. Finally, those involved in the scandalous misconduct must realize that their actions becoming public could hurt their reputation (if not worse, such as job loss, criminal prosecution, or other sanctions).[17]

Scandalmongering holds no appeal for me whatsoever. Bush and Cheney's removing the secrecy surrounding the problem areas I discussed in previous chapters would eliminate the potential of any of them becoming a scandal. If they don't, they have several inchoate scandals on their hands, since all the underlying ingredients are in place, including the right climate. From the preceding chapters, let me flag eleven potential areas of scandal: (1) Bush's character issues and (2) his prior business conduct — while the questions surrounding Bush's business dealings do not loom as large as Cheney's, they are far more serious than the Clintons' financial affairs, which were investigated for years and became a rolling scandal throughout his presidency. Much graver (no pun intended) is (3) Cheney's health and the failure to provide complete and truthful medical information. As for (4) Cheney's past business conduct, which the SEC is actively investigating (as is the French government), far more serious matters than Halliburton's accounting practices under Cheney are involved.* The SEC inquiry may include his getting rich, while other shareholders took a bath, because he knew about the financial problems with pending asbestos claims but failed to report this information. As the financial misconduct of Spiro Agnew (Nixon's vice president) has shown, unique problems arise with criminal wrongdoing at this level of government. A vice president may not be indictable because of the office he holds, and he may not be impeachable because it is not a high crime or misdemeanor under the constitutional standard. But whatever the case, Cheney's financial problems with Halliburton are more serious than the public is aware.

The ACLU has filed a lawsuit alleging (5) civil rights violations in squelching dissent at presidential and vice presidential appearances. This legal action may reach back into the White House, with the civil lawsuit also revealing criminal behavior. Another lawsuit involving (6) Bush's executive order dismantling the Presidential Records Act may show that his illegal actions (presidents cannot overturn laws with executive orders) were actually intended to cover up for his father or members of his own administration who served in the Reagan or Bush I administration. Then there are all the big campaign contributors. The distinction between bribery and gifts of money called campaign contributions is blurry at best, and (7) extraordinary secrecy surrounds more than just the development of a national energy policy that benefited contributors. There are also myriad contributors who are benefiting from the Bush II administration's concealing of business, environmental, health, and safety

---

*At the time of this writing it is too early to tell whether the French inquiry into Halliburton's involvement in bribing foreign officials to obtain business will directly involve Cheney. But he is one of the targets of the inquiry.

information. Should a whistle-blower decide to stand up, scandal could follow.

Bush and Cheney failed in their efforts to block a 9/11 inquiry, and (8) if Cheney's stall in addressing terrorism had an ulterior motive, or Bush and Cheney negligently ignored warnings, it will be a horrid scandal, certainly worse than Watergate. Bush and Cheney's (9) failure to update the existing continuation of government planning (including the presidential succession law) already evidences nonfeasance, but if we learn they have improperly politicized the existing operational plans, it too could result in a scandal. They cannot keep literally hundreds of lower-level government employees from talking, and I can tell you a few of them are very suspicious. There are two other potential scandals, both extremely serious. Discovering how (10) Bush misled Congress regarding war with Iraq, and then turned around and violated the very law he had requested, can only be called what it is — a high crime or misdemeanor under the Constitution. Will Republicans hold him accountable? Of course not. But that does not change the reality of his actions, which history will not treat kindly, nor will his Democratic opponent in 2004. Finally, there is (11) the leaking of Valerie Plame Wilson's covert CIA identity, which is being investigated and which, as I have explained, I have little doubt will be solved — but most likely not until after the November 2004 election. Quite correctly, *Hardball* host Chris Matthews and Republican National Committee chairman Ed Gillespie have both described the underlying offense as "worse than Watergate," and given that the criminal leak has not been flushed out, it has the potential of gathering other Watergate-like attributes.

John Thompson's study of political scandal resonates for me because of his appreciation, and explanation, of the essential role of the news media in modern political scandals. The media are part and parcel, both as a catalyst and critic, of bringing the scandal to life and keeping it alive. It is not that the media need to uncover the misconduct, although they often do; more often they need only report the information developed by others, from whistle-blowers to government investigators, and go with it. And when so reporting, find it unacceptable if not reprehensible. At present, the media are ever expanding. News reporting is no longer limited to radio, television, newspapers, and magazines. Internet chat rooms, blogging, and online reporting and commentary are changing the way Americans get their information, thereby changing the "mediation" (to use a John Thompson term) of scandals. For Bush and Cheney, this is not good.

Today the nation is deeply divided politically.*[18] Scandal sensitivity (another Thompson term) of widely unpopular and polarizing presidents is obviously higher than for those who are the opposite. For instance, Gerald Ford (with the Nixon pardon) and Jimmy Carter (with problems of his budget director, chief of staff, and brother) had scandals, but neither man was seriously damaged because they were not personally disliked as presidents. Nor was Ronald Reagan, who (with his vice president, secretary of defense, attorney general, and top national security advisors) survived the most serious abuse of presidential power scandal since Watergate. George H. W. Bush, not a discordant man, was only tainted by Iran-Contra, never badly tarnished. But Nixon, Clinton, and now Bush were divisive

---

*I have found no actual poll figures on Bush-haters, yet the reports of it continue. For example, syndicated columnist Molly Ivins wrote, in a column titled "Call Me a Bush-Hater" that "Robert Novak is quoted as saying in all his forty-four years of covering politics, he has never seen anything like the detestation of Bush. Charles Krauthammer managed to write an entire essay on the topic of Bush-haters in *Time* magazine as though he had never before come across a similar phenomenon."

presidents. For such leaders, there are no truly effective scandal firewalls once a fouling virus has infected their presidency and become known. There's also the matter of the news media. Bush's disdain for them and his harsh treatment of them have created a reservoir of ill will — not unlike Nixon did — should trouble erupt.

I make no pretense as a prognosticator. But I can recognize gathering storm clouds. If Bush gets through the 2004 election campaign and is reelected, his scandal jeopardy will continue, if not become aggravated should Republicans lose control of either the House or Senate (both of which, like the country, are almost equally divided) in either '04 or '06. But as serious as several of these developing scandals may be — and many of them are quite serious — as mentioned at the outset, the Bush-Cheney secrecy and style of governing carries with it potential consequences that are far worse than any political scandal. Their secret presidency is a dangerous threat to democracy in an age of terrorism.

Too Secretive and Bellicose for Fighting Terror

Since 9/11, Bush and Cheney have done a lot of muscle flexing and war making but absolutely nothing to prepare and educate the American public for a catastrophic terror attack. If they would stop playing politics with terrorism and get down to the serious business of dealing with it realistically (by bringing the rest of the world along as partners rather than as pissants), at the top of any plan would be preparing Americans for a worst-case situation. That they have failed to do so — along with their general handling of terrorism — suggests they see such a dire state of affairs as merely another political opportunity to further their hidden agenda. Just as they resisted acting for nine months on warnings about domestic terror, they have failed for over two and a half years to take some of the terror out of terrorism.

Do they not realize that the mix of their "let's kick ass" attitude — both at home and abroad — and the intrinsic nature of our democracy actually plays into the hands of terrorists? Their "look how tough we are" posture on everything actually entices terrorists to up the ante toward a worst-case scenario. Indeed, this administration is surely Osama bin Laden's dream team, given its governing techniques. This statement requires explanation.

University of Minnesota law professor Oren Gross has studied these broad but basic implications of terrorism and our nation's vulnerabilities. In the *Yale Law Journal* he explains the "fundamental conundrum" facing any democracy in dealing with terrorism.[19] "The ideals of democracy, individual rights, legitimacy, accountability, and the rule of law suggest that even in times of acute danger, government is limited, both formally and substantively, in the range of activities it may pursue in order to protect the state."[20] Thus, the great danger posed by terrorism for our democracy is not that terrorists can defeat us with physical or military force but rather that "terrorism presents its real threat in provoking democratic regimes to embrace and employ authoritarian measures that (1) weaken the fabric of democracy; (2) discredit the government domestically as well as internationally; (3) alienate segments of the population from their government, thereby pushing more people to support (passively, if not outright actively) the terrorist organizations and their causes; and (4) undermine the government's claim to the moral high ground in the battle against the terrorists, while gaining legitimacy for the latter." Professor Gross says, in effect, that the terrorists win if or when the United States becomes "less democratic."[21] Based on his analysis — with the exception so far of point 3 — the terrorists are making remarkable strides. If this is a fair measure of who is winning or losing the war on terrorism, and I believe it is (although that is not the purpose for which it was written), then we are losing. We are less democratic today than before 9/11. An even more serious terrorist attack will exacerbate each of these potentials, and given the Bush and Cheney approach, we may lose the war.

In 1987, the late Justice William J. Brennan Jr. (an Eisenhower appointee) lamented about the predictable nature of his country during war, noting, "After each perceived security crisis ended, the United States has remorsefully realized that the abrogation of civil liberties was unnecessary. But it has proven unable to prevent itself from repeating the error when the next crisis came along."[22] General Franks is wise to worry about what will happen to our Constitution if (or when) we learn that a terrorist organization has one or more WMD.

If there is no agreement about the allocation of powers under the Constitution regarding the roles of Congress and the president in foreign affairs, then there is even less agreement about the powers of the president in times of emergency. Before terrorists get their hands on weapons that can cause greater casualties than 9/11 and shred our Constitution, Americans should be told what could happen during such times (martial law, civil courts closed, government-controlled markets, price controls, curfews, dragnet roundup of suspects, military tribunals, elections canceled, etc.). It is not necessary to divulge classified national security information to discuss such matters generally. But should it not be for Americans to decide what they want their government to do if there is a catastrophic terror attack, just as they did, in effect, during the Cold War? Terrorism works by surprise. It is the responsibility of leaders to educate the nation and eliminate as much of the surprise as possible.

They have made no effort to do so. On the contrary, it has been a ceaseless presidential power grab since winning the office by a fluke.

C. Boyden Gray, White House counsel for Bush's father, has said that Bush senior "wanted to leave the office a little more powerful when [he] left it" and that Bush feels the same as his father.[23] Once again, the son is trying to do what the father failed to accomplish, with Cheney showing him how. As Arthur Schlesinger Jr. showed three decades ago, the imperial presidency is built on aggressive presidential actions in the name of national security. The line between matters foreign and domestic has long been indistinguishable, and the exercise of presidential power has likewise conflated. Understanding this reality, Nixon employed it to bestow his presidency with extraconstitutional powers. Bush and Cheney have adopted a similar stratagem. Watergate at its core was — pure and simple — a power struggle. It was the legislative and judicial branches seeking to keep the chief executive's powers in check, with the Fourth Estate exercising its powers — albeit belatedly — by informing the American public. Nixon, of course, lost this great battle — a fact for which we all must be thankful. Now Bush and Cheney have picked up where Nixon left presidential power. They seek to free the presidency of all restraints. They want to implement their policies — a radical wisdom they believe serves the greater good — unencumbered by those who view the world differently. So did Nixon. Bush and Cheney believe that the goodness of their motives justifies whatever action they believe necessary — even at the short-term expense of the health, safety, and welfare of a few thousand Americans, not to mention the lives of innocent foreigners, the "collateral damage" of modern warfare. So did Nixon. But as his writings and later interviews show, Nixon

learned from his mistakes. Bush and Cheney have ignored that —
and the lessons of Watergate.

It is difficult to trust a co-presidency hell-bent on enhancing
its powers through secrecy, demanding that it be held unaccountable, and willing to mislead the nation into a war (as part
of a hidden agenda for America's world domination). It appears
that Bush and Cheney will keep Americans in the dark about
dilemmas facing democracy in times of catastrophic crisis; they
will dumb the nation down through their official silence. So
when the moment comes and terrorists surprise America with an
even greater spirit-shattering attack than 9/11, Bush and Cheney will simply push aside the Constitution they have sworn to
uphold, inflame public passions with tough talk to rally support
(as television news runs endless loops of whatever the disaster, as
if no one has seen it, while sensationalizing the event with the
24/7 coverage that the terrorists so crave), and take this country
to a place it has only been once. For eleven weeks during the
outset of the Civil War, President Lincoln became what scholars have euphemistically called a constitutional dictator. But with
terrorism it will likely not be so brief. Bush once quipped, "If
this were a dictatorship, it'd be a heck of a lot easier, just so long
as I'm the dictator."[24] George Bush, however, is no Abraham
Lincoln.

Before we get there, however, hopefully the indecent secrecy
of the Bush-Cheney presidency, its failure to play by the rules of
traditional political behavior, and its refusal to address important issues will still be matters worthy of consideration during
the 2004 presidential campaign. These are issues that really cannot be ignored. Listen, if you will, to what Dick Armey had to
say at his farewell address at the National Press Club, upon leaving his long career in Congress and his post as House majority

leader. He was not speaking as a Republican or as a partisan but rather as a Ph.D. and onetime university professor, a man able to cut through the political noise and provide a sincere, learned, and wise warning. He braced all Americans about the "awful dangerous seduction of sacrificing our freedoms for safety against this insidious threat [of terrorism] that comes right into our neighborhoods." Armey said, "We the people had better keep an eye on . . . our government. Not out of contempt or lack of appreciation or disrespect, but out of a sense of guardianship." He added, "Freedom is no policy for the timid. And my plaintive plea to all my colleagues that remain in government as I leave it is, for our sake, for my sake, and for heaven's sake, don't give up on freedom!"[25]

George Bush and Dick Cheney have ignored Dick Armey's warning. It is not an accident that I have raised these concerns at this time; too few others have done so. No American wants the terrorists to win because of unnecessary presidential secrecy, our own collective stupidity, and the failure of our leaders to lead.

Appendix I

On January 28, 2003, when delivering his State of the Union address, President George W. Bush made his case for going to war with Iraq the heart of his presentation. The gist of his argument calling for the removal of Saddam Hussein by force is found in eight purported facts Bush provided to Congress. Based on material available in the public record, it is apparent that Bush provided conspicuously distorted, deceptive, and false information.

Purported Bush Fact 1: "The United Nations concluded in 1999 that Saddam Hussein had biological weapons materials sufficient to produce over 25,000 liters of anthrax — enough doses to kill several million people. He hasn't accounted for that material. He has given no evidence that he has destroyed it."

Bush's Source: He cites the 1999 United Nations Special Commission (UNSCOM) report to the U.N. Security Council. This report, however, is based on "estimates," not established facts, in which UNSCOM expressed varying degrees of confidence. In addition, UNSCOM never made the claim that Bush attributes to it. Instead, the report mentions only precursor materials ("growth media") that might be used to develop anthrax, and only by making a number of dubious additional assumptions can anyone reach the "over 25,000 liters of anthrax" that the president reported to Congress. Earlier the same month, in a

January 23 document, the State Department similarly cited the UNSCOM report, although noticeably more accurately than the president: "The U.N. Special Commission concluded that Iraq did not verifiably account for, at a minimum, 2160 kg of growth media. This is enough to produce 26,000 liters of anthrax." (The Department of State does not explain how it projected a thousand liters more than the president.) And two days after the State of the Union, in testimony before the Senate Foreign Relations Committee, Deputy Secretary of State Richard L. Armitage addressed the UNSCOM estimates in a more truthful light: as a reference to the "biological agent that U.N. inspectors *believe* Iraq produced." (Emphasis added.) In short, the president transformed UNSCOM estimates, guesses, and approximations into a declaration of fact, which is a deception.

Purported Bush Fact 2: "The United Nations concluded that Saddam Hussein had materials sufficient to produce more than 38,000 liters of botulinum toxin — enough to subject millions of people to death by respiratory failure. He hasn't accounted for that material. He has given no evidence that he has destroyed it."

Bush's Source: Again he cited the same UNSCOM report. Again he transformed estimates, or best guesses — based on the work of the UNSCOM inspectors and informants of uncertain reliability — into solid fact. His own State Department, however, more accurately referred to the same information as "belief," not fact: "Iraq declared 19,000 liters (of Botulinum toxin) [but the] UN *believes* it could have produced more than double that amount." (Emphasis added.)*

---

*See U.S. Department of State, "Iraq's Hidden Weapons: Failing to Disclose and Disarm," at www.state.gov/r/pa/ie/rls/19723.htm.

Purported Bush Fact 3: "Our intelligence sources estimate that Saddam Hussein had the materials to produce as much as 500 tons of sarin, mustard, and VX nerve agent. In such quantities, these chemical agents also could kill untold thousands. He has not accounted for these materials."

Bush's Source: Here, at least Bush admitted that he was drawing upon *estimates* — but this time, he left out other important qualifiers that would have signaled the uncertainty his own "intelligence sources" felt about these purported facts. In October 2002, a CIA report claimed that Iraq "has begun renewed production of chemical warfare agents, *probably* including mustard, sarin, cyclosarin, and VX." Bush omitted the "probably." The CIA also added still more caveats: "More than 10 years after the Gulf war, *gaps* in Iraqi accounting and current production capabilities *strongly suggest* that Iraq maintains a stockpile of chemical agents, *probably* VX, sarin, cyclosarin, and mustard." (Emphases added.)* If Bush's speechwriters initially included such caveats, they were removed, showing remarkable disregard for congressional and public intelligence, as well as the truth.

Purported Bush Fact 4: "U.S. intelligence indicates that Saddam Hussein had upwards of 30,000 munitions capable of delivering chemical agents. Inspectors recently turned up 16 of them, despite Iraq's recent declaration denying their existence. Saddam Hussein has not accounted for the remaining 29,984 of these prohibited munitions. He has given no evidence that he has destroyed them."

Bush's Source: Here he vaguely cited "U.S. intelligence" for this information, but it appears to have first come from

---

*See U.S. Central Intelligence Agency, "Iraq's Weapons of Mass Destruction Program" (Oct. 2002), at www.cia.gov/cia/reports/iraq_wmd/Iraq_Oct_2002. htm.

UNSCOM. If so, he has doubled the number of existing munitions that might be, as he argued, "capable of delivering chemical agents." UNSCOM's report, in its declassified portions, suggests that inspectors "supervised the destruction of nearly 40,000 Chemical munitions (including rockets, artillery, and Aerial bombs 28,000 of which were filled)." Their best estimate was that there were 15,000 — not 30,000 — artillery shells unaccounted for. The CIA's October 2002 report also acknowledges that "UNSCOM supervised the destruction of more than 40,000 chemical munitions." No declassified information supports Bush's report to Congress that 30,000 munitions capable of delivering chemical weapons remain unaccounted for. Nor has any news organization found evidence for the validity of Bush's claim. Where did Bush's number come from? It is difficult not to believe it was invented.

Purported Bush Fact 5: "From three Iraqi defectors we know that Iraq, in the late 1990s, had several mobile biological weapons labs. These are designed to produce germ warfare agents, and can be moved from place to place to evade inspectors. Saddam Hussein has not disclosed these facilities. He has given no evidence that he has destroyed them."

Bush's Source: The three informants have still not been identified — even though the administration now has had the opportunity to offer asylum to them and their families and then disclose their identities, or at least enough identifying information for the public to know that they actually exist and see why the government was prone to believe them. Bush's handpicked inspectors have not explained who these defectors were, either. Moreover, there is serious doubt that *any* mobile weapons labs have been found. Although the CIA claimed that two such labs had been located, Iraqi scientists say the labs were to produce hydrogen for weather balloons. No other Iraqi scientists, or others with reason to know, have been found to contradict their claim. In addition, the State Department publicly disputed the CIA (and DIA) claim that such weapons labs have been found. As with his other State of the Union statements, Bush presented belief as fact and projected a certainty that was entirely unjustified.

Purported Bush Fact 6: "The International Atomic Energy Agency confirmed in the 1990s that Saddam Hussein had an advanced nuclear weapons development program, had a design for a nuclear weapon and was working on five different methods of enriching uranium for a bomb."

Bush's Source: The International Atomic Energy Agency (IAEA) did provide some information to this effect, but the IAEA's own source was Iraq itself. According to Garry B. Dillon, the head of IAEA's Iraq inspection team in 1997–99, Iraq was begrudgingly cooperating with UNSCOM and IAEA inspections until August 1998. Moreover, a crucial qualifier was left out: whatever the program looked like in the early or mid-1990s, by 1998, the IAEA was confident it was utterly ineffective. As Dillon further reported, as of 1998, "there were no indications of Iraq having achieved its program goals of producing a nuclear weapon; nor were there any indications that there remained in Iraq any physical capability for production of amounts of weapon-usable nuclear material of any practical significance."* Later, IAEA's January 20, 2003, update report to the

---

*See the IAEA report at www.iaea.or.at/worldatom/Periodicals/Bulletin/Bull442/article3.pdf.

U.N. Security Council repeated the very same information Dillon had reported. It is deceptive to report Iraq's early 1990s effort at a nuclear program without also reporting that the attempt had come to nothing as of 1998. It is even more deceptive to leave this information out and then to go on — as Bush did — to suggest that Iraq's purportedly successful nuclear program was now searching for uranium, implying that it was operational when it was not.

Purported Bush Fact 7: "The British government has learned Saddam Hussein recently sought significant quantities of uranium from Africa."

Bush's Source: Countless news media accounts have now shown that the uranium story was untrue — and that at least some members of the Bush administration knew it to be false. I shall highlight only the relevant information. Cheney had questions about the Niger uranium story, so the CIA dispatched Joe Wilson, a former ambassador knowledgeable about Africa (and whose wife was a CIA covert agent dealing with weapons of mass destruction), to learn the truth and he found that it was counterfeit information. Wilson advised the CIA and State Department that the Niger story appeared untrue. Presumably Cheney learned these facts. Bush's use of the Niger uranium claim was removed from an October 7, 2002, speech because it was believed unreliable, but come the State of the Union, it had risen from the grave. No new evidence contradicting Wilson's assessment had emerged. Indeed, only days after Bush's State of the Union, Colin Powell refused to use this information in his United Nations speech — although he was reportedly pushed to do so by Cheney's staff — because he did not deem it reliable. It is hard not to believe that Bush's top advisers were aware of this hoax but assumed they could get away with it.

Purported Bush Fact 8: "Our intelligence sources tell us that [Saddam Hussein] has attempted to purchase high strength aluminum tubes suitable for nuclear weapons production."

Bush's Source: He was apparently referring to the CIA's October 2002 report, but again, all the CIA's qualifiers were left out, thus transforming a statement of belief into one of purported fact. The CIA report stated that "Iraq's aggressive attempts to obtain proscribed high-strength aluminum tubes are of significant concern. All intelligence experts agree that Iraq is seeking nuclear weapons and that these tubes could be used in a centrifuge enrichment program. *Most* intelligence specialists assess this to be the intended use, but *some believe* that these tubes are probably intended for conventional weapons programs." (Emphases added.) By January 20, 2003, the IAEA — which has more expertise than the CIA in the matter — had completed its investigation in Iraq of the aluminum tubes. It concluded that, as the Iraqi government claimed, the tubes had nothing to do with nuclear weapons; rather, they were part of a conventional rocket program. Thus, eight days before Bush's address, the IAEA stated in its report to the U.N. Security Council, "The IAEA's analysis to date indicates that the specifications of the aluminum tubes recently sought by Iraq appear to be consistent with reverse engineering of rockets. While it would be possible to modify such tubes for the manufacture of centrifuges, they are not directly suitable for such use." So Bush's claim that the tubes were "suitable for nuclear weapons production" — when only a week earlier, the IAEA, which is in the business of knowing such facts, plainly said that they were not — was false. Today, of course, with no nuclear facilities having been found in Iraq, it is clear that the information the IAEA provided was correct.

Appendix II

Two groups have long been at the forefront of efforts to reduce government secrecy: the news media and scientists. In reviewing stories about government secrecy back to the early 1900s, I found that initially it was only journalists who were concerned about this issue — and they were instrumental in getting Congress involved. But serious attention to government secrecy did not occur until the late 1950s. At about the same time, American scientists became concerned with excessive government secrecy, in the name of national security. Such secrecy was restricting the free flow of information vital to the scientific community, where scientists both test and build on the work of their colleagues. Therefore, it is not surprising to find journalists and scientists still among the most actively concerned about excessive secrecy, using the Internet to make their findings and information widely available.

Two sources are particularly helpful, consistently follow the latest developments, and do more than their fair share to help keep government open. These nonprofit public service organizations welcome contributions (both financial and important information relating to government secrecy):

Federation of American Scientists
1717 K Street, NW, Suite 209
Washington, D.C. 20036

Voice: (202) 546-3300
Fax: (202) 675-1010
E-mail: fas@fas.org

Steven Aftergood, at the Federation of American Scientists, prepares a daily (except weekends) newsletter digesting breaking news and updated information relating to secrecy. His FAS website on secrecy is one of the best, and without political spin: www.fas.org/sgp/index.html.

The Reporters Committee on Freedom of the Press
1815 North Fort Meyer Drive, Suite 900
Arlington, VA 22209
Voice: (800) 336-4243 or (703) 807-2100
E-mail: rcfp@rcfp.org

The Reporters Committee tracks a broad array of issues important to journalists. It watches government secrecy closely, providing comprehensive studies that can be downloaded (see www.rcfp.org/index.html), and its "Behind the Home Front" daily chronicle of news about homeland security and military operations affecting newsgathering, access to information, and the public's right to know is extremely helpful to those concerned about excessive government secrecy. (See www.rcfp.org/behindthehomefront.)

Below are listed websites maintained by organizations concerned with excessive government secrecy. This list is based on material initially assembled by Steven Aftergood, which I have modified slightly. With the FAS, the Reporters Committee, and the following, it is possible to remain aware of the federal government's restrictions on the public's right to know:

- **The Memory Hole** collects and publishes elusive records and documents that have been withdrawn from the public domain. (See www.thememoryhole.org.)
- **Cryptome** offers a good collection of new official and unofficial documents on security policy, updated regularly. (See http://cryptome.org.)
- **GlobalSecurity.org** provides resources on national security policy, including secrecy. (See www.globalsecurity.org.)
- **Project on Government Oversight** undertakes independent investigations to promote openness and government accountability. (See www.pogo.org.)
- **Electronic Privacy Information Center** offers declassified documents and insights relating to cryptography policy, privacy, and related issues. (See www.epic.org.)
- **Freedominfo.org** offers news about freedom of information efforts around the world. (See www.freedominfo.org.)
- **OMB Watch** provides resources, news, and analysis on the "right to know." (See www.ombwatch.org/info.)
- Public Citizen's **Freedom of Information Clearinghouse** includes resources about the Freedom of Information Act (see www.citizen.org/litigation/free_info), and its **BushSecrecy.org** offers information on Bush's secrecy policies (see www.bushsecrecy.org).
- **Access Reports** provides news and expert analysis on freedom of information policy. (See www.accessreports.com.)
- **The James Madison Project** was established to promote government accountability and the reduction of secrecy, as well as to educate the public on issues relat-

ing to intelligence and national security. (See www. jamesmadisonproject.org.)

- **FOI.net** provides resources on national and foreign freedom of information law. (See www.foi.net.)
- The FAS provides links to **Selected Agency FOIA Sites.** (See www.fas.org/sgp/foia/index.html#foia.)
- **CIA Center for the Study of Intelligence** provides its point of view on many secrecy issues. (See www.odci. gov/csi.)

Chapter Notes

PREFACE

1. For example, the *American Heritage Dictionary* (1985 edition) defines *Watergate* as "a scandal that involves officials violating public . . . trust through perjury, bribery, and other acts of abuse of power in order to keep their elective or appointive positions"; *Webster's Third New International Dictionary* (1993 edition) defines *Watergate* as "a scandal usually involving abuses of office and the compounding of wrongdoing through a cover-up"; and the *Merriam-Webster Online Dictionary* (2003 edition) defines it as "a scandal usually involving abuses of office, skullduggery, and a cover-up."

2. Everett Edward Mann, Jr., *The Public Right to Know Government Information: Its Affirmation and Abridgement* (doctoral dissertation, Claremont Graduate School, 1984), 216.

3. Sissela Bok, *Secrets: On the Ethics of Concealment and Revelation* (New York: Vintage, 1989), 171.

4. John Zogby, "Whatz New?" Zogby International (Sept. 7, 2000) at www.zogby.com/news/ReadNews.dbm?ID=259.

5. Marvin R. Shanken, "General Tommy Franks," *Cigar Aficionado* (Nov./Dec. 2003), 75, 90.

CHAPTER ONE: SURPRISINGLY NIXONIAN

1. For a particularly good example, see cub reporter Alexandra Pelosi's documentary, "Journeys with George," which Home Box Office aired on November 5, 2002.

2. Molly Ivins and Lou Dubose, *Shrub: The Short but Happy Political Life of George W. Bush* (New York: Vintage Books, 2002), 182–83.

3. Years later I learned I was not the only person whom Davis asked about Karl Rove, for Nixon's deputy campaign director, Jeb S. Magruder, was also quizzed about him. See Hamilton Fox, Memorandum to Files, "Interview with Jeb S. Magruder," September 4, 1973, Watergate Special Prosecution Force, National Archives and Records Administration.

4. *Dallas Morning News,* March 4, 2001.

5. George W. Bush, *A Charge to Keep* (New York: Morrow, 1999); Ivins and Dubose, *Shrub; Time, Newsweek,* and *U.S. News & World Report* (Jan.–Oct. 2000).

6. Richard Brookhiser, "President Bush Finds His Voice," *New York Times* (Aug. 11, 2001), A-15.

7. According to writer-editor Michael Kinsley (who follows this research closely), Bush's purported moral anguish was simply "pandering" to his political base while "sacrificing the future of many American citizens for short-termed political advantage." Michael Kinsley, "Taking Bush Personally," *Slate* (Oct. 23, 2003). Others say there are more than ten cell lines.

8. For example, James P. Pinkerton, "Bush's War Strategy Looks Like a Steal of Nixon's," *Newsday* (Nov. 18, 2003), at www.newsday.com, and Dana Milbank, "The Making of a President: The Nixon in Bush," *Washington Post* (Nov. 25, 2003), A-27.

9. David Frum, *The Surprise Presidency of George W. Bush* (New York: Random House, 2003), 20, 76–77, 91.

10. Dan Balz, a reporter for the *Washington Post,* has interviewed Bush on many occasions since 1994. Balz told a conference assessing Bush's presidency about Bush's asking him if he was trying to trick him and about Bush's articulate explanation of his decisions following 9/11, when he was familiar with the subject. Transcript of Bush Conference, Woodrow Wilson School (Princeton University, Apr. 25, 2003), 2–5.

11. Jeanne Cummings, transcript of Bush Conference, Woodrow Wilson School, 13.

12. Johanna Neuman, "With Bush, the Social Swirl Comes to a Dizzying End," *Los Angeles Times* (May 26, 2003), A-1.

13. Michael Elliott and James Carney, "How We Got There: First Stop,

Iraq," *Time* (Mar. 31, 2003), 175. ("F—— Saddam. We're taking him out," Bush is quoted as saying to Condi Rice before three U.S. senators.)

14. Cummings, transcript of Bush Conference, Woodrow Wilson School, 12–13.

15. Thomas B. Edsall, " GOP Battler Lee Atwater Dies at 40," *Washington Post* (Mar. 30, 1991), A-1.

16. Perry Bacon Jr., John F. Dickerson, Michael Duft, Eric Boston, Mark Thompson, Karen Tumulty, Douglas Walter/Washington; Sally B. Donnelly/Casper; and James Carney, "7 Clues to Understanding Cheney," *Time* (Jan. 6, 2003), 98.

17. John W. Dean, "*GAO* v. *Cheney* Is Big-Time Stalling: The Vice President Can Win Only If We Have Another *Bush* v. *Gore*-Like Ruling," *FindLaw's Writ* (Feb. 1, 2002), at http://writ.news.findlaw.com/dean/20020201.html; "Cheney Should Stop Stalling," *New York Times* (Feb. 11, 2002), A-27; and "More than Just His Location Remains Undisclosed: Why Dick Cheney's Secrecy Scheme for Pre-9/11 Information Makes No Sense," *FindLaw's Writ* (May 24, 2002), at http://writ.news.findlaw.com/dean/20020524.html.

18. John W. Dean, "Ignore Nixon at Your Peril: An Open Letter to Karl Rove," *FindLaw's Writ* (May 10, 2002), at http://writ.news.findlaw.com/dean/20020510.html.

19. James Madison, letter to W. T. Barry, Aug. 4, 1822, in Gaillard Hunt, ed., *The Writings of James Madison*, vol. IX (New York: G. P. Putnam's Sons, 1910), 103.

20. See, e.g., Curt Gentry, *J. Edgar Hoover: The Man and the Secrets* (New York: W. W. Norton, 1991), 223–73, and Anthony Summers, *Official and Confidential: The Secret Life of J. Edgar Hoover* (New York: G. P. Putnam's Sons, 1993).

21. Stanley I. Kutler, *The Wars of Watergate: The Last Crisis of Richard Nixon* (New York: Knopf, 1990), 78.

22. William Bundy, *A Tangled Web: The Making of Foreign Policy in the Nixon Presidency* (New York: Hill and Wang, 1998), xiii.

23. Ibid., 519, citing Robert Gates, *From the Shadows: The Ultimate Insider's Story of Four Presidents and How They Won the Cold War* (New York: Simon & Schuster, 1996), 49.

24. Bundy, *A Tangled Web*, 520.

25. Richard Nixon, *RN: The Memoirs of Richard Nixon* (New York: Grosset & Dunlap, 1978), 511–515.

26. See Jonathan Aitken, *Pride and Perjury* (London: HarperCollins, 2000).

27. Jonathan Aitken, *Nixon: A Life* (Washington: Regnery Publishing, 1993), 423, 424.

28. Bob Woodward, *Bush at War* (New York: Simon & Schuster, 2002), 145–46, 259, 282, 344.

CHAPTER TWO: STONEWALLING

Epigraph from presidential tape-recorded conversation, March 22, 1973, Old Executive Office Building.

1. "The Tsongas Problem," *National Review* (Dec. 28, 1992), 11.

2. David Brock, "How I Almost Brought Down a President," *Guardian* (Mar. 12, 2002), G-2.

3. Robert Schmuhl, "Presidential Perplexity: What's Public? What's Private?" *Society* (Nov. 2000), 96.

4. *Nixon* v. *Administrator of General Services*, 433 U.S. 425 (1977) (the Court balanced the public interest in performance of the president's official duties against the invasion of the president's personal privacy).

5. See generally Joel B. Grossman and David A. Yalof, "The 'Public' versus the 'Private' President: Striking a Balance between Presidential Responsibilities and Immunities," *Presidential Studies Quarterly* (Fall 1998), 821.

6. See, e.g., Donald R. Kinder, Mark D. Peters, Robert P. Abelson, and Susan T. Fiske, "Presidential Prototypes," *Political Behavior* 2:4 (1980), 315, 319 (Table I).

7. Martha T. Moore, "Bush TV Ad Attacks His Opponent's Credibility," *USA Today* (Sept. 7, 2000), 12-A.

8. Lois Romano and George Lardner Jr., "1986: A Life-Changing Year; Epiphany Fueled Candidate's Climb," *Washington Post* (July 25, 1999), A-1.

9. *Time* (Feb. 22, 1999), 38.

10. Scott Baldauf, "Compassionate Conservativism, Bush Style," *Christian Science Monitor* (Jan. 19, 1999), 1.

11. Bush, *A Charge to Keep* (New York: Perennial, 2001), 134.

12. On Nixon's secret use of Dilantin, see Anthony Summers with Robyn Swan, *The Arrogance of Power: The Secret World of Richard Nixon* (New York: Viking, 2000), 317–18.

13. Romano and Lardner, "1986: A Life-Changing Year." (The journalist was Al Hunt and his wife, Judy Woodruff, who were with their four-year-old son in a Dallas restaurant in early 1986; two weeks later, after learning Hunt was understandably upset by Bush's actions, Bush called Hunt and apologized. He had been drinking at the time of the incident.)

14. Ibid.

15. See, e.g., Jane Ely, "Enough Niceness to Almost Be Detestable," *Houston Chronicle* (June 6, 1999), 2.

16. Richard Cohen, "With a Name Like Bush," *Washington Post* (June 15, 1999), A-33.

17. Byron York, "George's Road to Riches," *American Spectator* (June 1999).

18. David Corn, "Bush and the Billionaire: How Insider Capitalism Benefited W.," *Nation* (July 17, 2002).

19. Suzan Mazur, "How Bush Got Bounced from Carlyle Board," *Progressive Review* at http://prorev.com/bushcarlyle.htm.

20. Bush, *A Charge to Keep*, 198.

21. Micah Morrison, "Vetting the Frontrunners I — George W. Bush: From Oil to Baseball to the Governor's Mansion," *Wall Street Journal* (Sept. 28, 1999), A-26.

22. Bill Minutaglio, *First Son: George W. Bush and the Bush Family Dynasty* (New York: Three Rivers Press, 1999), 238.

23. Bush, *A Charge to Keep*, 204.

24. York, "George's Road to Riches."

25. "New Sign of Cheney as No. 2 Contender," *New York Times* (July 24, 2000), A-14.

26. Steve Sternberg, "Doctors, Poll Say Cheney Health OK," *USA Today* (July 25, 2000), 1-A.

27. Lawrence K. Altman, "The 2000 Campaign: The Medical Factor; For Most Part, Doctors Concur on Cheney," *New York Times* (July 25, 2000), A-21.

28. Judy Keen, "Doctor Offers Clean Bill of Health," *USA Today* (July 26, 2000), 9-A.

29. Lawrence K. Altman, "The 2000 Campaign: The Medical Factor; Doctors Assert Cheney Leads Vigorous Life, Despite Ills," *New York Times* (July 26, 2000), A-19.

30. Steven A. Holmes, "Cheney in Hospital with Mild Heart Attack," *New York Times* (Nov. 23, 2000), A-1.

31. *Larry King Live*, Nov. 22, 2000, Transcript no. 00112200V22.

32. Luisa Dillner, "Time to Take It Easy: Dick Cheney Has Already Had Four Heart Attacks and a Quadruple Bypass," London *Guardian* (Mar. 8, 2001), 15 (quoting Gaynor Dewsnap of the British Heart Foundation).

33. Lawrence K. Altman, "Counting the Vote: Doctor's World; Cheney's Heart Attack Renews Debate on Checking Health of Candidates," *New York Times* (Nov. 24, 2000), A-43.

34. William Safire, "The Telltale Heart," *New York Times* (Nov. 30, 2000), A-35.

35. Marlene Cimons (of the *Los Angeles Times*), "Secrecy on Cheney's Health Worries Doctors; They Say Latest Illness Raises Concerns about His Ability to Serve," *Milwaukee Journal Sentinel* (Nov. 27, 2000), 9-A.

36. "Cheney Back on the Job, but Health Questions Linger," *USA Today* (Nov. 29, 2000), 14-A.

37. Joan Vennochi, "Doctors Can Ponder the Medical Questions; Politicians Can Ponder the Political Ones. Vice President Dick Cheney Should Answer These Ethical Ones," *Boston Globe* (Mar. 9, 2001), A-23.

38. Dana Milbank, "The Chairman and the CEO; In Incoming Corporate White House, Bush Is Seen Running Board, Cheney Effecting Policy," *Washington Post* (Dec. 24, 2000), A-1.

39. Susan Page (of *USA Today*), "Bush's Prime Minister; But Cheney's the Man Who Would Not Be President," *Seattle Times* (Mar. 6, 2001), A-3.

40. "Excerpts from Cheney Health Remarks," *New York Times* (June 30, 2001), A-11.

41. Carl T. Hall and Mark Sandalow, "Cheney Says He May Need Heart Device," *San Francisco Chronicle* (June 30, 2001), A-1.

42. Dave Saltonstall, "Health Risks Still a Possibility," *New York Daily News* (July 1, 2001), 5.

43. Abraham McLaughlin and Francine Kiefer, "With Latest Cheney Operation, White House Edges Toward Greater Disclosure," *Christian Science Monitor* (July 2, 2001), 2.

44. Jonathan D. Glater, "Five Questions for Harry J. Pearce; An Honesty Policy on Executive Illness," *New York Times* (July 8, 2001), III-4.

45. Susan Ferraro, "W's Pick May Have Heart for Campaign," *New York Daily News* (July 25, 2000), 6.

46. Ulysses Torassa, "Angioplasty Had Side Effect," *San Francisco Chronicle* (Mar. 6, 2001), A-13.

47. Robert E. Gilbert, *The Mortal Presidency: Illness and Anguish in the White House* (New York: Basic Books, 1992), 1.

48. Phillip H. Melanson with Peter F. Stevens, *The Secret Service: The Hidden History of an Enigmatic Agency* (New York: Carroll & Graf Publishers, 2002), 334.

49. Nicholas von Hoffman, "This President Spoke for the People of the World," *Newsday* (Dec. 9, 2003), at www.newsday.com/news/opinion/ny-vphof093576583dec09,0,1483117.story.

50. Fred Barnes, "A Ridge Too Far?: Will Bush Select the Pro-Choice Pennsylvania Governor as His Running Mate?" *Weekly Standard* (May 15, 2000), 8.

51. Adam Nagourney and Frank Bruni, "The 2000 Campaign: The Selection; Gatekeeper to Running Mate: Cheney's Road to Candidacy," *New York Times* (July 28, 2000), A-1.

52. Gary McWilliams, "Dick Cheney Ain't Studyin' War No More," *Business Week* (Mar. 2, 1998), 84.

53. Ibid.

54. Kenny Bruno and Jim Valette, "Cheney & Halliburton: Go Where the Oil Is," *Multinational Monitor* 22:5 (May 2001), 22.

55. Christopher Marquis, "Over the Years, Cheney Opposed U.S. Sanctions," *New York Times* (July 27, 2000), A-21.

56. Transcript, ABC News, *This Week* (July 30, 2000).

57. Lowell Bergman, Diana Henriques, Richard Oppel Jr., and Michael Moss, "Cheney Has Mixed Record in Business Executive Role," *New York Times* (Aug. 24, 2000), A-1.

58. Colum Lynch, "Halliburton's Iraq Deals Greater Than Cheney

Has Said: Affiliates Had $73 Million in Contracts," *Washington Post* (June 23, 2001), A-1.

59. Nicholas Kristof, "Revolving-Door Master," *New York Times* (Oct. 11, 2002), A-33.

60. Ron Nessen, *It Sure Looks Different from the Inside* (Chicago: Playboy Press, 1978), 230.

61. Lawrence F. Kaplan, "From Russia with Loans — What Dick Cheney Has Been Doing All These Years," *New Republic* (Aug. 7, 2000), 22.

62. According to the USACC (at www.usacc.org), Cheney resigned in November 2001.

63. George W. Bush, "Letter to Congressional Leaders Transmitting a Report on Assistance to Azerbaijan," *Weekly Compilation of Presidential Documents* 39:14 (Washington: Government Printing Office, 2003), 398.

64. Statement by the press secretary, Feb. 21, 2003.

65. "List of Countries with Troops in Iraq," Associated Press (Nov. 13, 2003).

66. "Nepotism in Central Asia" (editorial), *New York Times* (Oct. 27, 2003), A-22.

67. Bergman, et al., "Cheney Has Mixed Record in Business Executive Role," idem., A-1.

68. Adam Clymer, "Cheney, Trying to Remove Issue, Promises to Forfeit Stock Options," *New York Times* (Sept. 2, 2000), A-1.

69. CNN (October 6, 2000) at www.cnn.com/2000/ALLPOLITICS/stories/10/05/vp.debate.

70. Rega pointed out the falsity of Cheney's claim. "Halliburton was identified as a potential participant in 10 loans or loan guarantees — valued at a total of $1.8 billion — awarded by the U.S. Export-Import Bank," Rega reported. But even his fast fact checking disclosed that from "1996 through 1999, the U.S. Defense Department granted Halliburton contracts valued at about $1.8 billion, according to department records. The Pentagon ranked Halliburton the No. 17 recipient of 'prime contract awards' in fiscal 1999, with $657.5 million. In 1998, the company received $285.8 million in contracts, $290.5 million in 1997 and $573.6 million in 1996, the records showed." See John Rega, "USA: Government Ties Helped Cheney and Halliburton Make Millions," *Bloomberg News* (Oct. 6, 2000) at www.corpwatch.org.

71. Byron York, "Get Cheney: Democrats Try to Hang the Veep with Halliburton," *National Review* 54:14 (Aug. 12, 2002).

72. Jeff Gerth and Richard Stevenson, "Cheney's Role in Acquisition under Scrutiny," *New York Times* (Aug. 1, 2002), A-1.

73. See 15 U.S.C. §§ 78ff(a), 78j(b), and 78u-1.

74. Allan Sloan and Johnnie L. Roberts, "Sticky Business," *Newsweek* (July 22, 2002), 26.

75. Bill Saporito, "The Rap on Bush and Cheney," *Time* (July 22, 2002), 22.

76. Gerth and Stevenson, "Cheney's Role in Acquisition under Scrutiny."

77. Spencer Ackerman and Franklin Foer, "The Radical: What Dick Cheney Really Believes," *New Republic* (Dec. 1 & 8, 2003), 19.

CHAPTER THREE: OBSESSIVE SECRECY

1. Abraham McClaughlin, "Transition: A Vice President-Elect with 'Big Time' Clout," *Christian Science Monitor* (Dec. 20, 2000), at http://search.csmonitor.com/durable/2000/12/20/p1s2.htm. (Presumably, McClaughlin is referring to the presidential transitions of Ford, Reagan, and Bush I — going in and going out, except that for Bush I he apparently was not involved in the White House exit; otherwise, this would have been his seventh.)

2. David A. Kaplan, *The Accidental President: How 413 Lawyers, 9 Supreme Court Justices, and 5,963,110 (Give or Take a Few) Floridians Landed George W. Bush in the White House* (New York: William Morrow, 2001), 229–30.

3. Gerald R. Ford, *A Time to Heal: The Autobiography of Gerald R. Ford* (New York: Harper & Row Publishers, 1979), 324.

4. Nessen, *It Sure Looks Different from the Inside*, xii and 249.

5. Lucius Lomax, "W.'s Paper Chase: Bush Attempts to Have His State Papers Declared Federal Property," *Austin Chronicle* (Sept. 28, 2001), at www.austinchronicle.com/issues/dispatch/2001-09-28/pols_feature2.html.

6. Alison Leigh Cowan, "Father's Library Can Hold Bush Papers, If Door Is Ajar," *New York Times* (May 4, 2002), A-8.

7. Office of the Attorney General, State of Texas, John Cornyn, May 3, 2002, Opinion No. JC-0498 Re: Interpretation of Texas Govern Code

section 441.201 concerning the official records of a former governor, at www.oag.state.tx.us/opinopen/opinions/op49cornyn/jc-0498.htm.

8. Lucius Lomax, "Closing Texas' Open Records: What Bush Doesn't Want You to Know," *Austin Chronicle* (Nov. 8, 2003), at www.austin chronicle.com.

9. Alan Berlow, "The Texas Clemency Memos," *Atlantic Monthly* (July/ Aug. 2000), at www.theatlantic.com/issues/2003/07/berlow.htm.

10. Philip Shabecoff, "Ford Aides Reported Critical of White House Staff," *New York Times* (May 11, 1976), 22.

11. Philip Shabecoff, "Ford's Primary Losses Divide White House Staff as Factions Trade Charges of Laxity," *New York Times* (May 25, 1976), 18.

12. Ibid.

13. Eric Schmitt, "The Armchair General: Richard Bruce Cheney," *New York Times* (July 26, 2000), A-19.

14. Edward Walsh, "Bush Sets Key Role for a Longtime Family Foot Soldier," *Washington Post* (Nov. 28, 2000), A-25.

15. Ibid.

16. Elaine Sciolino, "Contesting the Vote: Selecting the Players; Washington Insider and Family Loyalist Poised for Job of Bush Chief of Staff," *New York Times* (November 28, 2000), A-23.

17. Jeanne Cummings, "Card Is Quiet Enforcer at White House," *Wall Street Journal* (July 28, 2003), A-4.

18. Ibid.

19. Nessen, *It Sure Looks Different from the Inside*, 252.

20. Gregg Zoroya and Judy Keen, "He Puts Words in Bush's Mouth," *USA Today* (Apr. 10, 2001).

21. See, e.g., Jack Nelson, "U.S. Government Secrecy and the Current Crackdown on Leaks," Joan Sorenstein Center on the Press, Politics and Public Policy: Working Paper Series (Fall 2002), at www.ksg. harvard.edu/presspol/publications/Nelson.pdf.

22. John W. Dean testimony, Hearings Before the Senate Committee on Presidential Campaign Activities (June 25, 1973), 918.

23. U.S. Senate, *The Final Report of the Senate Select Committee on Presidential Campaign Activities*, Report No. 93-981, 93rd Congress, 2nd Session (Washington: Government Printing Office, 1974), 201–2.

24. See www.commondreams.org/news2003/0923-11.htm, and Dave Lindorff, "Keeping Dissent Invisible: How the Secret Service and the

White House Keep Protestors Safely Out of Bush's Sight — and Off TV," *Salon* (Oct. 16, 2003).

25. Jeffrey Collins, "Bush Protestor Faces Charges in S.C.," Associated Press (July 18, 2003). Note: The criminal statute being used is 18 U.S.C. §1752(a)(1)(ii).

26. Thirty-four amici curiae briefs were filed to reverse Morison's conviction, including those of CBS, ABC, NBC, the *Washington Post*, the *New York Times*, and the *Los Angeles Times*, not to mention every news-media-related trade and professional association. See *U.S. v. Morison*, 844 F.2d 1057 (1988).

27. For example, the existence of a secret deep-sea salvage operation to recover a sunken Soviet submarine, believed to carry hydrogen-warhead missiles, cryptographic information, and code books, was discovered by *Los Angeles Times* reporters in the summer of 1974. CIA director William Colby requested that the information not be published, explaining that premature disclosure could tip off the Soviets and prevent the "single biggest intelligence coup in history." Even so, the *Los Angeles Times* published the story, and when Soviet vessels soon arrived, the CIA was forced to abandon the operation. Leaks have also caused deaths. In 1975, *Counterspy* magazine printed a leak from disenchanted former CIA agent Phillip Agee, identifying the CIA's station chief in Athens, who was soon assassinated. Leaks force presidents to tighten security, as did President Jimmy Carter in the summer of 1980, when highly classified information about the "stealth" bomber surfaced publicly. House Investigations Subcommittee of the Committee on Armed Services, 96th Congress, 2nd Session, Report on Leaks of Classified National Defense Information — Stealth Aircraft, H.R. No. 30 (1981).

28. Daniel Patrick Moynihan, *Secrecy* (New Haven: Yale University Press, 1998), 94–95.

29. See Felicity Barringer, "Federal Worker Sentenced for Passing On Information," *New York Times* (Jan. 16, 2003), A-18. See also R. Robin McDonald, "U.S. Attorney 'Sending a Message' to Those Who Leak Information," *Fulton County Daily Report* (Jan. 15, 2003), which appears to have first reported the story, which was reprinted by Law.com.

30. Section 641 of Title 18.

31. Section 1030(a)(4) of Title 18.
32. Sections 1343 and 1346 of Title 18.
33. Richard C. Leone and Greg Anrig Jr., eds., *The War on Our Freedoms: Civil Liberties in an Age of Terrorism* (New York: Public Affairs, 2003), 237–38.
34. Peter Johnson, "Bush Has Media Walking a Fine Line," *USA Today* (Mar. 7, 2003).
35. Helen Thomas, interview with Andrew Denton, "Enough Rope with Andrew Denton," *ABC Online*, episode 26 transcript, at www.abc.net.au/enoughrope/stories/s941661.htm.
36. Elisabeth Bumiller, "Trying to Bypass the Good-News Filter," *New York Times* (Oct. 20, 2003).
37. Matt Born, "Bush Snarls as White House Pack Closes In," London *Telegraph* (May 31, 2002).
38. Howard Kurtz, "What Bush Said and When He Said It," *Washington Post* (Oct. 1, 2001), C-1.
39. Wynton C. Hall, " 'Reflections of Yesterday': George H. W. Bush's Instrumental Use of Public Opinion Research in Presidential Discourse," *Presidential Studies Quarterly* 32 (Sept. 2002), 537.
40. Lewis L. Gould, *The Modern American Presidency* (Lawrence, Kans.: University Press of Kansas, 2003), 211.
41. Hall, "Reflections of Yesterday," 540–41.
42. Ibid., 532.
43. Ibid., 555.
44. Bob Davis, "Presidential Perceptions: Early Opinions Often Turn Out Wrong," *Wall Street Journal* (Feb. 9, 2001), A-12.
45. Elisabeth Bumiller, "Keepers of Bush Image Lift Stagecraft to New Heights," *New York Times* (May 16, 2003), A-1.
46. Dana Milbank, "A Baghdad Thanksgiving's Lingering Aftertaste," *Washington Post* (Dec. 12, 2003), A-35.
47. Gary L. Gregg II, "Crisis Leadership: The Symbolic Transformation of the Bush Presidency," *Perspectives on Political Science* 32:3 (Summer 2003), 143.
48. I have written numerous columns on this subject. See www.findlaw.com and the source material at the GAO website (www.gao.gov/press/wvc.html) and the House Government Operations Subcommittee

on Government Reform website (www.house.gov/reform/min/inves_ energy).

49. Dick Cheney, letter to the Honorable George W. Bush, President of the United States, May 16, 2001, at www.whitehouse.gov/energy. All letters and materials quoted are found on these websites, unless otherwise cited.

50. Craig Aaron, "Power Rangers," Tompaine.com (Nov. 23, 2003), at www.tompaine.com/feature2.cfm/ID/9465/view/print.

51. For example, Cheney told *Fox News Sunday* that he would not give Democrats in Congress or the GAO "a listing of everybody I meet with, of everything that was discussed, any advice that was received, notes and minutes of those meetings." Cheney added, "Now, that would be unprecedented in the sense that that's not been done before. It's unprecedented in the sense that it would make it virtually impossible for me to have confidential conversations with anybody." "Cheney Says Won't Turn Over List of Energy Meetings," Associated Press (Jan. 27, 2002). By mid-August, Comptroller Walker wrote Cheney a letter and, without calling him a liar, noted that what Cheney was claiming the GAO was seeking was not correct. See www.gao.gov/aug17let.pdf.

52. T. J. Halstead, "The Law: *Walker* v. *Cheney:* Legal Insulation of the Vice President from GAO Investigations," *Presidential Studies Quarterly* 33:3 (September 2003), 647.

53. See *In re Cheney*, 334 F.3d 1096 (July 8, 2003).

54. Mark J. Rozell, *Presidential Power, Secrecy, and Accountability* (Lawrence, Kans.: University Press of Kansas, 2002), 55–56.

55. Dan Eggen and Mike Allen, "Bush Backs Ashcroft in Records Dispute; Justice Has Resisted Releasing Files," *Washington Post* (Sept. 6, 2001), A-21.

56. William A. Orme Jr., "Marc Rich Aided Israeli Official," *New York Times* (Feb. 22, 2001), A-21.

57. Neil A. Lewis, "Clinton and Barak Discuss Rich Pardon in a Transcript," *New York Times* (Aug. 21, 2001), A-15.

58. Joshua Micah Marshall, "Bush's Executive-Privilege Two-Step," *Salon* (Feb. 7, 2002), at www.salon.com.

59. House Government Reform Committee, "Everything Secret Degen-

erates: The FBI's Use of Murderers as Informants" (Nov. 2003), at http://reform.house.gov/GovReform/News/DocumentSingle.aspx? DocumentID=1885 (p. 141).

60. Charles Tiefer, "Executive Privilege Overclaiming at the Justice Department," testimony, House Government Reform Committee, *Federal Document Clearing House Congressional Testimony* (Feb. 6, 2002).

61. House Government Reform Committee, "Everything Secret Degenerates," 139.

62. Gary L. Gregg II and Mark J. Rozell (ed.), *Considering the Bush Presidency* (Oxford: Oxford University Press, 2004), 133.

63. See the Presidential Recordings and Materials Preservation Act, Public Law 93-526 (Dec. 19, 1974), 88 Stat. 1695.

64. See www.archives.gov/about_us/basic_laws_and_authorities/ presidential_records.html.

65. Nelson, Testimony, Hearings on Oversight of the Presidential Records Act.

66. Marcy Lynn Karin, "Out of Sight, but Not Out of Mind: How Executive Order 13,233 Expands Executive Privilege While Simultaneously Preventing Access to Presidential Records," *Stanford Law Review* 55 (Nov. 2002), 553–54.

67. Nelson testimony, Hearings on Oversight of the Presidential Records Act.

68. Senator Jeff Bingaman, "Statement on Introduced Bills and Joint Resolutions," *Congressional Record*, Senate (July 31, 2003), S10621 (statement on introduction, with Senator Graham of Florida, legislation to repeal and revoke Executive Order 13233).

69. American Library Association, "Ongoing List of Historical Works That Would Have Been Affected by Executive Order 13233," at www.ala.org. (A small sample of the list includes *Abuse of Power* by Stanley Kutler, *A Few Good Men* by Evan Thomas, *America's First Families* by Carl S. Anthony, *America in the King Years* by Taylor Branch, *Chief Justice* by Ed Cray, *Deliver Us from Evil* by William Shawcross, *FDR* by Jean Edward Smith, *George Bush* by Herbert Parmet, *Grant* by Jean Edward Smith, and *John Adams* by David McCullough.)

70. Quotations from an unpublished paper (a work-in-progress) by Nancy Kassop, "George W. Bush and the Presidential Records Act" (on file with author).

71. For an overview of the broader constitutional implications of Bush's actions, which may also suggest that Bush is seeking to make new law by overturning the Presidential Records Act of 1978, see Jonathan Turley, "Presidential Papers and Popular Government: The Convergence of Constitutional and Property Theory in Claims of Ownership and Control of Presidential Records," *Cornell Law Review* 88 (Mar. 2003), 651; for a justification of Bush's radical actions, see Erik Paul Khoobyarian, "Student Comment: Reinterpreting the Apparent Failure of the Presidential Records Act and the Necessity of Executive Order 13233: Denying Historians Access or Protecting the PRA?" *Santa Clara Law Review* 43 (2003), 941. (Note: Mr. Khoobyarian favors executive privilege and secrecy rather than Congress's efforts to make presidential papers available for the public to better understand their democracy.)

72. Christopher H. Schmitt and Edward T. Pound, "Keeping Secrets: The Bush Administration Is Doing the Public's Business Out of the Public Eye. Here's How — and Why," *U.S. News & World Report* (Dec. 22, 2003), at www.usnews.com/usnews/issue/031222/usnews/22secrecy.htm.

CHAPTER FOUR: SECRET GOVERNMENT

1. Ackerman and Foer, "The Radical," 19–20.

2. George E. Reedy, *The Twilight of the Presidency* (Cleveland: World Publishing, 1970), 18.

3. Michael A. Genovese, "The Transformations of the Bush Presidency: 9/11 and Beyond," *The Presidency, Congress, and the War on Terrorism: Scholarly Perspectives,* University of Florida Conference (Feb. 3, 2003), at www.clas.ufl.edu/users/rconley/conferenceinfo.htm.

4. Ibid.

5. Richard Brookshire, "The Mind of George W. Bush," *Atlantic Monthly* (Apr. 2003), 55. Brookshire, who expresses concern about his imagination, also says that "George W. Bush, No. 43, is not an easy man to write about. He . . . is not well spoken."

6. Eric Schmitt, "Cheney Assembles Formidable Team," *New York Times* (Mar. 2, 2001), A-8.

7. Patrick E. Tyler, "U.S. Strategy Plan Calls for Insuring No Rivals Develop," *New York Times* (May 8, 1992), A-1.
8. David Armstrong, "Dick Cheney's Song of America: Drafting a Plan for Global Dominance," *Harper's* (Oct. 2002), at www.findarticles. com/cf_dls/m1111/1829_305/92589441/pl/article.html.
9. Tyler, "U.S. Strategy Plan Calls for Insuring No Rivals Develop," A-1.
10. Ibid. Buchanan would again go after what he called the "Wolfowitz memorandum" in his 1999 book, *A Republic, Not an Empire: Reclaiming America's Destiny*, realizing that this plan had not gone away.
11. Ackerman and Foer, "The Radical,"19.
12. See the Project for the New American Century, at www.newamerican century.org/index.html.
13. "Rebuilding America's Defenses," at www.newamericancentury.org/ RebuildingAmericasDefenses.pdf, pp. 51–52.
14. Henry Kissinger, notwithstanding some fundamental problems with neoconservatism, called this work by his friend (and employing his finest Kissingerian diplomatic equivocation) a "seminal treatise"; on the other hand, Gore Vidal, focusing on the various authors, found them "in the grip of a most unseemly megalomania, speaking for no-one but political hustlers within the Washington beltway." See http:// www.bbc.co.uk/bbcfour/documentaries/profile/robert-kagan.shtml.
15. Robert Kagan and William Kristol, eds., *Present Danger: Crisis and Opportunity in American Foreign and Defense Policy* (San Francisco: Encounter Books, 2000), viii, 4.
16. This, of course, is an ongoing effort. See David Rennie, "Neocons Gone Wild: Hawks Tell Bush How to Win War on Terror," *London Daily Telegraph* (Dec. 31, 2003), citing Richard Perle and David Frum, *An End to Evil: How to Win the War on Terror.*
17. Ibid.
18. Ackerman and Foer, "The Radical," 20.
19. Ibid. Elizabeth Drew, a highly perceptive and experienced Washington journalist, has confirmed the neocons' new power and influence within the Bush II administration by identifying the principal activists. Ms. Drew, writing in the June 12, 2003, *New York Review of Books*, reported that they have a "formidable alliance" composed of "Richard Perle, who until recently headed the Defense Policy Board (he's still a member) . . . ; James Woolsey, who has served two Democratic and

two Republican administrations [and] was CIA director during the Clinton administration . . . ; Kenneth Adelman, a former official in the Ford and Reagan administrations [both Woolsey and Adelman are currently members of the Pentagon's Defense Policy Board] . . . ; Paul Wolfowitz, the deputy secretary of defense and the principal advocate of the Iraq policy followed by the administration; Douglas Feith, the undersecretary of defense for policy, the Pentagon official in charge of the reconstruction of Iraq; and I. Lewis ("Scooter") Libby, Vice President Cheney's chief of staff. Two principal allies of this core group are John Bolton, undersecretary of state for arms control (though he opposes arms control) and international security affairs, and Stephen Hadley, the deputy national security adviser." Ms. Drew added that "Cheney himself and Defense Secretary Donald Rumsfeld can be counted as subscribing to the neocons' views about Iraq." Cheney and Rumsfeld, though not declared neoconservatives, have long shared many (if not most) of the neocons' beliefs.

20. I am a longtime reader of *Commentary* and the *Weekly Standard*, two principal publications for neoconservative thinking. In addition, in undertaking this project, I re-read Irving Kristol's *Reflections of a Neoconservative: Looking Back, Looking Ahead* (New York: Basic Books, 1983) and read several works by or about Leo Strauss.

21. Congressman Paul slightly modified his floor speech when he posted these key elements on his website at www.house.gov/paul/tst/tst2003/tst071403.htm.

22. Irving Kristol, "The Neoconservative Persuasion: What It Was and What It Is," *Weekly Standard* 008 (Aug. 25, 2003).

23. Dr. Rice was joined in tutoring Bush by Paul Wolfowitz, a neocon, and at the time the dean of Johns Hopkins School of Advanced International Studies, who had worked with Cheney at Defense and, as he later said, found himself and Cheney on the same intellectual wavelength; Richard Armitage, hawkish but a man who is comfortable with both neocons and realists, having served as assistant secretary of defense for international security affairs during the Reagan presidency, and is a close friend of Colin Powell; Robert Blackwill, a realist, a former dean of Harvard's Kennedy School of Government, and a special assistant for national security affairs on the Bush I National Security Council (and Rice's boss when she was there); Stephen Hadley, a neo-

con who had worked for Cheney at Defense as an assistant secretary
for international security policy; Richard Perle, a neocon who during
the Reagan administration was an assistant secretary of defense for international security policy as well; Dov Zakheim, probably a neocon,
given his active involvement with the Project for the New American
Century, who served in the Reagan administration at Defense, as
deputy undersecretary of planning and resources (his areas of expertise are Western Europe, the Middle East, and East Asia, and particularly domestic Israeli politics); and Robert Zoellick, probably a
neocon, given his relationship with the Project for the New American
Century, and undersecretary of state for economic affairs and White
House deputy chief of staff for Bush senior. In short, there was a decided neoconservative hard-line tilt to the tutors, a fact that would
have a significant impact on American foreign policy. This information
is drawn from three dozen sources, including the underlying source
for the members of the team from Ivo H. Daalder and James M. Lind-
say, *America Unbound: The Bush Revolution in Foreign Policy* (Washington: Brookings Institute Press, 2003), 17–34. Determining the
political philosophy of the Vulcan tutors was done, as best as possible,
by searching records and talking with journalists familiar with the
players. Not all neocons, it seems, acknowledge their beliefs publicly.
24. Sarah H. Wright, "Speaker Analyzes the Early Going for Bush," *Tech
Talk* (Mar. 8, 2001), at http://web.mit.edu/newsoffice/tt/2001/mar08/
lemann.html.
25. Ackerman and Foer, "The Radical," 17.
26. "Excerpts from Bush's Remarks on National Security and Arms Policy," *New York Times* (May 8, 2000), A-21.
27. Frank Bruni with Michael Cooper, "Bush Camp Sees Unrest as Vali-
dation of Its Views," *New York Times* (Oct. 13, 2000), A-1.
28. Alison Mitchell, "Gore and Bush Unite in Vowing Retaliation Against
Terrorism," *New York Times* (Oct. 13, 2000), A-13.
29. "Clinton Warned Bush of bin Laden Threat," Reuters (Oct. 15,
2003).
30. Ronald Kessler, *The CIA at War* (New York: St. Martin's Press, 2003),
195.
31. Michael Elliott, "They Had a Plan," *Time* (Aug. 12, 2002), 28.
32. George Tenet, testimony, "Written Statement for the Record of the

Director of Central Intelligence Before the Joint Inquiry Committee," Oct. 17, 2002, at www.cia.gov/cia/public_affairs/speeches/2002/
dci_testimony_10172002.html.

33. The *Washington Post* (Feb. 1, 2001) set forth the other members of the
Commission on National Security/21st Century: "lawyer and former
commerce undersecretary Lionel H. Olmer; former representative
Lee H. Hamilton (D-Ind.), director of the Woodrow Wilson International Center; business executive and former Air Force secretary Donald B. Rice; Norman R. Augustine, chairman of Lockheed Martin
Corp.'s executive committee; Anne Armstrong, a Nixon and Ford
administration official and former ambassador to Britain; John R.
Galvin, former supreme allied commander for Europe; Council on
Foreign Relations President Leslie H. Gelb; former NBC diplomatic
correspondent John Dancy; James R. Schlesinger, a former energy
and defense secretary and CIA director; former U.N. ambassador Andrew Young; and retired Adm. Harry D. Train." In addition, Newt
Gingrich, former Speaker of the House, served on the commission.

34. "Road Map for National Security: Imperative for Change," *The Phase
III Report of the U.S. Commission on National Security/21st Century*
(Feb. 15, 2001), viii.

35. Joseph Perkins, "Those Who Would Lay the Blame on America Are
Wrong," *San Diego Union-Tribune* (Sept. 14, 2001), B-9 ("Hart dared
to suggest this week that the Bush administration failed to heed the
commission's prediction this past January. . . . 'Frankly, the White
House shut [the commission] down,' Hart said").

36. George W. Bush, "Domestic Preparedness Against Weapons of Mass
Destruction," Statement by the President, May 8, 2001.

37. Secretary of State Colin Powell, testimony, Senate Appropriations
Committee: Subcommittee on Commerce, Justice, and State, the Ju-
diciary, and Related Agencies, Federal Document Clearing House
Congressional Testimony (May 8, 2001).

38. Mike Allen, "Bush Seeks to Restrict Hill Probes of Sept. 11," *Washington Post* (Jan. 30, 2002), A-4.

39. James Risen, "White House Drags Its Feet on Testifying at 9/11
Panel," *New York Times* (Sept. 13, 2002), A-12.

40. "Perspectives: Senator Richard C. Shelby," *New York Times* (Sept. 10,
2002), A-14.

41. "Inquiry into 9/11 Won't Interfere with Anti-Terror War," *USA Today* (May 21, 2002), A-12.

42. Jeanne Cummings, "Kissinger to Lead Probe of Sept. 11," *Wall Street Journal* (Nov. 29, 2002), A-4.

43. Shaun Waterman, "9/11 Families Seek Curb on Probe Officer," *Washington Times* (Oct. 6, 2003), at www.washingtontimes.com.

44. Philip Shenon, "Administration Faces Subpoenas from 9/11 Panel," *New York Times* (Oct. 26, 2003), A-1.

45. Deborah Solomon, "Questions for Tom Kean: Want to Know a Secret?" *New York Times Magazine* (Jan. 4, 2004), at www.nytimes.com/2004/01/04/magazine/04QUESTIONS.html.

46. Not surprisingly, there are literally hundreds of websites either raising — or more responsibly, trying to knock down — conspiracy theories on 9/11. The questions I've posed are drawn from Michael I. Niman, "9/11 Conspiracy Tales: This Much We Know to Be True . . . ," *Humanist* 62:2 (Mar./Apr. 2002), 18; Jim Bittermann, "French Buy Into 9/11 Conspiracy," CNN.com (June 26, 2002); Chris Harris, "Conspiracies and Coverups Made Easy," *Peacework* 29:328 (Sept. 2002), 24; Dean Schabner, "What Consensus? Conspiracy Theorist Immune to the Widespread Support for War on Terror," ABCNews.com (Apr. 17, 2002); Michael Meacher, "This War on Terrorism Is Bogus," *Guardian* (Sept. 6, 2003); and David Corn, "When 9/11 Conspiracy Theories Go Bad," AlterNet.org (Mar. 1, 2002).

47. Anti-Defamation League, *Unraveling Anti-Semitic 9/11 Conspiracy Theories* (New York: Gorowitz Institute, 2003).

48. See U.S. Army, Military District of Washington, at www.mdw.army.mil/welcome.html.

49. Barton Gellman and Susan Schmidt, "Shadow Government Is at Work in Secret; After Attacks, Bush Ordered 100 Officials to Bunkers Away from Capital to Ensure Federal Survival," *Washington Post* (Mar. 1, 2002), A-1. This article served as the basis for my explanation of what was done on September 11, 2001, which really did not become widely known until Gellman and Schmidt pulled together the story and found that COG had become permanent.)

50. 3 U.S.C. §§19(a), (b) and (d)(1) (with cabinet succession following the age ranking of the department he or she heads: secretaries of State,

Treasury, and Defense, attorney general — with the secretary of Homeland Security recently placed before the secretaries of Interior, Agriculture, Commerce, Labor, Health and Human Services, Housing and Urban Development, Transportation, Energy, Education, and Veterans Affairs).

51. Laura Myers, "Former Russian Official Says Military Lost Track of 100 Nuclear Bombs," Associated Press (Sept. 4, 1997); "Insider Notes from United Press International," United Press International (Oct. 5, 2001). See also Bob Port and Greg B. Smith, "'Suitcase Bomb' Allegedly Sought; Bin Laden Eyes Russian Stockpile," *New York Daily News* (Oct. 3, 2001), A-3, and Rupert Cornwell, "The Nuclear World: Time to Take Stock; A Terrorist's Bomb in a Suitcase Is Probably the Greatest Nuclear Threat to America," London *Independent* (Aug. 21, 1999), 4.

52. Ruth Wedgwood, "Al Qaeda, Military Commissions, and American Self-Defense," *Political Science Quarterly* 117:3 (Fall 2002), 357.

53. The May 2003 report of the Commission on Continuity of Government, and an outline of the commission's work, is online at www.continuityofgovernment.org.

54. Sharon Begley with Lynette Clemetson, Adam Rogers, Steven Levy, Peter McGrath, Joanna Chen, and William Underhill, "What Price Security?" *Newsweek* (Oct. 1, 2001), 58.

55. David Cole, "The New McCarthyism: Repeating History in the War on Terrorism," *Harvard Civil Rights-Civil Liberties Law Review* 68 (Fall 2003), 2. See also David Cole, *Enemy Aliens: Double Standards and Constitutional Freedoms in the War on Terrorism* (New York: New Press, 2003).

56. Several websites have been created to report and monitor these activities; among those I have found particularly informative are www.aclu.org; www.buzzflash.com; www.markarkleiman.com; www.talkingpointsmemo.com; and see also Appendix II.

57. ACLU, "Privacy," at www.aclu.org/Privacy/Privacy.cfm?ID=11054&c=130.

58. ACLU, "List of Communities That Have Passed Resolutions," at www.aclu.org/images/template/leftSafeandFree.jpg.

59. ACLU, "Conservative Voices Against the USA Patriot Act Part I," www.aclu.org/SafeandFree/SafeandFree.cfm?ID=12632&c=206. See also Part II.

CHAPTER FIVE: HIDDEN AGENDA

1. Richard F. Grimmett, "U.S. Use of Preemptive Military Force: The Historical Record," Congressional Research Service Document RS21311 (Sept. 18, 2002), at http://usinfo.state.gov/journals/itps/1202/ijpe/pj7-4grimmett.htm. Regarding the Spanish-American War, Grimmett explains, "The Spanish-American War is unique in that the principal goal of United States military action was to compel Spain to grant Cuba its political independence. An act of Congress passed just prior to the U.S. declaration of war against Spain explicitly declared Cuba to be independent of Spain, demanded that Spain withdraw its military forces from the island, and authorized the president to use U.S. military force to achieve these ends. Spain rejected these demands, and an exchange of declarations of war by both countries soon followed. . . . The circumstances surrounding the origins of the Mexican War are somewhat controversial in nature — but the term 'preemptive' attack by the United States does not apply to this conflict." The United States joined the Afghanistan Northern Alliance in ousting the Taliban.

2. George W. Bush, "State of the Union Address," *Weekly Compilation of Presidential Documents* (Jan. 29, 2002), 133–39.

3. George W. Bush, "Commencement Address at the United States Military Academy in West Point," *Weekly Compilation of Presidential Documents* (June 1, 2002), 944–48.

4. John Lewis Gaddis, "A Grand Strategy of Transformation," *Foreign Policy* (Nov./Dec., 2002), 50 (sidebar).

5. See *The National Security Strategy of the United States of America* (Sept. 2002), 13–16, at www.whitehouse.gov/nsc/nss.html.

6. James J. Wirtz and James A. Russell, "U.S. Policy on Preventive War and Preemption," *Nonproliferation Review* (Spring 2003), at http://cns.miis.edu/pubs/npr/vol10/101/wirtz.pdf.

7. Writers such as Paul Krugman of the *New York Times*, E. J. Dionne and Dana Milbank of the *Washington Post*, Harold Meyerson of the *American Prospect*, and Eric Alterman at the *Nation* are among the better-known political commentators who have addressed Bush's lying. (A Google search of Bush "lies" or "lying" will produce over 350,000

hits). Innumerable websites and bloggers have addressed Bush's untruthfulness, with sites like BuzzFlash.com, SmirkingChimp.com, Bushlies.net, Bushwatch.com, and Dailyhowler.com regularly featuring the latest dissembling. Several recent books deal with Bush's lying, including Al Franken's *Lies: And the Lying Liars Who Tell Them — A Fair and Balanced Look at the Right*, Jim Hightower's *Thieves in High Places*, Joe Conason's *Big Lies*, Molly Ivins and Lou Dubose's *Bushwhacked: Life in George W. Bush's America*, Michael Moore's *Dude, Where's My Country*, Lakshmi Chaudhry, Christopher Scheer, and Robert Scheer's *The Five Biggest Lies Bush Told Us About Iraq* and David Corn's *The Lies of George W. Bush*. This does not, by any means, exhaust the sources; rather, these are places where I found material, examined it, and discovered that the charges of Bush's extensive lying were valid. A few Bush defenders, such as Byron York (*National Review* Online, and *National Review*, June 16, 2003), have made arguments that charges of Bush's lying are misplaced or less-than-verifiable. But no one has undertaken to refute the complete, and hefty, list of Bush lies — a list that seems to grow. I randomly examined many of the charges of lying and found no viable defense or explanation for an unconscionable amount of false information. I have not, however, attempted to write a book on Bush's lying, other than as it relates to his secrecy. While I believe that the sources listed above are solid in their assertions, I have relied principally on the work of Washington journalist David Corn.

8. David Corn, *The Lies of George W. Bush: Mastering the Politics of Deception* (New York: Crown, 2003).

9. James P. Pfiffner, "The Contemporary Presidency: Presidential Lies," *Presidential Studies Quarterly* 29 (Dec. 1999), 903.

10. Dana Milbank, "For Bush, Facts Are Malleable," *Washington Post* (Oct. 22, 2002), A-1.

11. James Risen, "Prague Discounts an Iraqi Meeting," *New York Times* (Oct. 21, 2002), A-1; see also Louis Fisher, "Deciding on War Against Iraq," *Perspectives on Political Science* 32 (Summer 2003), 135.

12. Steve Inskeep, "Morning Edition," National Public Radio (Sept. 3, 2002), at http://proquest.umi.com/pqdweb?index=295&did=00000 0352186731&SrchMode=1&sid.

13. Reviewing respected publications privy to such information showed

that, at best, Saddam Hussein was years away from nuclear capability, which is not "fairly soon," as claimed by Cheney in August. Cheney provided no source for his information. For example, the assessment of two experts in the field: "It has been four years since UN weapons inspectors operated in Iraq, however, and *it is now difficult to assess* Iraq's capabilities with precision. It is therefore prudent to *assume* that Iraq has or will soon have biological and chemical weapons and *that it may, within a matter of years, acquire nuclear weapons.*" Daryl G. Kimball, "The Task of Disarming Iraq," *Arms Control Today* (Sept. 2002), 2; and "U.S. and foreign intelligence agency reports . . . indicated that Hussein was working faster toward a nuclear weapons inventory and *could have such before year 2005.*" Marvin Leibstone, "America Takes on Iraq," *Military Technology* (Sept. 2002), 8 (emphasis added for both.)

14. Karen DeYoung, "Bush Cites Urgent Iraqi Threat," *Washington Post* (Oct. 8, 2002), A-21.

15. Fisher, "Deciding on War Against Iraq," *Perspectives on Political Science.*

16. Joseph Cirincione, Jessica T. Mathews, and George Perkovich, *WMD in Iraq: Evidence and Implications,* Carnegie Endowment for International Peace (Jan. 2004), 8. This study is available online at www.ceip.org/files/Publications/IraqReport3.asp.

17. Elisabeth Bumiller, "President to Seek Congress's Assent over Iraq Action," *New York Times* (Sept. 5, 2002), A-1.

18. David e. Sanger, "Beating Them to the Pre-War," *New York Times* (Sept. 28, 2002), B-7.

19. Recorded and reported by the *New York Times* (Oct. 3, 2002), A-14.

20. John McCarthy, "Senators Were Told Iraqi Weapons Could Hit U.S.," *Florida Today* (Dec. 17, 2003), at www.floridatoday.com/!NEWSROOM/localstoryN1216NELSON.htm. The falsity of this assertion is reported in *WMD in Iraq,* 40–42.

21. George W. Bush, "Address to the Nation on Iraq from Cincinnati, Ohio," *Weekly Compilation of Presidential Documents* (Oct. 14, 2002), 1716.

22. Dana Milbank and Claudia Deane, "Hussein Link to 9/11 Lingers in Many Minds," *Washington Post* (Sept. 6, 2003), A-1.

23. Jim VandeHei and Juliet Eilperin, "Congress Passes Iraq Resolution: Overwhelming Approval Gives Bush Authority to Attack Unilaterally," *Washington Post* (Oct. 11, 2002), A-1.

24. See Charles J. Hadley, "Powell's Case for Iraq War Falls Apart 6 Months Later," Associated Press (Aug. 10, 2003), at www.fortwayne. com/mld/fortwayne/news/local/6502258.htm?

25. See Joint Resolution, Public Law 107-243, Oct. 16, 2002, at www. broadbandc-span.org/downloads/hjres114.pdf.

26. As one legal scholar has noted regarding such resolutions: "Under traditional principles of statutory construction, these provisions have no binding legal effect. Only material that comes after the so-called 'resolving clause' — 'Resolved by the Senate and House of Representatives of the United States of America in Congress assembled' — can have any operative effect. Material set out in a whereas clause is purely precatory. Such material may be relevant for the purpose of clarifying ambiguities in a statute's legally operative terms, but in and of itself such a provision can confer no legal right or obligation." Michael J. Glennon, "Presidential Power to Wage War Against Iraq," *Green Bag* (Winter 2003), 183. (Note: *Precatory* means "having the nature of prayer, request, or entreaty; conveying or embodying a recommendation or advice or the expression of a wish, but not a positive command or direction." *Blacks Law Dictionary*, 6th ed. It is for this reason that members of Congress seldom focus on the whereas clauses.)

27. Adriel Bettelheim, "Presidential Power," *CQ Researcher* (Nov. 15, 2002), 8.

28. The relevant provisions of section 3 (b) (1) and (2) of Public Law 107-243 are set forth below:

Section 3 (b) PRESIDENTIAL DETERMINATION

— In connection with the exercise of the authority granted in subsection (a) to use force the President shall, prior to such exercise or as soon thereafter as may be feasible, but no later than 48 hours after exercising such authority, make available to the Speaker of the House of Representatives and the President pro tempore of the Senate his determination that

(1) reliance by the United States on further diplomatic or other peaceful means alone either (A) will not adequately protect the national security of the United States against the continuing threat posed by Iraq or (B) is not likely to lead to enforcement of

all relevant United Nations Security Council resolutions regarding Iraq; and

(2) acting pursuant to this joint resolution is consistent with the United States and other countries continuing to take the necessary actions against international terrorists and terrorist organizations, including those nations, organizations, or persons who planned, authorized, committed or aided the terrorist attacks that occurred on September 11, 2001.

29. George W. Bush, "Letter to Congressional Leaders on the Conclusion of Diplomatic Efforts with Regard to Iraq," *Weekly Compilation of Presidential Documents* (Mar. 24, 2003), 341.
30. See "Report in Connection with Presidential Determination under Public Law 107-243," at www.c-span.org/resources/pdf/Report107_243.pdf.
31. A true congressional finding is found, for example, in the Equal Opportunity for Individuals with Disabilities Act at 42 U.S.C. §12101(a) — which clearly states that "the Congress finds that . . . ," for in fact Congress had so found based on its own inquiry.
32. "Report in Connection With Presidential Determination," 7.
33. Stephen F. Hayes, "Case Closed," *Weekly Standard* (Nov. 24, 2003), 20.
34. "Bush the Misleader," *Nation* (Oct. 13, 2003), 3.
35. Jeffery Goldberg, interview, "All Things Considered" (Feb. 4, 2003). Jeffery Goldberg is a writer for the *New Yorker.*
36. Ibid. "All Things Considered" host Robert Siegel stated: "*Newsweek,* by the way, quotes German police documents this week as saying he's [referring to Zarqawi] much closer to Iran. See also *Newsweek* (Mar. 3, 2003), which further reported that Zarqawi had relocated to Iran in October 2001.
37. David e. Sanger, "Bush Reports No Evidence of Hussein Tie to 9/11," *New York Times* (Sept. 18, 2003), A-22.
38. George W. Bush, interview with Diane Sawyer, ABC News (Dec. 17, 2003), at http://abcnews.go.com/sections/primetime/US/bush_sawyer_excerpts_2_031216.html.
39. M. Weber, "Politics as a Vocation," in H. H. Gerth and C. W. Mills, eds., *From Max Weber* (New York: Oxford University Press, 1958), 113.

40. Elizabeth Holtzman, "Debate on Articles of Impeachment," *Hearings of the Committee on the Judiciary, House of Representatives*, 93rd Congress, 2nd Session (Washington: Government Printing Office, 1974), 494.

41. Henry P. Smith III, "Debate on Articles of Impeachment," *Hearings*, 503.

42. Robert W. Kastenmeier, "Debate on Articles of Impeachment," *Hearings*, 506.

43. U.S. Senate, *The Final Report of the Senate Select Committee on Presidential Campaign Activities*, Report No. 93-981, 93rd Congress, 2nd Session (Washington: Government Printing Office, 1974), 361–444.

44. Dana Milbank regularly calls attention to the excessive secrecy of the Bush-Cheney presidency. See, for example, Dana Milbank, "Under Bush, Expanding Secrecy," *Washington Post* (Dec. 23, 2003), A-19; "White House Web Scrubbing; Offending Comments on Iraq Disappear from Site," *Washington Post* (Dec. 18, 2003), A-5; "The Making of the President: The Nixon in Bush," *Washington Post* (Nov. 25, 2003), A-5; Dana Milbank and Mike Allen, "Release of Documents Is Delayed; Classified Papers to Be Reviewed," *Washington Post* (Mar. 26, 2003), A-15; Dana Milbank, "U.S. Withdraws from Missile Treaty," *Washington Post* (June 14, 2002), A-28.

45. Letter from Center for Auto Safety, Public Citizen, Consumer Federation of America, U.S. Public Interest Research Group, and Advocates for Highway and Auto Safety to Administrator, National Highway Traffic Safety Administration (Apr. 22, 2003), at www.autosafety.org/article.php?scid=93&did=789.

46. Robert F. Kennedy Jr., "Crimes Against Nature," *Rolling Stone* (Dec. 11, 2003), at www.rollingstone.com/features/nationalaffairs/featuregen.asp?pid=2154.

47. "Editorial: Undermining Environmental Law," *New York Times* (Sept. 30, 2002).

48. This material is based on Andrew Schneider, "White House Budget Office Thwarts EPA Warning on Asbestos-Laced Insulation," *St. Louis-Post Dispatch* (Dec. 29, 2002), at www.citizen.org/documents/zonolite.pdf.

49. This material is based on Elizabeth Shogren, "EPA's 9/11 Air Rating Distorted, Report Says," *Los Angeles Times* (Aug. 23, 2003), A-1; Lau-

rie Garrett, "EPA Misled Public on 9/11 Pollution: White House Ordered False Assurances on Air Quality, Report Says, *Newsday* (Aug. 23, 2003); Hillary Rodham Clinton, "Clinton Calls on President to Provide Answers Regarding EPA's Responses to 9/11 [Senate Floor Speech]," Sept. 5, 2003, at http://clinton.senate.gov; Winnie Hu, "Clinton to Block E.P.A. Nominee to Pressure Bush on Air Quality," *New York Times* (Sept. 7, 2003), A-18; and Carl Limbacher, "Hillary: I'll Block EPA Nominee Over 9/11 Air Scandal," *NewsMax.com* (Sept. 7, 2003), at www.newsmax.com/archives/ic/2003/9/7/82718.shtml.

50. This material is based on Mary H. Cooper, "Bush and the Environment," *CQ Researcher* (Oct. 25, 2002), and Mary H. Cooper, "Air Pollution Conflict: Will President Bush's New Policies Erase Past Gains?" *CQ Researcher* (Nov. 14, 2003).

51. "Assault on State's Air Rules," *Los Angeles Times* (Jan. 10, 2004), B-22.

52. William Sheehan, "Politics and Pollution," *New York Times* (Aug. 29, 2003).

53. Seth Borenstein, "Bush Giving Business a Boost; Environmental Rule Changes Fulfill Corporate Wish List," *Pittsburgh Post-Gazette* (Sept. 21, 2003), A-11.

54. Ibid.

55. Cooper, "Bush and the Environment," 874.

56. Stephanie Ebbert, "A Regional Approach to Global Warming: Romney Joins Group," *Boston Globe* (July 25, 2003), A-3.

57. Steve Connor, "Top Brit Scientist Says U.S. Climate Policy Bigger Threat to World than Terrorism," London *Independent* (Jan. 9, 2004), at http://news.independent.co.uk/world/americas/sotry.jsp?story=479418.

58. Robert Perks and Gregory Wetstone, "Rewriting the Rules, Year-End Report 2002: The Bush Administration's Assault on the Environment," *National Resources Defense Council: Environmental Legislation: In Depth: Report* (Jan. 2003), vi, at www.nrdc.org/legislation/rollbacks/rr2002.pdf.

59. Elizabeth Shogren, "Feds Opposing Bush on Environment Afraid to Speak Out," *Los Angeles Times* (Nov. 14, 2003), at www.protectamericaslands.org/pdfs/press_azcentral.pdf.

CHAPTER SIX: SCANDALS, OR WORSE

1. George W. Bush, press conference (Mar. 13, 2002), at www.whitehouse.gov/news/releases/2002/03/20020313-8.html.
2. See George W. Bush, "Memorandum for the Attorney General, Congressional Subpoena for Executive Branch Documents" (Dec. 12, 2001), at www.fas.org/sgp/bush/121201_execpriv.html.
3. "Iran Contra Affair: The Final Report — Excerpts: Majority, Minority Views of Committees," *Los Angeles Times* (Nov. 19, 1987), 16.
4. Ibid.
5. Edwin S. Corwin (as updated and revised by Randall W. Bland, Theodore T. Hindson, and Jack W. Peltason), *The President: Office and Powers, 1787–1984* (New York: New York University Press, 1984), 201.
6. Phillip R. Trimble, "The United States Constitution in Its Third Century: Foreign Affairs: Distribution of Constitutional Authority: The President's Foreign Affairs Power," *American Journal of International Law* (Oct. 1989), 750, 751.
7. William Safire, "Behind Closed Doors," *New York Times* (Dec. 17, 2003), A-35.
8. *Detroit Free Press* v. *Ashcroft*, 303 F.3d 681 (2002).
9. Quoted in Everett Edward Mann Jr., "The Public Right to Know Government Information: Its Affirmation and Abridgement" (Ph.D. dissertation, Claremont Graduate School, 1984), iv–ix and 1.
10. Quoted in Chalmers Johnson, *The Sorrows of Empire: Militarism, Secrecy, and the End of Republic* (New York: Metropolitan Books, 2004), 298.
11. John Orman, *Presidential Accountability: New and Recurring Problems* (New York: Greenwood Press, 1990), 145.
12. Gerald Wetlaufer, "Justifying Secrecy: An Objection to the General Deliberative Privilege," *Indiana Law Journal* 65 (Fall 1990).
13. Sissela Bok, *Secrets: On the Ethics of Concealment and Revelation* (New York: Vintage, 1989), 25.
14. Ibid., 26.
15. Ibid., 26.
16. See Irving L. Janis, *Group Think* (Boston: Houghton Mifflin, 1982). Janis looked at group decisions relating to Kennedy's Bay of Pigs, Truman's Korean War, the failure at Pearl Harbor, LBJ's escalation of the

Vietnam War, and Nixon's Watergate cover-up, all examples of fiascoes that were explained by the pitfalls of groupthink. On the other hand, when Janis examined the group decision making during JFK's Cuban missile crisis and Truman's formulating the Marshall Plan, groupthink had been avoided, with successful and sound decisions being made.

17. John B. Thompson, *Political Scandal: Power and Visibility in the Media Age* (Cambridge, UK: Polity Press, 2000), 1–30, 60–118. Note: Not only have I brutally compressed Thompson's fine scholarship, I've added my own description of his work. His material deserves better than I have given it here, for I have merely taken his effort, applied it to Bush and Cheney, added my own understanding of scandals, and reached my conclusions. I thank him for his groundbreaking study and apologize for the down and dirty use I have made of it.

18. Pew Research Center for the People and the Press, "The 2004 Political Landscape: Evenly Divided and Increasingly Polarized" (Nov. 5, 2003), at http://people-press.org/reports/display.php3?ReportID=196.

19. Oren Gross, "Chaos and Rules: Should Responses to Violent Crisis Always Be Constitutional?" *Yale Law Journal* 112 (Mar. 2003), 1011, 1030.

20. Ibid.

21. Ibid., 1030–31.

22. Quoted in ibid., 1020.

23. Alison Mitchell, "Cheney Rejects Broader Access to Terror Brief," *New York Times* (May 20, 2002), A-1.

24. Quoted in Johnson, *The Sorrows of Empire*, at 291.

25. Nat Hentoff, *The War on the Bill of Rights and the Gathering Resistance* (New York: Seven Stories Press, 2003), 15, 125.

Acknowledgments

Notwithstanding several years of reading and writing columns about George W. Bush and Dick Cheney, it was not until the spring of 2003 that I began thinking seriously about writing this book. It was about the time that I had the good fortune of finding a literary agent — through my screenplay-writing agent/ manger Rick Berg — when Lydia Wills joined the New York office of the Los Angeles–based firm Writers and Artists Agency, where she now heads up the literary department. Lydia has strong feelings about books and she believed this was a "must do" project, when I was thinking of all the reasons to do something else. Now that it is done, I am glad I listened to her good advice. Lydia guided the preparation of a proposal (the always-impossible task of explaining in some detail a book you've not yet written) and then placing it with an editor and publisher where she believed it belonged — editor Geoff Shandler at Little, Brown and Company.

From the outset, Geoff believed this story needed to be told and he has guided this "fast track" project from start to finish, planning and coordinating the countless tasks and people necessary to bring it to publication. Geoff's skilled pruning and polishing of my narrative greatly improved the book. Similarly, copyeditor Steve Lamont ironed away remaining wrinkles, and his fine work, like Geoff's, is reflected on every page. Their diligence and alacrity are greatly appreciated. As is the effort of the Little, Brown sales force, the unheralded front line for all authors, and the other professionals at Little, Brown, such as Liz Nagle and Michael Pietsch, who have been important to this book. Last, but not least, the index was prepared by Anne Holmes of EdIndex.

To gather the information about Bush and Cheney and their secretive White House, I spoke or exchanged e-mails with many people. As I mention in the Preface, they all were consulted on an off-the-record basis. While these sources were extremely helpful, with a vindictive presidency (which attracts like-thinking supporters), only yours truly should have to deal with any wrath if they are unhappy with the truth. So too with the advice, suggestions, and wisdom provided by half a dozen friends I asked to read the manuscript, who graciously set aside time in their busy lives to provide me with their thoughts — and doing so in a matter of days because of the compressed publication schedule. To both my off-the-record sources and private readers, I thank you all again. Needless to say, while I have checked and rechecked my facts and carefully deliberated on my conclusions, if there are any errors, they are mine and not of those who have assisted in this endeavor.

Index

About the Author

Before becoming counsel to the president of the United States in July 1970 at age thirty-one, John W. Dean was chief minority counsel to the Judiciary Committee of the U.S. House of Representatives, the associate director of a law-reform commission, and associate deputy attorney general of the United States. He served as Richard Nixon's White House lawyer for a thousand days.

Dean's previous books include *Blind Ambition: The White House Years, Lost Honor, The Rehnquist Choice, Unmasking Deep Throat—History's Most Elusive News Source,* and *Warren G. Harding.* He has written articles and essays on law, government, and politics for the *New York Times, Rolling Stone,* MSNBC, *Salon,* and many other publications. He writes a biweekly column for *FindLaw's* "Writ."

Dean recently retired from his successful career as a private investment banker, and now writes and lectures full-time. He lives in Beverly Hills, California, with his wife, Maureen.